Baedeker

Dubai
United Arab Emirates

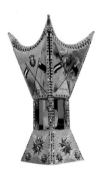

www.baedeker.com

Verlag Karl Baedeker

TOP ATTRACTIONS ★ ★

Besides sandy beaches, luxury hotels and huge shopping malls offering a vast array of goods, the UAE's museums and art galleries, medieval forts and lush green oases make a visit to Dubai and the neighbouring emirates an unforgettable experience.

1 ★ ★ Sharjah

With a variety of museums and art exhibitions, the capital of the Emirate of Sharjah is also the cultural capital of the United Arab Emirates.

The *Al Hisn Fort*, for instance, once the residence of the emirs of Sharjah and rebuilt in the original style, now houses a comprehensive museum on the Gulf region's history. The *Sharjah Art Museum* is not only home to the largest collection of primarily contemporary art in the United Arab Emirates; it also allows visitors to see painters and sculptors at work. ▶ page 235

2 ★ ★ Dubai

The Gulf metropolis, divided by Dubai Creek, is the sheikhdoms' main tourist destination. Explore the region's past at the *Dubai Museum* or visit the magnificent *Grand Mosque* in the Bastakiya quarter, which is not only worthwhile for the mosque's ornate interior design, but also informs about the basic principles of Islamic religious practices. *Heritage Village*, an open-air museum and recreated traditional souk, offers regular folklore events and arts and crafts for sale. In a magnificent setting outside the Burj Al Arab luxury hotel, the *Wild Wadi Water Park* – the largest water theme park in the Middle East –

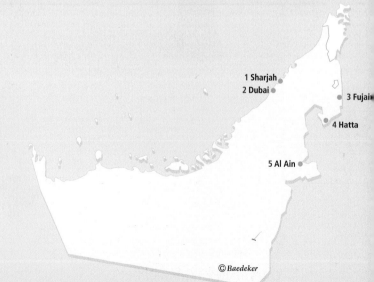

1 Sharjah
2 Dubai
3 Fujai
4 Hatta
5 Al Ain

© Baedeker

provides for fun in the pool. Dubai's *Gold Souk* with over 200 shops is one of the Emirates' top sights. ▶ **page 176**

3 ✶✶ Fujairah
Every Friday afternoon, the *Bull Ring* on the edge of town is a venue for the unusual spectacle of an Arabic bullfight. Near Badiyah, a few miles north of Fujairah, is a jewel of history and culture: the *Al Badiyah Mosque*, the oldest mosque in the country. ▶ **page 209**

4 ✶✶ Hatta Pools
The rocky cliffs south of the Hatta oasis carry water all year round, and number among the most impressive landscapes of the Emirate of Dubai. Feel free to have a dip! ▶ **page 205**

Dubai
The Jumeirah Beach Hotel is one of many luxury retreats.

Al Ain
4000-year old graves were discovered near the oasis.

5 ✶✶ Al Ain
Abu Dhabi's »garden city« is situated in the middle of a water-rich region at the foot of the Hajar Mountains.
Only a few miles away from the city, visitors can explore the most significant excavation site of the sheikhdom: Hili Archaeological Gardens, with graves and the remains of settlements from the over 4,000 year old Umm al-Nar culture.
 ▶ **page 156**

BAEDEKER'S BEST TIPS

A summary of the most interesting Baedeker tips included in this book: enjoy and experience the United Arab Emirates at its best.

▪ A paradise...
...and not just for herons and kingfishers. How about a visit to the mangrove reserve near the little town of the Khor Kalba on the Gulf of Oman?
▶ **page 21**

▪ Birdwatching in the desert
The small lake of Al-Wathba, situated around 40km/25miles south-east of Abu Dhabi, is a habitat for 200 bird species.
▶ **page 25**

▪ Visiting a mosque
Two of the most important and magnificent Dubai mosques are also accessible to non-Muslims. ▶ **page 30**

Dubai Shopping Festival
In January and February, it's all about bargain hunting in Dubai's shopping malls.

▪ Shisha for women
Dubai's »Apple« restaurant also allows women a puff on the water pipe.
▶ **page 73**

▪ Dinner Cruises
A truly special experience is having dinner while cruising across Dubai Creek, with a great view of the night-lit skyline of the metropolis. ▶ **page 79**

▪ Dubai Shopping Festival
With enough time and, of course, money, January and February are the best months to go bargain hunting. ▶ **page 98**

▪ Sandy Beach
The wonderful beach and glinting waters of the fishing town Al Aqqa, 15km/9mi south of the three-zoned town of Dibba, is an inviting spot for a swim. ▶ **page 129**

Jumeirah Mosque
Even non-Muslims can visit the Emirate's most beautiful mosque.

Medieval Arabia
The »Palace of the Queen of Saba« is concealed not far from Ras Al Khaimah.
► page 133

Bloodless bullfights
Besides Fujairah, the coastal town of Barka (Oman) is another place to see an Arabic bullfight. ► page 136

Animal snapshots
There are plenty of opportunities to take photos of the animals at the livestock market of Al Ain, which takes place every morning opposite the Al-Sharki Fort.
► page 161

»Around Dubai«
A rather unusual way to see the attractions of the city. ► page 199

Winter sports in Dubai
If it's too hot for shopping, why not cool off on the piste or in the ice rink?
► page 201

Mountain trips
Enjoy a swim below the waterfall in the Hajar Mountains. ► page 217

Very Special Arts Studios
Visit the art workshops in Sharjah, the UAE's »cultural capital«. ► page 240

Sharjah Women's Club
A relaxation paradise – for women only.
► page 249

Animal snapshots...
...galore at the livestock market in Al Ain.

Abra Tour
Dubai Creek can also be explored in a traditional water taxi.

Majlis Gallery
See whether the art shop at the Al Fahidi Roundabout in Dubai really is air-conditioned by just one wind tower.
► page 182

Abra-Tour
Take a boat tour on Dubai Creek with one of the traditional water taxis – for just a few pounds an hour. ► page 196

Desert shells
On Fossil Rock near the Al Dhaid oasis, discover 100 million year old fossils of sea snails and shells in the middle of the desert! ► page 250

Dreamland Aqua Park
Carefree pool fun in the fantastic water park near Umm al-Quwain.
► page 263

The abras, traditional water taxis, offer quick and inexpensive rides across Dubai Creek.
► page 196

BACKGROUND

PRACTICALITIES

TOURS

Gorgeous old silver jewellery, mainly from Yemen or Oman, offered at antique stores and souks
► page 103

Camels were the most precious property for nomadic Bedouins
► page 230

SIGHTS
from A to Z

Pricing Categories

Hotels
Luxury: from £135
Mid-range: £80 – £135
Budget: up to £80
For one night in a double room
(2 people) in the winter season.

Restaurants
Expensive = from £13
Moderate = £5 – £13
Inexpensive £5
For a three-course dinner

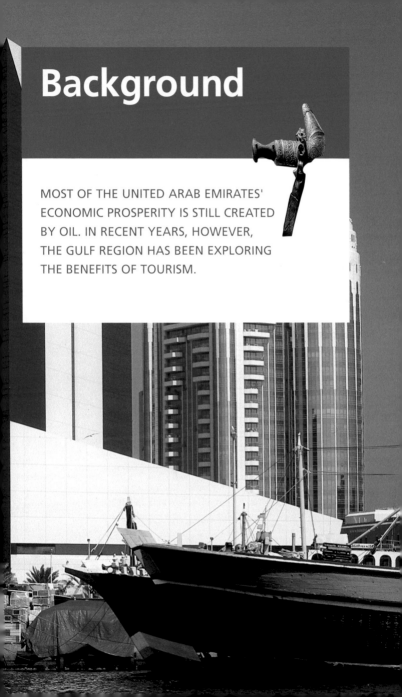

Background

MOST OF THE UNITED ARAB EMIRATES'
ECONOMIC PROSPERITY IS STILL CREATED
BY OIL. IN RECENT YEARS, HOWEVER,
THE GULF REGION HAS BEEN EXPLORING
THE BENEFITS OF TOURISM.

ARABIA'S TREASURES

»Allah u akbar« – at sunset the muezzin's call reverberates from hundreds of mosques. The entire city stops as from all directions men in white caftans come together to pray. Soon, however, everyone returns to their daily tasks. Despite the modernity brought about by its gigantic oil reserves, life in the UAE is still dominated by religion.

The United Arab Emirates (UAE; al-Imarat al-Arabiya al-Muttahida) is a federation of the emirates Abu Dhabi, Dubai, Sharjah, Fujairah, Ras al-Khaimah, Ajman and Umm al-Quwain. Situated east of the Arabian Peninsula, the subcontinent is bordered by the Gulf of Aden and the Arabian Sea in the south, the Gulf of Oman and the Arabian Gulf (also known as Persian Gulf) in the east and the Red Sea in the west. Founded in 1971, the federation is a third of the size of the UK – a little larger than Scotland – and is situated between Oman's Musandam Peninsula in the north-east and the Qatar Peninsula in the west. In the south, the country borders the Saudi Arabian Rub al-Khali Desert.

The emirates and big cities are connected by wide four and six-lane motorways, which are elaborately covered with greenery and lit at night. Signposting is excellent, written in both Arabic and English. The flow of motorway traffic approaching the cities

Coffee pot
Symbolic decoration; also for roundabouts

is maintained by means of bridges and underpasses as well as numerous roundabouts (abbreviated R/A).

The Black Gold Rush Brings Prosperity...

Only a few decades ago, the United Arab Emirates was among the poorest countries in the world. The desert soil made all kinds of agriculture impossible; there were hardly any schools, hospitals or asphalt streets. But everything changed when oil was discovered. The petrodollars were used to build a modern infrastructure: today the country's food self-sufficiency is largely guaranteed, and its health care system which counts among the best in the world, is for the most part free of charge to nationals.

Fine, white sand
The beaches of the UAE are only six hours away.

Water pipes
Try a water pipe with fruit-flavoured tobacco in one of the traditional coffee houses.

Spoilt for choice
In Gold Souk, all that sparkles is the genuine article.

Modern desert sport
The desert offers various activities to sports enthusiasts in the UAE.

Wild Wadi
Dubai's theme park has the longest water slide in Arabia.

Oases
More and more desert land is irrigated and used for agriculture.

The population enjoys all the conveniences of modern life without ever having to pay taxes. The dramatic development of the UAE is closely linked to one name: the late Sheikh Zayed bin Sultan Al Nahyan, Emir of Abu Dhabi, who ruled the Gulf country for thirty years.

...and Prosperity Brings Education

In the early 1950s the only educational institutions in the UAE were the mosque schools, or kuttabs, where boys were taught to read and write in order to recite the Qur'an. The first modern school was founded in Sharjah in 1953 with support from the British. The first school in Abu Dhabi opened in 1959, and when Sheikh Zayed came to power, the first school for girls was founded here. The quality of education has rapidly improved since compulsory education finally became statutory in 1972.

The country's first university was founded in 1977 in Al Ain (Abu Dhabi); before that, students from the UAE went to study in Great Britain or the United States. The Ajman University of Science & Technology and the Gulf Medical College – both in Ajman – are funded by the central government, as is the University of Sharjah and the American University of Sharjah, which teaches economics. Generous grants allow all citizens of the United Arab Emirates to study abroad.

Burj Al Arab
The luxury hotel has become one of Dubai's hallmarks.

Tourist Paradise

It is only a six-hour flight to escape the cold European winter. The sheikhdoms provide sunshine galore, wide sandy beaches, bright colourful landscapes and the crystal clear water of the Arabian Gulf. Furthermore, tourists and business travellers appreciate the relaxed atmosphere and the Emirates' high level of security. It is absolutely safe to roam the city streets, even after dark.

Facts

The United Arab Emirates consists of seven sheikhdoms, which were unified as one federal state in December 1971. Despite being a desert nation, the various emirates feature a surprisingly broad variety of landscapes.

Nature

Natural Environments

The United Arab Emirates is situated in the eastern part of the **Arabi-an plate**. This enormous landmass once covered the southern hemisphere before splitting into several pieces during the Mesozoic Era (250–265 million years ago). When the plates collided in the Tertiary Period (65 million years ago) the sediments of the Tethys Ocean were thrust upwards to form mighty mountain ranges. A separation of the Arabian and the African plates created the Red Sea and the Syrian rift, which today extends from the Ghab basin, through the Jordan rift valley, to the Gulf of Aqaba. According to recent scientific study, the Arabian plate is slowly drifting northward. It has been calculated that the plate has shifted around 100km/62mi over the last 100 million years.

Geology

> ## Baedeker TIP
>
> ### Living desert
> Explore the fascinating beauty and vibrancy of the unique desert ecosystem by visiting the exhibitions and outdoor enclosures of Sharjah Desert Park between Sharjah and Al-Dhaid (Sharjah Airport Road, Dhaid Highway, Junction no. 8).

Around two thirds of the United Arab Emirates is made up of **sandy desert**. The rest of the country is covered by **rocky desert** and savannah-type **semi desert**. The sandy desert consists mainly of **dunes**, which move with the wind away from the sea, constantly building new formations up to 150m/492ft high.

Deserts, dunes and mountains

The **Hajar Mountains** are situated along the Oman border in the eastern part of the United Arab Emirates, reaching heights of up to 1,000m/3,281ft. Steep canyons and wide valleys are characteristic of this rugged limestone mountain range. Rainfall and ground water supplies on the western side have led to the settlement of the region, with agricultural areas such as Masafi and ► Hatta. On the eastern side, a 5km/3.1mi-wide plain stretches out to the ocean. As an extension of the Omani Batinah plain in the southern Fujairah Emirate, it is particularly fertile.

◄ *Hajar Mountains*

The coastline is distinctive in its numerous off-shore islands and sandbanks. Off the coast of Abu Dhabi, there are around 200 of these small and sometimes miniature islands, ranging from sandbanks of just a few square metres to larger islands such as **Bani Yas** and **Umm al-Nar**, the latter of which is home to a significant archaeological site, as well as a refinery and a desalination plant. The coastline is charac-

Islands and inlets

← *The ruins of the Shimal fortress near Ras Al Khaimah are a reminder of the region's bellicose past.*

Dromedaries have adapted to the extreme desert climate.

terized by countless inlets or narrow creeks (khor), which sometimes extend far inland. Nearly all coastal towns of the Emirates are situated along these inlets.

Wadis   In the UAE and on the entire Arabian peninsula, there are no large rivers which carry water all year round. During the winter months, the seasonal rain water collects in the wadis or dry riverbeds, which sometimes grow briefly into raging torrents.

Groundwater reserves from greater depths first fostered the development of **oasis settlements**. Today, the mostly sandy Emirate of Abu Dhabi encompasses two extensive oasis regions, Al Ain and Liwa, both of which are used for agriculture, especially the latter.

While the oasis town of Al Dhaid supplies the Sharjah Emirate with agricultural products, the Emirate of Ras Al Khaimah uses the Digdagga oasis to raise cattle and grow dates. The Dibba oasis on the northern coast is shared by the sheikhdoms of Fujairah and Sharjah and the Sultanate of Oman.

Facts and Figures *United Arab Emirates*

©Baedeker

nited Arab
Emirates

Location
► Arabian Peninsula
► 22° to 26° north latitude and
52° to 56° east longitude

Area
► 77,700 sq km/30,000 sq mi (including
islands 83,600 sq km/32,280 sq mi)
► Neighbouring countries:
Saudi Arabia, Oman

Emirates
► Abu Dhabi, Ajman, Dubai, Fujairah, Ras
al-Khaimah, Sharjah, Umm al-Quwain

Capital city
► City of Abu Dhabi

Largest cities
► City of Abu Dhabi (470,000 residents),
City of Dubai (950,000 residents),
City of Sharjah (450,000 residents),
Al Ain (250,000 residents)

Form of government
► Federation
(since 2 Dec. 1971)

Head of state
► President:
Sheikh Khalifa Bin-Zayed al-Nahyan
(also Emir of Abu Dhabi)
► Prime Minister:
Sheikh Maktoum Bin-Rashid al-
Maktoum (also Emir of Dubai)

Population
► 3.7 millions

Population density
► 44 residents/sq km
(116 residents/sq mi)

Languages
► Arabic, English

State religion
► Islam

Economy
► Main sectors of the economy:
production of mineral oil and
natural gas, trade, tourism

Currency
► Dirham (Dh)
1 Dirham = 100 Fils

Time
► GMT + 4 hours
(during the summer:
GMT + 3 hours)

Water

Drinking water is an extremely precious resource in the United Arab
Emirates. Constant population growth has led to an enormous increase in the demand for already scarce water supplies. Furthermore,
the uncontrolled building of wells caused the groundwater level to
sink so dramatically that in 1992 the northern emirates prohibited
the drilling of additional wells. The building of desalination plants

Dubai's golf courses use up 4 million litres/1 million US gal of water every day.

was an attempt to satisfy the growing demand for water. Between 1970 and 1995, fresh water production increased from 5 million litres/1.3 million US gal to 212 million litres/56 million US gal per day, and with the implementation of a new desalination plant in Abu Dhabi, the »Al-Taweelah Plant«, the production of drinking water grew to 450 million litres/119 US gal per day.

In earlier centuries, a sophisticated **irrigation system** saw to it that spring water from the oases made landscapes thrive. Canals known as aflaj (singular: falaj), made either of stone or clay and later also of cement, carried precious water to the fields and gardens. However, these **artificial rivers** not only nurtured this »green paradise«, they also provided the drinking water supply for the population (▶Baedeker Special p. 214).

Flora

Vegetation in the UAE is sparse. Both in the coastal and the mountainous regions, the annual rainfall is not enough to support plant cover on the ground. Moreover, the salination of the desert allows only

The lush gardens and parks are popular as play areas and picnic grounds.

a few particularly resistant plants can thrive. The **acacia** is well adapted to the climate, as can be seen from its fine pinnate leaves and thin thorns. Equally resistant to the dry conditions is the fast-growing and originally Australian **eucalyptus tree**.

The branches of the umbrella tree, from the **Malvaceae** family (Thespesia populnea), form a dense, evergreen canopy resembling the shape of an umbrella. The species sprouts pretty, little yellow blossoms with red dots. Its fruit is not edible, even though they resemble apples.

 Millions of trees

- As part of a massive afforestation scheme, 140 million trees, including 40 million palm trees, have been planted throughout the Emirates. Date palm and olive trees not only enrich the landscape, they also ensure rich harvests. In ancient times, the extremely undemanding olive tree was highly valued as a cultivated plant.

One of the most flashy »newcomers« to the Arabian Gulf is the **Flamboyant tree**. Originally from Madagascar, between February and April it bears fiery red and orange blossoms.

As the United Arab Emirates became increasingly wealthy from oil sales, it began to **green the desert**. Trees and plants that are resistant to extreme heat, dryness and drought were imported.

By means of advertising campaigns, the government now tries to convince citizens of the importance of a green country. Schools organize special project weeks where children learn more about native and foreign vegetation, climatic zones and environmental protection.

Oryx antelopes have been successfully resettled.

Every year since 1981, 15 April has been »Tree Day«, a festive event with speeches, dance performances and the planting of numerous trees. The efforts have been a great success: so far, five percent of the land in the Emirate of Dubai has already been covered with greenery. The ultimate goal is eight percent, which corresponds with the inhabited area of the emirate.

Fauna

Besides dromedaries (▶ Baedeker Special p. 230), the UAE provides a habitat for around two dozen mammal species, some of which are endemic to the Gulf and some of which originate from other regions of the Arabian Peninsula and Africa. At the top of the food chain is the **leopard**, whose population has shrunk to only around a hundred animals. Indeed, there haven't been any leopard sightings in the UAE in quite some time. The elegant big cat mainly hunts in the mountainous regions of the Arabian Peninsula, and feeds on wild goats, rodents and birds.

Gazelles and antelopes
In the UAE, there are numerous species of gazelles and antelopes. The **Arabian mountain gazelle**, which is now only rarely found in the wild, lives primarily in mountainous regions. The **oryx antelope** is one of the most striking, but also most uncommon species.

In summer, the fur of this shy animal with two long, pointed horns turns almost completely white. The oryx antelope, once found across the entire Arabian Peninsula and North Africa, nearly became extinct as a result of excessive hunting. At the beginning of the 20th century, only few small herds lived in the Emirates, the Sultanate of Oman and Yemen. In Oman, the last of these animals to live in the wild were killed in 1972. Since then there have been attempts to resettle the oryx antelope, which has been added to the list of protected species. As part of a project financed by the World Wildlife Fund (WWF), animals bred in the

? DID YOU KNOW ...?

■ ... that the »mythical« unicorn is a creature that actually existed? In the 5th century BC Egyptians used to tie the horns of young oryx antelopes so that they would grow together as one. This is how the unicorn, the animal of legend, was »created«.

US have been resettled in several herds in Oman and the Emirates. Now there are over 1,000 animals living in the UAE.

The caracal lynx, or **desert lynx**, lives all across the Arabian Peninsula and mainly hunts at night for birds and small rodents. During the heat of day the caracal, which survives on very little water, hides in cool dens and retreats.

The **red fox** is the most common of foxes. The animal mainly lives in desert regions, but it can also be found at the edge of cities.

Desert hares and **jumping mice** are among those mammal species which can occasionally be spotted in the Sharjah Desert Park.

Other mammals

Reptiles are perfectly adapted to the Gulf's arid desert climate, which provides ideal living conditions for animals which are able to absorb warmth from their surroundings and survive for days without water. As a result, there are plenty of reptile species living in the UAE. The largest among the lizard family is the **desert monitor**, with a body length of over a metre (3 feet). The reptile with its serra-

> ## ! Baedeker TIP
>
> ### A paradise
> The mangrove reserve south of Fujairah at the Gulf of Oman is a paradise, and not only for aquatic birds. A plethora of coastal flora and fauna thrive in the brackish water area near the town of Khor Kalba. Equipped with a pair of binoculars, enough patience and a bit of luck, it is possible to observe herons, kingfishers and sea cows.

ted, spiky tail is harmless to humans and mainly feeds on small birds, mice and insects. Do beware of some snake species, however. Among the most venomous are the **horned viper**, which likes to sunbathe in the desert.

Bird life in the United Arab Emirates is enormously diverse. Colin Richardson, author of the standard reference book *The Birds of the United Arab Emirates*, lists more than 400 different species. During the winter half-year in Europe, migratory birds from Europe, Siberia and Central Asia rest here on their way to Africa and India.

Birds

The **greater flamingo** hibernates in Dubai Creek. Up to 2,000 of these majestic birds are counted each year, which makes Dubai the home of the largest flamingo colony on the Arabian Peninsula. Sheikh Muhammad bin Rashid Al Maktoum, Crown Prince of Dubai and a well-known bird-lover, regularly has the flamingos fed high-carotene food to help them keep their bright pink feathers.

Flamingos

Over the previous decades, the abundance of marine wildlife has been reduced by poor environmental conditions and increased fishing, yet divers and snorkelers are still presented with a varied and fascinating **underwater world**. Along the eastern coast of the United Arab Emirates, divers can fully appreciate the amazing world of the

Marine wildlife

Jockey and horse in deep concentration before the first race of the day

»THE NOBLEST ANIMAL OF ALL«

Bedouin works of art and tribal records show that horses were bred on the Arabian Peninsula as early as 2000 BC. Arabian thoroughbreds are considered the world's most beautiful horses; the rather small and delicate animals are intelligent, fast and very attached to people. This noble desert creature is particularly known for its stamina: it is said that a thoroughbred Arabian horse can easily gallop for seven hours without stopping.

Fast and tough

It must have been significant to the development of the Arabian horse's distinctive features that the Bedouins

»Then God took a handful of wind and created a chestnut-brown horse.«

hardly interfered with nature during breeding, despite the fact that only half of the year's foals survived the difficult climatic conditions on the Arabian Peninsula, with temperatures of over 50°C/122°F.

Systematic breeding of Arabian horses began in Spain after it was conquered by the Arabian army in the 8th century, and reached a climax in the 16th century in the region of what is now Poland. Polish breeding mares became so renowned that even the Spanish court purchased them.

Today Arabian horses are bred worldwide. Crossbreeding with other species has brought about the Anglo-Arab horse, which is particularly known for its speed and tenacity.

The horse myth

To the Bedouins and the Arabian nobility, horses are true »objects of desire«. Even the Qur'an praises the animals: »Then God took a handful of wind and created a chestnut-brown horse. He exclaimed: I create thee, Oh Arabian. To thy forelock, I bind Victory in battle. On thy back, I set a rich spoil and a Treasure in thy loins. I establish thee as one of the Glories of the Earth. I give thee flight without wings.«

According to old accounts, **Prophet Muhammad** took 100 horses with him on his departure from Mecca, but only five survived the strenuous journey. These five are believed to be the progenitors of all Arab horses. With his horse, *Burak*, Muhammad

Motto of the Dubai World Cup: once a winner, always a millionaire

also rode towards heaven. In the Dome of the Rock of Jerusalem a hoof print is still visible in the stone.

The sport of kings

Besides camel racing and falcon hunting, horse racing is considered the kings' sport in modern Arabian society. The four race tracks in the UAE host weekly races during the

world. Hosted by the Dubai Racing Club, the race is held every year in March and attracts members of the ruling families of Dubai and Abu Dhabi, as well as renowned breeders and race horse owners.

The horses are trained in luxury training stables. Sheikh Mohammed Bin-Rashid al-Maktoum, the UAE's prime minister, is owner of the Zabeel

od exclaimed: I create thee, Oh Arabian. To thy forelock, I bind tory in battle. On thy back, I set a rich spoil and a Treasure in thy ns. I establish thee as one of the Glories of the Earth. I give thee flight without wings.«   (Qur'an)

winter months. Usually six races are held during the course of one afternoon or evening; winners receive trophy money or other prizes.

Though admission is free, spectators have a chance to win as well. As in all Islamic countries, betting is prohibited in the United Arab Emirates; however, visitors can enter their favourite horse on a card, free of charge. Those who pick the winning horse for all races receive a cash prize from the host.

Dubai World Cup

With prize money of over US$6 million, the Dubai World Cup boasts the highest remuneration in the

Stables. Around 140 horses are cared for by an equal number of keepers, while two dozen jockeys prepare them for their performance on the racetrack.

The animals are kept in air-conditioned stables. Their feed – including honeyed oats and vitamin power drinks – are flown in from overseas. The paths between the stables are covered with synthetic flooring to prevent hoof or leg injuries. Veterinarians and horse dentists are on call around the clock.

The 2007 Dubai World Cup was won by *Invasor*, ridden by Fernando Jara and owned by Sheikh Hamdan bin Rashid Al Maktoum.

Flamingo colony in front of modern Dubai's skyline

Indian Ocean with its tropical corals and exotic fish. The **coral reefs**, covered with colourful brain and plate corals, are particularly stunning. Divers are surrounded by whole colonies of fragile seahorses and, at times, even come across the odd **reef shark**.

Water snakes Be careful with venomous water snakes, which occasionally appear. The various species include the **annulated sea snake**, which can reach a length of up to 3m/9.8ft.

Sea cows The sandy ocean floor all along the western shore of the Emirates is only rarely deeper than 30m/98ft and often covered with sea-grass – ideal living conditions for the rare sea cow, which belongs to the Sirenia family. The Arabs also call it Arous al-Bahr, **»bride of the sea«**. These 3m/10ft-long mammals can reach an age of 70 years old and weigh around 500kg/1,100lb. They feed on plants and live in herds of four to ten animals. Today, the sea cow is a protected species, and the approximately 5,000 animals living in the Arabian Gulf consitute the world's second largest sea cow population after Australia.

Dolphins and whales It is also possible to see dolphins and whales in the Emirates' waters. There are almost two dozen species in the Arabian Gulf and the Indian Ocean, including humpback whales, blue whales, fin whales and false killer whales.

There are numerous animal protection organizations in the UAE. **Animal protection**
The Sharjah Desert Park, for example, was founded in 1992. It now
also includes a museum, which familiarizes visitors with the desert
ecosystem and its inhabitants.

The National Avian Research Center (NARC) aims to preserve rare   ◄ NARC
bird species in the United Arab Emirates. At their research centre in
Sweihan, Abu Dhabi, birds from
the zoos of Dubai, Al Ain and the
private zoos of the royal families
are bred and then transferred to
nature reserves. The NARC's essential goal, however, is to breed the
houbara, the bird which is the
Arabs' preferred choice of prey for
falcon hunting. This timid desert
bird can be found in all arid zones
of the earth.

The **Arabian Leopard Trust** (ALT)
is a non-governmental organization whose aim is to explore and
improve the living conditions of
endangered desert animals.

> **!** *Baedeker* TIP
>
> **Bird-watching in the desert**
> Situated in a mangrove swamp just a few miles
> south of Dubai is the Khor Dubai Wildlife
> Sanctuary, the most important bird sanctuary in
> the Emirates. Another sanctuary is located right
> in the middle of the desert: Al Wathba Lake,
> around 40km/25mi south-east of Abu Dhabi City
> along the Al Ain Truck Road. Some 200 bird
> species live and breed at this 5 sq km/1.9 sq mi
> lake. For more information call the Emirates Birds
> Records Committee in Dubai, tel. 04/3 48 52 77.

Population · Politics · Economy

Nationals and Expatriates

The local Arab population, who refers to itself as nationals or locals,   **Locals**
are of Bedouin origin. Even up until the early sixties, more than half
of the population led nomadic lives. The individual emirates were
founded according to ancient tribal regions which had developed
over centuries. Today, the emirates' inhabitants comprise the members of several tribes, primarily the nomadic **Bani Yas** and the seafaring **Qawasim** who ruled the Gulf region from the 18th century.
The Qawasim's preferred tribal area was in the region of Ra's al-
Khaymah; the Sharjah settlement, however, also dates back to this
tribe. Originally from central Arabia, the Bani Yas always settled
around the oases of Liwa during the summer months and eventually
founded Abu Dhabi.

Of the UAE's population, 85% consists of foreigners, and they are   **Expatriates**
the reason, besides oil, for this new state's current wealth. It is the
expatriates (foreign workers) who keep the system in the Gulf running: most of the work in the UAE is done by foreigners. Local families often hire several foreign cleaning ladies, nannies and a chauf-

Nationals strolling along Abu Dhabi's Corniche

feur, in addition to a gardener – mostly from India or Sri Lanka – and a chef from Pakistan or Yemen. Bankers and managers from larger firms or hotels are originally from Europe or the US, while managers from small or mid-sized firms may also come from Arab countries and Asia. Technicians are usually from Europe and the US, as are physicians, though they increasingly come from Egypt and Jordan. Hotel staff is either Indian or Filipino, while arduous manual labour is done by Ceylonese, Pakistanis, Indians or Bengalis.

In the course of nationalizing the job market, Dubai made an attempt in 1996 to reduce the number of foreigners, and expelled 250,000 foreigners from the country. A rash decision, as it quickly turned out – hotels and restaurants were soon understaffed and construction building projects were delayed or even stopped: as a result, the measure was postponed. Now education schemes, awards and other incentives are offered to get the local population to work.

»Blood is thicker than water«

■ This Arab saying describes the family ties upon which the Bedouins' social life is grounded. Particularly in Arab circles of power, blood relations are of fundamental importance. Even members of the ruling families of Maktoum (Dubai) and Nahyan (Abu Dhabi) who are not in political power profit from their membership of the clan, at least financially – receiving a generous appanage.

Multicultural Dubai Dubai is distinctly multicultural: the emirate's foreign population originates from 136 countries, primarily from India, Pakistan, Sri

Expatriates building a dhow, the Arabs' traditional trading ship

Lanka, the Philippines, Egypt, Lebanon and Palestine. The overwhelming majority is forced to live in the Emirates without their wives or relatives. An immigrant worker's family receives a residence permit only with a minimum salary of 4,000 dirham per month as well as a written declaration of consent from the employer. However, foreign workers are willing to accept such restrictions, as the tax-free wages in the UAE are many times higher than what they would earn in their home country. In addition, residents of the Emirates are entitled to free health care.

Religion

Islam, the youngest of the five world religions, is the country's state religion. The Islamic confession of faith proclaims: »I bear witness that there is no god but Allah, and Muhammad is his messenger«, which in Arabic is: »La illaha illa Allah, Muhammad rasul Allah.« **State religion**

The emergence of the world religion of Islam is closely linked to the life of **Prophet Muhammad** who was born in Mecca in 570 as Abu al-Qasim Muhammad ibn 'Abd Allah ibn 'Abd al-Muttalib. At the age of 25, he married the 40-year old merchant's widow Khadija, his former employer. As a caravan leader, he frequently underwent long journeys and occupied himself with religious topics. In 610, »God's Prophet« Muhammad began preaching the messages that the archangel Gabriel had revealed to him. Part of this new doctrine, which Muhammad had founded, was his claim to worship only one god, to **Emergence of Islam**

Female students on campus at the American University in Sharjah

In the Emirates, mostly only visiti Saudi Arabian we who are veiled.

LIVING WITHOUT THE VEIL

The United Arab Emirates and Bahrain are considered the most liberal countries on the Arabian Peninsula. Unlike in conservative Saudi Arabia, where women must wear a veil when in public, they are not required to in the UAE. They can move freely and also study abroad. More than half of all university students in the country are female.

The Western media usually portrays Arab women as oppressed and without any rights. Furthermore, Gulf visitors from Western countries who see women wearing a face mask or veil jump to the conclusion that they have low social status.

According to **Islamic law**, a man may have four wives; however, with the exception of the upper class and government circles, monogamy is preferred, if only for financial reasons. The Qur'an states that each of a man's wives must be given the same property and rights.

In most Arab countries, girls stay unveiled only until puberty

While men represent the family in public, women are the guardians and keepers of the home. They administer their own capital and live a self-determined life, in accordance with the prevailing morals and values.

Marriage and family

Marriage and family have always had **absolute priority** in the lives of Arabs. In the Arab upper class, it is still mostly the parents who choose the groom as a wedding is primarily a matter between families and not so much of the two individuals involved.

The proposal is made by the father of the groom. He and the bride's family negotiate on the dowry, which on average amounts to 100,000 AED (£13,500). From the state's wedding fund, instigated by late President Sheikh Zayed in order to restrict marriages with foreign partners, all married couples from the UAE are given a house and 70,000 AED (£9,500).

Domestic sphere

In Islam, the home is traditionally a sphere of absolute privacy, a kind of untouchable, sanctified world. This also explains why an Arab woman should always wear a veil when she leaves her home. By covering herself, she can then take the protectiveness of her home outside.

The Arab expression for house is »dar«, and means private living space. On the Arabian Peninsula, it is deemed indecent to inquire about the health of wives or daughters. The proper and discreet way is to inquire about the well-being of the house, including all family members.

Everyday life

A woman's most important contacts are her female relatives and friends. When it comes to everyday life in the Emirates, local women are still only vaguely present for tourists and visitors. If at all, they are seen in the lobbies of luxury hotels or in the air-conditioned and shiny chrome shop-ping malls of Dubai and Abu Dhabi. While most women wear the latest fashion, they like to cover their clothes with a black abaya garment.

Women's Federation

A woman's daily routine is subject to a steady rhythm: they spend most of the day housekeeping and raising their children. However, they still have plenty of free time as it is customary to have foreign house servants.

The courses organized by the **UAE Women's Federation** are very popular, with subjects including a wide range of art history, art education and languages. The renowned organization was founded by the late president's wife, Sheikha Fatma Bint-Mubarak. She strongly believes that women should take part in all sections of economy and culture. The UAE is therefore unique among the Gulf States in the fact that women can hold positions in the armed forces and work in many other occupations.

free the slaves and to give alms. The initially small number of Muhammad's followers was opposed by an increasing number of Meccan citizens who feared that this new doctrine would worsen their financial position, as they were supposed to pay the regular alms tax while no longer profiting from the »heathen« pilgrimages to the pre-Islamic Kaaba shrine. Eventually, Muhammad left Mecca on 15 July 622 to settle further north in the city of Yathrib (Medina). This date also marks the beginning of the Islamic calendar. In 630, after the victory in Badre over the citizens of Mecca, Muhammad returned to the city and made it the centre of his new religion.

The Prophet's revelations are written in the **114 suras** of the **Qur'an**. Believers recognize it as »the literal word of God«. The Qur'an provides guidance in nearly all aspects of life, from health care to marriage, even inheritance issues and disputes with neighbours.

! **Baedeker TIP**

Visiting a mosque

Generally, mosques are not accessible to non-Muslims. Dubai provides a unique opportunity for visiting an Arabic house of God. The Centre for Cultural Understanding organizes regular guided tours for tourists through the Grand Mosque and Jumeirah Mosque, two of the most important and beautiful buildings in the city (bookings Sat–Wed 9am–2pm, Thu 11.30am–2pm, Beach Centre, Level 2, Jumeirah Beach Road, tel. 04 / 3 44 77 55 or directly at the meeting point on Thu and Sun at 10am at Jumeirah Mosque).

Basic duties of Islam   The **submission to God**, which is also what Islam literally means, secures believers an afterlife in paradise. This, however, means that the Qur'an commandments must be observed, particularly the five basic duties: the creed of Islam, the five daily prayers, observing the fasting rules during the month of Ramadan, almsgiving and the pilgrimage to Mecca.

Ramadan   During Ramadan, the ninth month of the Islamic calendar, every Muslim must fast according to the laws of the Qur'an, as prescribed by the second sura. This means that between sunrise and sunset no one is allowed to eat, drink or smoke. Excluded from these laws are the sick, children, pregnant women, travellers and hard labourers. The fasting period lasts 29 days and ends with a three-day celebration of breaking the fast, »Eid al-Fitr«.

Mosques   Usually, mosques may not be entered by non-Muslims, even though these buildings – unlike Christian churches – are not sacred but purely meant as **congregation rooms**. The term mosque is derived from the Arabic word »masjid«, meaning to bow or to kneel in prayer.
The most important place in a mosque is the **»mihrab«**, which is built into the **qibla wall**. It is a semi-circular niche, which is finely ornamented in accordance with its significance. As proscribed by the

Oil wealth also brought numerous magnificent mosques to the Emirates.

Qur'an, the qibla indicates the location of the niche and the direction of prayer, facing towards Mecca. Also, every mosque has a **minaret**, a tower from where the muezzin, the caller, reminds his fellow believers to pray five times a day. Even the floor is important: rugs provide protection during prayer, as it is obligatory for the forehead to touch the floor several times. In order to meet the requirements of the ritual cleansing before each prayer, every mosque must always provide a source of water.

Although every town can have several mosques, there is one mosque – the Friday Mosque or Grand Mosque – which is the spiritual centre and is usually much bigger than the other mosques.

◀ Friday Mosque

The Islamic faith can be divided into two major religious denominations, which developed as a result of a dispute over the rightful successor of Muhammad. Besides the Qur'an, Sunni Muslims refer in their doctrine to the »sunnah«, the religious principles and laws taught by Prophet Muhammad. Elected successors, i.e. not related by blood, are also considered legitimate successors to Muhammad. The Shiites are regarded as the religious followers of the fourth Caliph Ali, son-in-law and cousin of Muhammad. They only accept direct descendants of Muhammad as the rightful successor of the Prophet.

Sunnis and Shiites

Glimpse into a prayer room of a mosque

Religious denominations in the UAE ▶ Around 80% of the Arab population in the UAE are Sunni Muslims; 20% follow Shia Islam. While the citizens of Abu Dhabi are nearly all Sunnis, Dubai is shared by Sunni (65%) and Shiite (35%) Muslims. The Emirates' east coast is mainly inhabited by Shiite communities.

Islamic calendar The Islamic calendar is based on the **lunar calendar**. One year consists of 354 or 355 days, i.e. eleven days shorter than the solar year of the Gregorian calendar. According to the Christian calendar, the Islamic calendar began on 15 July 622, in the year of the **Hijra**, when Prophet Muhammad withdrew from Mecca and settled in Medina. The year 2005 of the Gregorian calendar, for example, corresponds to the years 1425/1426 AH (anno hegirae) according to the Islamic calendar. The twelve lunar months are defined by the Qur'an, and each of them comprises 29 or 30 days.

Freedom of religion In the United Arab Emirates foreign workers are guaranteed freedom of religion, which means that there are also Christian churches and Hindu temples in Abu Dhabi, Dubai and Sharjah.

State and Society

Form of state and government On 2 December 1971, the United Arab Emirates was established as a **federal state** consisting of the seven emirates Abu Dhabi, Dubai, Sharjah, Ajman, Ras al-Khaimah, Umm al-Quwain and Fujairah. The state is governed by the Supreme Council of Rulers, made up of

United Arab Emirates Map

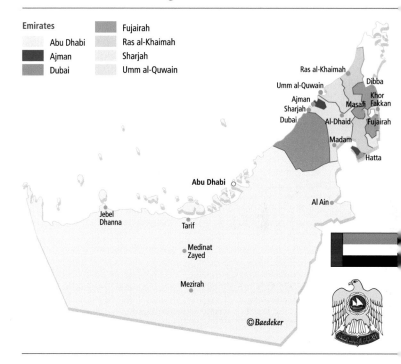

Emirates

Abu Dhabi
Ajman
Dubai
Fujairah
Ras al-Khaimah
Sharjah
Umm al-Quwain

Ras al-Khaimah
Umm al-Quwain
Ajman
Sharjah
Dubai
Dibba
Khor Fakkan
Masafi
Al-Dhaid
Fujairah
Madam
Hatta
Abu Dhabi
Al Ain
Jebel Dhanna
Tarif
Medinat Zayed
Mezirah

©Baedeker

the seven emirs. The Supreme Council determines the political direction and governs with support from the Council of Ministers, which is headed by the Vice President, and consists of 21 ministers with portfolios.

The Emir of Abu Dhabi, **Sheikh Khalifa Bin-Zayed al-Nahyan**, is President of the United Arab Emirates and Chairman of the Council of Rulers. The Prime Minister is **Sheikh Maktoum Bin-Rashid al-Maktoum**, the Ruler of Dubai. Each of the individual emirates are also run by ministries, which are mostly headed by a member of the royal family.

While the seven rulers attempt to reach consensus for the UAE, each emirate is run by an individual feudalistic government: the emir issues decrees, usually with the aid of one or more counsellors. Parties, unions and other forms of political participation of citizens are prohibited in the UAE. Within the framework of the federation, however, the sovereignty of the individual emirates is still very extensive. Common politics and legislation are restricted to foreign affairs and defence policy, matters of health and education, as well as sections of economy and law.

Welfare state   The citizens of the UAE live in a large welfare state. The ruling families distribute part of their wealth among their subjects and thereby
maintain their satisfaction and approval for political actions. The army, ministries and authorities are the most important employers for
the local population, whose remunerative working day usually ends
at around 2pm.

According to the tradition of Arab countries, the respective rulers always lend an ear to all questions and issues of their subjects. The
»open door« policy of government theoretically offers all citizens of
the United Arab Emirates the op-
portunity to discuss issues in person with the ruler of the emirate
or even with the president of the
country.

The United Arab Emirates signed
the Founding Charter of the **Gulf
Cooperation Council** (GCC) with
Bahrain, Oman, Kuwait, Qatar and
Saudi Arabia in Abu Dhabi in
1981. The goal of this union was
cooperation in the areas of foreign,
security and economic policy. The
political principles of the GCC are
defined by the Supreme Council,
which consists of the six heads of
state. It meets once a year and on
special occasions. The rotating presidency is held by one of the
member states on an annual basis.

A brief lesson in colours

■ The UAE flag consists of a vertical red band
covering the left third of the flag, and three
horizontal bands of green, white and black
(top to bottom). Green is found on most
Arabic flags. The first flag of Islam was also
green, which is said to date back to the
green of the Prophet Muhammad's turban.
Red is the colour for Arabic nationality, and
white was the prevailing colour for flags of
Arabic sheikhdoms in the 19th century. Black
is an element of the pan-Arab flag, created in
1918, and therefore an element of many
Arab national flags.

Judiciary   In the United Arab Emirates, legislation is largely based on Islamic
law, the **Sharia**. Traditionally, it is the sheikh's responsibility to pass
judgment. Legal cases involving foreigners, however, are almost
without exception tried before a court of law, according to principles
of law and order.

Economy

It was Allah who brought **oil** to the Emirates – to faithful Muslims,
at least, it is obvious that Allah gave his loyal followers black gold in
order to help them find fortune and happiness. The young state does
in fact owe its excellent economic circumstances to oil and gas, and
its population never needs to worry about money. The per-capita income in the United Arab Emirates is about 22,000 US dollars.

However, there are considerable differences between the individual
emirates in terms of general wealth and the deposits and quantity of
the extracted oil and gas. Abu Dhabi owns the largest oil and gas reserves, followed by the sheikhdoms of Sharjah and Dubai.

The United Arab Emirates is the founding member of **OPEC** (Organization of Petroleum Exporting Countries), which was established in 1974. While only a few years ago oil production and export were the key economic factors in the Gulf region, new business opportunities are now being opened up. Increasingly important for business development are oil-independent sectors, which make up nearly three quarters of the gross national product of the United Arab Emirates. In Dubai in particular, the diversification of the national economy is well advanced: commerce, industrial production and tourism make up about 90% of the gross national product.

Agriculture

At first glance, agricultural efforts seem rather futile in the face of the lack of water, the sandy desert, ground and its continuous salination, and the summer temperatures of up to 50°C/122°F. To counteract such miserable soil conditions, fruit and vegetables are grown in a mixture of sand, imported fertile soil and peat. For a number of years, agricultural research centres have been funded to experiment with hardy plants that can thrive even under the extreme climatic conditions of the Arabian Peninsula.

Due to the extensive **greening** of the desert, the agricultural area of the UAE has increased from 18,000ha/44,478ac in 1972 to more than 300,000ha/741,300ac to date. Meanwhile, the United Arab Emirates has become an exporter of fruit and vegetables, and in recent years even exports its grain production surpluses.

The World Trade Centre is the focus of business activity in Dubai.

Parallel to increased areas of cultivation and larger annual harvests, several canning factories have been established. The marketing of tomato ketchup and tinned tomatoes has been particularly successful – nearly half of the production is exported to Europe and to neighbouring Arab countries.

Dairy farming is also enormously successful in the UAE. Today, a total of around 30,000 cattle are reared to cover the population's demand for dairy products.

Dairying

Liwa Oases: enough water makes even the desert turn green.

Poultry farms Poultry farms are widely spread across the UAE and supply produce for both domestic and international markets.

Fishing The fishing waters of the Arabian Gulf are considered rich in both the amount of fish and the variety of different species. The annual fishing harvest amounts to about 80,000 tons. Most of the 20,000 tons of exported fish are tuna, mackerel and crab.

Oil and Gas

Genesis of oil Oil is found anywhere in the world where there is sedimentary rock. Millions of years ago, this rock formed from organic and inorganic sediment under immense pressure. Its numerous cavities were filled with individual oil drops, which had developed over millions of years from residual plant and animal microbes living in water. Dead organisms sank to the bottom of the sea where, as a result of oxygen deprivation, they did not dissolve, but instead created digested sludge. Anaerobic bacteria – which as the name suggests do not require oxygen – turned this digested sludge into oil, which was then covered by sediment. When the Earth's surface hardened, the oil was first pressed into the cavities of the sedimentary rock, then squeezed through until it reached impermeable rock layers, where it formed deposits (▶p. 38).

There is considerable variation regarding the amount of oil in each emitate: **Abu Dhabi** owns 94% of all deposits and produces about 84% of the UAE's output, followed by **Dubai** with approximately 14% of the production. In Sharjah, oil was found only in 1974, and much less than originally hoped. Moreover, oil that is produced on the Sharjah island of Abu Musa must be shared with Iran, which has claimed the island ever since 1974. But Sharjah also has large natural gas reserves, which are used to run the local light industry, which includes gas-driven public transport vehicles.

Oil deposits

? DID YOU KNOW ...?

- ... that the UAE owns about 10% of the world's known oil reserves? After Saudi Arabia and Iraq, the third largest reserves on the planet are located here. Studies have revealed that the country's oil reserves amount to an estimated 98 billion barrels. Based on the volume of current output, these reserves will last for more than 100 years.

Industry

The Emirate of Sharjah dominates industry with around half of the industrial production in the United Arab Emirates. The industrial areas of **Layya** and **Al Saja'a** now have the necessary infrastructure to

Sharjah's industry

Port Rashid – Dubai's gigantic trans-shipment hub

OIL PRODUCTION

Approx. 10% of the world's known oil reserves are located in the territory of the United Arab Emirates; only Saudi Arabia and Iraq have even larger reserves. The people here are convinced that it was Allah himself who brought oil to the countries of this region, and bestowed wealth upon them. It is true that the annual income per capita of $22,000 is enormous, considering the UAE would be one of the world's poorest countries if it wasn't for the oil.

① Oil rig
The most significant part of an oil production plant is the oil rig. Drill poles of up to 9m/9.9yd each and screw-thread connections are driven up to 10,000m/10,940yd underground. If the pressure of the oil deposit is big enough, the oil is pumped to the surface. If the pressure is not enough, water or steam is pumped through additional bore holes in order to make the oil rise to the top.

② Hoist
All drill poles hang on a hoist attached to the steel frame of the oil rig.

A tough job: workers on the oil derrick in the Dubai desert

③ Settling tank
First, a sieving procedure removes rough debris from the extracted mineral oil which is then channelled into the settling tank where the sediment (e.g. sand) settles to the bottom.

④ Mud pump
The settled sediment on the tank floor is removed. What remains is pure crude oil, which is channelled through pipelines for further processing.

⑤ Drive units
Engines with a power of up to 4,000 kW start rotating a tray (»lazy Susan«), which is linked to the drill poles. These drill poles are then driven into the ground with an attached boring tool.

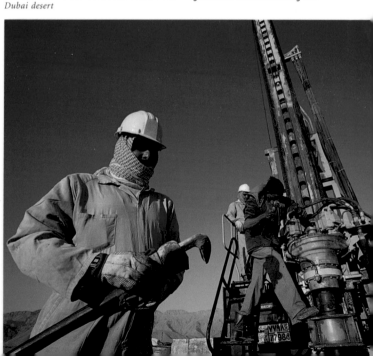

Jumeirah Beach Hotel is synonymous with luxury beach holidays in Dubai.

Today, the comparatively liberal Emirate of Dubai attracts the most visitors. For years, the country has been tapping international tourism as a lucrative source of revenue by building luxurious hotels.

Abu Dhabi is currently making great efforts to participate in international tourism. It has founded its own airline (Etihad Airways), undertaken a costly modernization of the city, and planned and built the kind of new hotels which cause a sensation, including the luxury Emirates Palace Hotel (ill. p.150).

History

Until recently, the United Arab Emirates did not invest in historical research and archaeological excavation. Therefore many periods of its national history remain largely unexplored.

Archaeology in the UAE

The UAE is still quite new to scientific research of the country's pre- and early history. Before oil was discovered, it was mainly foreign research institutions which conducted archaeological studies in the Arabian Gulf. Today, the now wealthy countries have funds of their own.

Archaeological exploration of the emirates began in 1953, with a discovery on **Umm al-Nar**, a small island off the coast of Abu Dhabi. The many flints found in the sand, which were once employed as tools, gave the island its name: Umm al-Nar, meaning »**mother of fire**«. Today, this expression is synonymous with the period between 2500 and 1800 BC. Ancient settlements were discovered; ceramics, jewellery and weapons were found in communal graves. Numerous gravestones displaying drawings of camels were an indication that even at this early point in time, pack animals were domesticated in the Gulf.

Early History
(4000 BC – 6th century AD)

4000–2000 BC	Mesopotamian settlements on the east coast of the Arabian Peninsula
1000 BC	Incense trade with Oman leads to the expansion of settlements inland.
2nd century AD	With the breaching of the Marib dam, more settlers move to the area of the present-day UAE.

First settlers

The first inhabitants of the Arabian Peninsula were presumably hunters and gatherers who lived in this area toward the end of the **Old Stone Age** (17000–8500 BC). The earliest settlements in the area of the UAE, from around 4000 BC, were located in Ras al-Khaimah. Round stone graves found north of the Khatt hot springs, as well as flint tools and arrowheads, give an indication of an ancient culture. Grave findings on the island of Umm al-Nar are evidence for extensive trade relations of an already developed civilization. During the **Bronze Age** (2000–1300 BC), the area of what is now known as the United Arab Emirates was the main supplier of bronze to Mesopotamia (Iraq). Archaeological excavations have shown that the traditional »arish« style of housing was already in use then.

← *Dubai's history comes to life at the National Museum.*

The Hili Tomb in Al Ain is the most important archaeological site in the country.

Mesopotamia Mesopotamia, the country situated between the Euphrates and Tigris rivers, is one of the most ancient civilizations of Arabia. Apart from references in the Old Testament mentioning a thriving region, nothing was known about this early society for a long time. In 1765, the German geographer Carsten Niebuhr discovered cuneiform writings in the Persian imperial city of **Persepolis** that were composed by the Archaemenid kings Darius (521–485 BC) and Xerxes (485–465 BC). The texts were deciphered in 1802 by linguist Georg Friedrich Grotefend. Eventually thousands of clay tablets were found, which belonged to Assurbanipal, King of Assyria (668–626 BC), and included accounts of the Sumerians, Assyrians and Babylonians. The Babylonian-Assyrian cuneiform tablets of the Mesopotamians also revealed information about ancient civilizations in the Gulf region.

Sumerians As early as 3200 BC, the Sumerians, a non-Semitic people, settled in Mesopotamia and established city states along the lower reaches of the Euphrates and Tigris rivers. In 2900 BC, the Sumerians developed cuneiform writing, which is considered the oldest known form of written expression. Cuneiform was written on clay tablets, and the symbols were carved in with styluses.

Akkadians Around 2350 BC Semitic Akkadians started to settle in Mesopotamia. They founded the harbour city of Akkad, which also became the Akkadian capital, and traded with numerous remote cities and nations. Clay tablets include accounts of King Sargon of Akkad, who boasted that fully loaded ships from Meluhha, Dilmun and Magan berthed at his harbour. Meluhha was located in Pakistan, Dilmun was a region in the western part of the Arabian Gulf, and Magan was located in the area of what is now the UAE and Oman.

Along the Gulf coast, people settled in village communities surrounded by protective walls. One of the most significant sites from the Bronze Age is Shimal, in the Emirate of Ras al-Khaimah. Several communal graves were discovered here as well as in Qusais, Jumeirah and along the hills of Jebel Hafit near Al Ain.
Shimal

In Ad Door near Umm al-Quwain stand the **ruins** of a **temple** from around 100 BC, in the vicinity of which pottery from India and Mesopotamia as well as Roman glassware have been found.
Ad Door

The Islamic Empire
(6th century – 15th century)

570	Birth of Prophet Muhammad
622	Beginning of the Islamic calendar and the Islamization of South Arabia
632	Death of Prophet Muhammad
644	Written summary of the Qur'an
661	Sunni and Shia schism

Islam, the youngest of the great monotheistic world religions, was first preached by **Muhammad Ibn Abd Allah** (570–632), later known as Prophet Muhammad, a merchant from Mecca. The year 622, when Muhammad and his followers retreated to Medina, also marks the beginning of the Muslim calendar. After Muhammad's death in 632, his father-in-law, **Abu Bakr**, was made his successor (632–634) and first caliph.
Development of Islam

In 635, the Arabian Peninsula became fully Islamized after the Battle at Dibba, a region which today belongs to the Emirate of Fujairah, and where local tribes had initially rejected the new religion. When Ali, cousin and son-in-law of Muhammad, became the fourth caliph in 656, the centre of Islam shifted from Medina to Iraq. With Ali's assassination in 661, Islam split into the two rival religious groups of **Shiite** and **Sunni** Muslims (►p. 31); the caliphate moved from Arabia to Damascus and with it the centre of Muslim power. The Holy Cities remained only spiritual centres.

*Caliph
Harun al-Rashid*

The elected caliph was succeeded by the **Umayyad** dynasty, which produced a total of 14 caliphs. In 750, it was overthrown by the Abbasid dynasty in Baghdad, which ruled until 1258. During the reign of **Harun al-Rashid** (786–809), one of the most famous Abbasid caliphs, Islamic culture became increasingly sophisticated.

For almost a thousand years, the harbour city of **Julfar** dominated the history of what is now known as the United Arab Emirates. The first references to this city can be found in Arab chronicles, which give accounts of a Mesopotamian army that stopped there in 696 on its way to Oman. In the following centuries, the city became a frequent site of battle. In 942, Julfar troops succeeded in freeing the cities of Baghdad and Basra from Persian invaders. Chinese and Vietnamese potsherds found in Julfar are indications of the extensive Asian trade of Arab sailors.

Portuguese Period
(16th century / 17th century)

1507	The Portuguese conquer Muscat (Oman) and erect forts on the eastern coast of the Arabian Peninsula.
1618	Founding of the British East India Company on the southwest coast of Yemen
1680	The Dutch establish trading posts on the Arabian Gulf.

Portugal as a colonial power

In 1498, the Portuguese discovered the sea route to India. Nothing now stood in the way of their territorial expansion in Arabia. In 1507, they conquered Muscat and gained control of the entrance to the Arabian Gulf, the Strait of Hormuz. Numerous forts were erected along the coast, but unlike Oman, the Portuguese found the southern part of the Gulf coast insignificant and useless for their strategic purposes. The European colonial power only occupied what is now called **Khor Fakkan** whose deep natural harbour aroused Portugal's interest. From there, they dominated the coast until far into the 17th century.

Many of the late medieval forts have been rebuilt or restored.

The great power of the Portuguese didn't stop piracy along the Gulf coast, but it did diminish it considerably. The pirates were members of the Qawasim tribe, whose settlement area was in what is now the Sheikhdom of Ras al-Khaimah. In the early 19th century the **Qawasim** owned a fleet of over 800 ships crewed by about 20,000 men. Slavery also thrived: Central African captives were carried off to gathering points along the coast where slave traders sold them to South Arabia.

Piracy on the Gulf Coast

◄ Slavery

Trucial States (17th century – 20th century)

18th century	Bedouins settle on the coasts of what is now the UAE.
1761	Foundation of Abu Dhabi
1841	Protectorate Treaties between the Emirates and Great Britain
1958	Oil is found in Abu Dhabi.
1971	Foundation of the United Arab Emirates

Great Britain's influence on the Gulf coast must be viewed in connection with the world power's increasing commitment to India. In 1608, the first ship of the British East India Company landed at the

Influence of Great Britain

Dubai at the estuary of Al-Khor in 1950

coast of the subcontinent. After the establishment of a **trading hub**, the British quickly began to explore the Gulf region. Under Shah Abbas, Persia allied itself with the East India Company in 1622, which led to the British successfully ousting the Portuguese from the Gulf region.

Development of the Sheikhdoms

During the 18th century, the Sheikhdoms of **Umm al-Quwain**, **Ajman** and **Sharjah** became the new settlements of the Bedouin tribes in the hinterland. Then **Abu Dhabi** was founded in 1761; and in 1833, under Sheikh Maktoum, Bedouins from the Bani Yas tribe first settled along the creek of **Dubai**.

»Pirate Coast«

When British ships were repeatedly attacked by the **Qawasim**, Europeans began referring to the Gulf region as the »Pirate Coast«. With support from the Sultan of Oman, the British government dispatched several warships. In 1819, they attacked Ras al-Khaimah, the Qasimi base, and burnt down forts in Umm al-Quwain, Ajman, Sharjah and Dubai. Eventually Great Britain and the Qawasim tribe negotiated. In the treaty of 1820, the rulers of the sheikhdoms on the Arabian Gulf agreed to stop raiding ships of the East India Company; in return, the British offered the sheikhdoms military protection. Several other truce treaties and agreements followed.

»Trucial Coast«

Due to the lack of clearly defined borders and a comprehensive country name, the emirates on the Arabian Gulf came to be called the **Trucial Coast**. In 1892, the sheikhdoms signed **»Exclusive Agreements«** thereby committing to deny other states the right to settle along their coasts, which was practically equivalent to status as a British protectorate.

In 1951, the British founded the »Trucial States Council«, the »Council of Emirs«, where controversial political issues were discussed. Nearly two decades later, in 1968, the British began to withdraw from all regions »east of Suez«, which suddenly forced the emirates to make decisions about their political future; vastly differing interests had to be taken into account. Great Britain urged them to form a federation.

The Council of Emirs in the 1970s

Eventually, on the initiative of Abu Dhabi and Dubai, the **United Arab Emirates** was formed on 2 December 1971, as a federation of states including the seven sheikhdoms of Abu Dhabi, Dubai, Sharjah, Ajman, Ras al-Khaimah, Umm al-Quwain and Fujairah.

The neighbouring sheikhdoms Qatar and Bahrain, which until then had also been under the British protectorate, decided to establish states of their own. Bahrain proclaimed independence on 15 August 1971, Qatar on 1 September in the same year.

»Trucial States Council«

Art and Culture

Islamic culture has bestowed upon the world a highly developed form of decorative art. The variety of techniques is extensive. The most significant among them, however, is calligraphy with its various scripts and arabesques.

Islamic Art

In the Islamic world, painting and sculpture are less significant art forms than the richly ornamental decorative art. Besides floral and geometrical motifs, this art form mainly employs Arabic writing, as Islamic law forbids the visual representation of God or people. In the Qur'an, however, there is no indication of such a prohibition; it is actually based upon a declaration by Muhammad that men and animals may be created by God alone.

Ornamentation

The art of calligraphy has always been highly valued in the Islamic world and is considered far more important than any other fine art, for »nothing is more rewarding than to write down God's words«. The formula »bismi allah« (»in the name of Allah«) is used repeatedly, as are the words »Allah« and »Muhammad«, in numerous different ways. Besides the sura of the Qur'an, lines of poetry, famous names and significant dates are also rendered in calligraphy. Almost every building in the Islamic world has some form of **calligraphy decoration** – lines of writing in flowing styles are used to frame windows, doors and niches. For scripts there is a distinction between italics and the older, kufic form of writing, which was simpler, less curved and therefore particularly suitable for writing on parchment or stone. The close connection between calligraphy and geometry becomes evident in the proportions of calligraphy, which vary according to geometrical figures and principles.

Calligraphy

◄ Kufic and italic writing

Alongside calligraphy, the arabesque was a preferred artistic form of expression. The decorative pattern contains **plant forms**, primarily tendrils, forming intricate lines in great numbers and variations. Floral forms are often combined with geometrical structures or characters.

Arabesque

Islamic Architecture

Arches have dominated the structures of Islamic architecture since the construction of the Great Mosque in Damascus in the early 8th century. During the same period, Islam's **decorative architecture** developed out of the building style in which columns were connected to form arcades, so that the area in between the arches could be decorated with ornaments and patterns, both vertically and horizontally. Mosque architecture always follows consistent decorative principles. The interior, usually covered by a dome, is decorated with ornaments and characters and often laid out with several layers of rugs. The **minaret** is a slender and often richly decorated tower rising above the mosque, from which the muezzin calls the faithful to prayer five times per day.

Mosques

← *Arabian gold jewellery is also richly ornamented.*

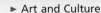

The key elements of the interior architecture are the prayer niche facing Mecca (**mihrab**) and the pulpit (**minbar**). There is often also an outer courtyard of the mosque, usually surrounded by arcades, which is where the facilities for ritual washing are located.

Islamic architecture typically developed on a local basis. Unlike in medicine or music, architecture was not considered an academic discipline, but a trade – knowledge that could be learnt by everyone. As builders were not organized into guilds and didn't tend to travel, knowledge about construction was hardly ever exchanged within the Arab world.

The design of **residential buildings** is based on the **principles of sacral architecture**. While the exterior seems fairly unadorned, the interior of the building unfolds in almost prodigal splendour. Arab housing areas and settlements are much more secluded than western cities or villages, and therefore largely hidden from passing tourists. The seemingly chaotic streets and alleys are arranged every which way, often ending in cul-de-sacs or narrow courtyards, but the

Filigree patterns cover the minarets and domes of mosques.

apparent chaos is there for a reason: the alleys which end suddenly in a complex of interlocking houses allow residents and clans the privacy they desire.

Furnishing ► To western tourists, Arab homes often seem surprisingly large. The extensive houses, however, also accommodate the numerous in-laws of a family, including their children. Small windows provide protection from the hot and often hostile environment outside, while the thick walls keep the rooms cool in summer. One room is reserved exclusively for men, the **mafraj**, which is traditionally located on the top floor. Here, the men of the house lounge on rugs and cushions after an opulent meal, drink tea and smoke a water pipe, while the ladies sit together in the rooms reserved for women. Even today, this tradition is still prevalent.

Free-standing defence towers were often extended and turned into mighty forts.

Forts

Even before the common era, settlers from the Umm al-Nar period erected stone towers, most likely used for observation and defence. With the Islamization of the Arabian Peninsula in the 7th century, the number and size of **watchtowers** increased. They were round and consisted partly of a very solid stone foundation, while the rest of the tower was made of air-dried mud bricks. The entrance was located on the level of the first floor and could only be reached via ladders or ropes. Over time, several towers were connected by stone or mud walls and created a **safe fortress** with an interior courtyard.

◀ Sanctuaries

Soon the Emirates had an extensive network of forts, which were often located on a hill or in the mountains overlooking the villages and oases. However, it proved necessary to extend the protected area in order to provide a sanctuary for citizens in the event of attack. The forts were increasingly based around water; living and storage rooms were built, as well as stables, and the interior courtyard was extended. Some forts were even traversed by a canal system, the aflaj (▶ Baedeker Special p.214), to irrigate the garden.

◀ Representational buildings

In the 17th century, defence buildings that were originally designed as forts also came to be used as **governors' residences** for the imam or emir. They included representative rooms, some of which where decorated with ceiling paintings and carvings. The mighty wooden gates to the fortress were decorated with iron and brass nails.

Of many forts, only the stone foundations as well as a few collapsed mud walls have remained. Today, these ruins are considered national monuments and have been elaborately restored using only original materials.

Arts and crafts

Ceramics are mainly produced in the Emirate of Ras al-Khaimah.

Silver jewellery has a long and important tradition in Arab countries. The silver **Maria Theresia thaler**, which was introduced in South Arabia in the 18th century, was used as payment for coffee and remained the valid currency in Yemen until 1968, but also served as material for creating masterpieces of filigree art. The 28g/1oz coin with a portrait of the Austrian Empress, first minted in 1741, was often incorporated into pieces of jewellery. Opulent earrings, necklaces and belts were adorned with corals and ochre and milk-coloured amber.

Variety of shapes ► Besides the traditionally Arabic and Islamic shapes, silversmiths took inspiration from the Asian and African cultures, incorporating finely crafted petal or leaf shapes. This filigree effect was increased by one special characteristic of the precious metal: silver oxidizes very quickly. Even when silver is polished, the dents in the finely chased jewellery keep their dark stains. The resulting three-dimensional effect gives silver its particular charm.

Gold jewellery is usually sold by weight.

In the neighbouring state of Oman silver jewellery is still very popular. In the silver city of **Nizwa**, dozens of silversmiths are still processing the precious metal using traditional methods. One centuries-old tradition has it that silver jewellery possesses magical powers. **Amulets** are said to protect their wearers from doom or the »evil eye«. Even children were given an amulet, a tradition which is to this day still widely practised on the Arabian Peninsula.

In parallel with changing tastes over the past decades, the silversmiths of the Emirates have become **goldsmiths**.

The centuries-old design tradition meant for oxidized silver brings about different results when applied to gold. For this reason, Arab gold jewellery hardly ever appeals to European tastes. Only very few workshops have developed a simpler vocabulary of design more suitable for gold.

Tradition is kept alive, and not just on national holidays.

Ceramics are mainly produced in Ras al-Khaimah. The local red clay   **Ceramics**
is processed into ceramic vessels for storing food, as well as jars, pots,
cups and mugs. **Mabkhar**, clay pots that are used as incense burners,
make popular souvenirs.

Arab Folklore

Folk music (► Baedeker Special p.56) and folk dance play a significant role at most traditional celebrations, particularly at weddings.
Aside from a few exceptions such as the »hair dance«, performed by
young, unveiled women in colourful dresses, it is only the men who
dance. The groups aren't fixed; every man is invited to participate.
The dancers move in a line or circle and clap their hands to the
rhythm of the drums or a tambourine.

Traditional Clothing

Traditional clothing in the Arabian Gulf is influenced by religious   **Male clothing**
laws and climate. The male population of the United Arab Emirates
prefers the »**dishdasha**«, an ankle-length, long-sleeved white caftan –
also coloured or striped in winter – usually made of cotton. For special occasions, a black or brown cape-like garment, embroidered

Strong emotions are roused by the masters of musical nuance.

Traditional m... dance in a m... ern setting

THE WONDERFUL WORLD OF MUSICAL NUANCE

Music has always been highly appreciated in Arab culture, aptly expressed by the words »tarab« (music) and »mutrib« (singer), originally meaning joy or giver of joy. Even when reciting Qur'an verses, the melodiousness of the presentation is important. In fact, numerous well-known Arab singers started their career as Qur'an reciters.

Distinct Arabic music only emerged after the establishment of Islam, as a new musical tradition evolved over the course of the 7th and 8th centuries with Byzantine, Greek and Indian influences as well as elements from an Arab-Semitic musical culture.

Foreign world of sound

Unlike the western 12-tone system, the Arab system comprises more than 24 tones. To European ears used to the 12-tone system, a melody with more than twelve tones within one octave and with intervals smaller than a semitone may sound rather foreign. One major difference from European music is the size of the interval, which to those accustomed to European music sounds rather like »sharp« intonation.

Sigah and Saba ...

Another element of Arabic music is heterophony: the multiple variation of a song or melody. Those who can deliver unique interpretations are considered creative musicians, or even composers.

... love and pain

Arab music theorist al-Faruqi compares the tool of artistic ornamentation to the principle of musical improvisation: »Just like using an unlimited amount of motifs to create visual arabesques, the musical vocabulary of improvisational Arab instrumental or vocal artists is practically unrestricted.« Furthermore, Arabic music is based on the principle of »maqam«. Originally the term only referred to the place where music was played. Today maqam expresses the improvisational method for carrying a melody, and also which vocal style, rhythm and instruments are used for the performance. The maqam is also associated with particular emotions: »bayati« stands for life energy and joy, »sigah« for the feeling of love, and »saba« for pain and sadness.

In Syria and Iraq, there are more than one hundred traditional »maqamat«. Experienced listeners can recognize the underlying maqam even by hearing just the beginning of a musical performance.

Impact on Europe

Arabic music was also brought to Europe via Mauritanian Spain. Whether at the Sicilian court of Frederick II or at the dukes' courts in Christian Spain – Arab singers and musicians were always welcome and popular guests.

by choosing a particular maqam, which depends on the mood and material.

However, since westernization has also penetrated Arabic music, the once widespread singing techniques are slowly disappearing, as is the traditional ensemble consisting of four to six instruments: lute (ud), zither (kanun), reed pipe (nay), violin (kamancheh), tambourine (daf) and goblet drum (darbakeh).

Now modern compositions even make use of European instruments, upon which it is almost impossible to play

»Arab musicians can choose from an unlimited vocabulary of musical motifs.«   (al-Faruqi)

European music also adopted elements from Arabic singing and melody, as can be seen by the impact on troubadour poetry.

The end of originality?

Today a performer's repertoire comprises folklore, national and love songs. The music interprets the lyrics

traditional Arabic music. The consequence of this was a transformation which ultimately meant rhythmic simplification. In recent years, Arabic music has been greatly compromised to match international tastes by incorporating western dance rhythms and melodies. But maybe the move westwards will attract even more listeners.

with a wide golden border, is worn over it. The head is always covered by a white, loosely worn scarf, a **keffiyeh** or **ghutra**, which is held by a black wool rope known as a **agal**; a small skull-cap, a **taqia**, helps hold the scarf in place.

Curved dagger

Men wear the traditional curved dagger only on special occasions. Just a few decades ago, the **curved dagger**, its blade beautifully decorated with silver thread or disks, was an essential part of the outfit. The handle of the dagger, often decorated with silver, is made of horn, animal bone or – in the case of the more valuable specimens – of ivory. Daggers that are sold to tourists mostly have a plastic handle; the blade, once made of steel, now often consists of sheet metal and is hollow and blunt. The matching belt used to be made of leather with silver embroidery, and is now of plastic with brocade-like trim.

Local girl wearing festive garments

A typical garment for women is the **»kandoura«**, a long dress with elaborate embroidery on the neckline, sleeves and hem. Over the kandoura, women often wear a rectangular cloth, the **thaub**, with holes for the head and arms; underneath the kandoura they wear long trousers (**sirwal**) with embroidery on the hem. Outside the house, women dress in a long black cloak, called the »abaya«,»abba« or »shaili«.

In Dubai, Abu Dhabi and Sharjah only older women cover their faces, while women in other emirates prefer long silk veils. A shiny, black, sometimes golden mask covering eyebrows, nose and mouth (**burqa**) is mainly worn by women from Saudi Arabia and Qatar visiting the Emirates.

Henna painting

Henna paintings are part of the traditional jewellery for Gulf women, which are worn for special occasions such as weddings, births and religious holidays. The powder of the henna bush is mixed with frag-

Henna tattoos: exotic souvenir of an Arabian holiday

rant oils and essences and processed to form a reddish paste. Hands, arms, feet and legs are then painted with artistic patterns symbolizing beauty, purity and fertility. The jewellery-like tattoo stays on the skin for several days or weeks until it fades. Today, numerous cosmetic studios offer female tourists the chance to decorate their hands with traditional henna paintings.

Famous People

In the past, Arab sailors explored the world, but it was often European scientists who explored the deserts. Today, it is the sheikhs who control their country's future.

Ahmed Bin-Majid (1432–1500)

Born in Julfar in 1432, Shihab al-Ahmed Bin-Majid al-Najdi was one **Navigator** of the best navigators in the Arab world. He went to a Qur'an school and later studied geography, astronomy and Arabic literature.

Majid, who titled himself »Lion of the Sea« and helped the Portuguese find their way to Mauritius, was recruited up by the Portuguese explorer Vasco de Gama in 1498 to join him on his journey to India from the African west coast. Majid navigated around the Cape of Good Hope, sailed north along the east coast of Africa and crossed the Indian Ocean. He documented his knowledge of seafaring in dozens of books. *The Benefits and Principles of Oceanography*, published in 1489, is an early reference work about the origins of navigation, compasses and astronomical meteorology.

Ibn Battuta (1304–1377)

Journeying further than any of his contemporaries, Ibn Battuta lived **Legal scholar** to travel: he covered a total of 120,000km/73,000mi. The faithful Muslim's greatest ambition was to see the most significant places of the Islamic world with his own eyes.

Born in Tangier in 1304, a jurist from a wealthy family, Ibn Battuta first travelled the world at the age of 21. Over the next 30 years he travelled continuously to India, the Maldives, China and Africa. After a visit to Mecca in 1326/1327 Ibn Battuta took the sea route from Jeddah (Saudi Arabia), along the Red Sea coast to Aden (Yemen). From there he continued via Salalah and Sur (Oman) to the east coast of what is now the UAE. In his accounts he describes that, in the spirit of Allah, he meets fellow Muslims everywhere; they support him and help him in emergencies. His longest journey, between 1333 and 1346, was through India,

Ibn Battuta on his travels

where for some of the time he worked as a judge for the Sultan of Delhi. His last journey in 1355/1356 was a risky crossing of the Sahara desert, from Tangier to Mali

← *For many years, Sheikh Zayed bin Sultan Al Nahyan ruled the desert state as President of the UAE.*

and Timbuktu. It was the Sultan of Morocco who finally urged Battuta to dictate an account of his extensive travels and experiences to a scholar, compiled in a book titled *Rihla* (journeys). Ibn Battuta died in 1377 (according to other sources 1369) in his birthplace, Tangier.

Sir Wilfred Thesiger (1910–2003)

Explorer

To this day, the desert crossings of Sir Wilfred Thesiger are an inspiration to anyone travelling in Arabia. The embodiment of the eccentric British world traveller, Thesiger received an excellent education: born on 3 June 1910 in the Ethiopian capital Addis Ababa he attended Eton College and Magdalen College, Oxford, and later pursued a career in the government administration of Sudan. Thesiger first travelled to the Arabian Peninsula in 1945. He began his first desert crossing in Salalah (Oman), and travelled across the wide Rub al-Khali desert to Doha (Qatar). Four years later Thesiger was the first European to cross the dreaded Wahibah Sands east of Oman. With *Arabian Sands*, his book about his second desert crossing, he gained international fame. He was knighted in 1995. On invitation of the Sultan of Oman and the President of the UAE, he returned to South Arabia in the years 1977, 1990 and 2000 where he received several honorary awards.

Sheikh Zayed Bin-Sultan al-Nahyan (1917–2004)

First President of the United Arab Emirates

The ruler of the Emirate of Abu Dhabi was also the late Head of State and President of the United Arab Emirates. Born in Al Ain in 1917 (or 1918), his al-Nahyan family is a member of the Al Bu Falah section of the Bani Yas Bedouin tribe, to which the Dubai dynasty also belongs. Between 1946 and 1966 Sheikh Zayed held the post of governor of the east province of the Abu Dhabi Emirate. After a revolt in 1966 his brother Sheikh Shakhbout Bin-Sultan al-Nahyan succeeded the emir, who had been in power since 1928.

Sheikh Zayed contributed significantly to the establishment of the UAE in 1971 and became its first President the same year; his office was confirmed by the Supreme Council of Rulers every five years. He knew how to balance the emirates' opposing interests within the federation, even if it meant »buying« the smaller emirate's approval. The border conflicts between Saudi Arabia and Oman were settled mainly through his efforts. His generosity in sharing the blessings of the »black gold« with the population also fostered social peace.

Social interests inclined him to found the first school for girls in 1966, and mandatory education finally became statutory in 1972. The elaborate and expensive landscape management of the Abu Dhabi Emirate also dates back to the emir's initiative, as do numerous social benefits for the sick or disabled, widows, and those intending to marry. The generous benefits of the UAE welfare system are practically financed by the Emirate of Abu Dhabi. In 1975 the ruler's wife, Sheikha Fatima Bint-Mubarak, founded the Abu Dhabi Women's Society, which still today runs a handicraft cooperative in the capital. Sheikh Zayed died on November 2nd, 2004. His eldest son, Sheikh Khalifa Bin-Zayed al-Nahyan, became his successor.

Sheikha Lubna Khalid Sultan al Qasimi

For many young women in the Emirates, Sheikha Lubna Al Qasimi is a role model. The popular Minister of Economy and Planning is the UAE's first woman minister ever, and moreover occupies a key senior position in government.

Government minister

A member of the Al Qasimi royal family, the ruling family of Sharjah, Lubna was a voracious reader as a girl and a keen pupil at school. She excelled in her studies, going on to study computer science at the age of 17, and gaining her Bachelor of Science from the University of California. Returning home, she started a career as a computer programmer, working long hours and eschewing the privilege her background could have provided. She subsequently held a variety of senior positions, and in 2000 became the head of the Tejari, the UAE's leading electronic business-to-business marketplace. In 2001 Lubna headed the executive team responsible for e-government initiatives in Dubai's public sector. In November 2004, she assumed her position in the cabinet – the first woman in the Emirates' history to achieve this.

Despite her Western education, Lubna wears the black abaya and shayla robes traditional for Emirate women. Today, she is one of the UAE's most influential figures, and admired to the extent that, during public appearances, young women approach her to have their photographs taken with her, tell her their dreams – and ask for career advice.

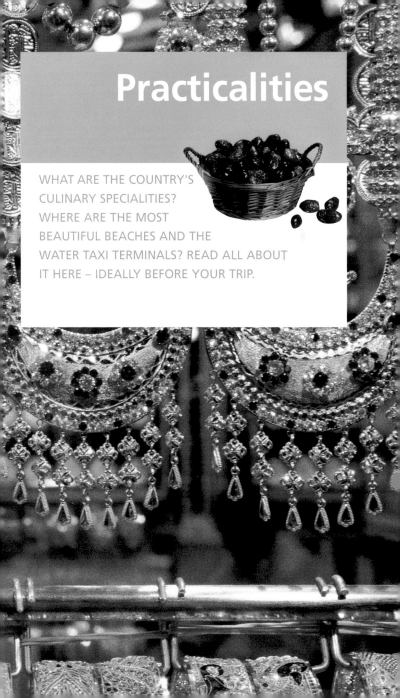

Practicalities

WHAT ARE THE COUNTRY'S
CULINARY SPECIALITIES?
WHERE ARE THE MOST
BEAUTIFUL BEACHES AND THE
WATER TAXI TERMINALS? READ ALL ABOUT
IT HERE – IDEALLY BEFORE YOUR TRIP.

Accommodation

Hotels

International luxury hotels can be found in the larger cities and at the beaches of the United Arab Emirates. They offer first-class service, pools and often a private beach with many choices of water sports. Fitness, tennis and other leisure facilities are usually included. There are also many mid-range hotels which are less expensive than in Europe. Dubai has approximately 270 hotels with 30,000 beds. Abu Dhabi and Sharjah also have sufficient hotels; however, the selection is smaller in the other four emirates.

Rest houses   Inexpensive rest houses, which roughly correspond to two-star or three-star hotels and are also suitable for a stay of several days, can be found in the ► oases of Liwa, Medinat Zayed, Sweihan, Remah and in Ain Al-Faydah near ►Al Ain.

Prices   Hotel prices vary between the emirates; they are highest in Dubai and Abu Dhabi. There are also significant price fluctuations depending on the season. Prices go up on Islamic holidays, and are at their lowest during the summer. In resort and beach hotels and also in

Elegant accommodation on Dubai Creek – the Sheraton Hotel

The ultimate holiday at the Burj al-Arab luxury hotel on Dubai's coast

some inland hotels, room prices are higher on Thursdays than on other days of the week. Four-star and five-star hotels are often less expensive when booking an all-inclusive trip. 5 to 10% taxes and a service charge of 10 to 15% are normally added to the room price.

Youth Hostels

Youth hostels (bait al-shabab) can be found in Abu Dhabi, Al Ain, Dubai, Sharjah, Fujairah and Ras al-Khaimah. Accommodation requires an international youth hostel pass, which is available for 75 AED. Men and women sleep in separate rooms; one night costs between 20 and 40 AED per person. With a family pass, couples and families can book a room of their own. The hostels are very pleasant and run by energetic, bustling staff.

Camping

Although campsites don't exist in the UAE, camping in the wild is widely practiced. Just look for a spot away from the settlements and pitch a tent. Camping is allowed everywhere except for beaches. Avoid the wadis (dry river beds) in winter as they may flood from sudden rainfall.

YOUTH HOSTEL INFORMATION

▶ **UAE Youth Hostel Association**
Al-Qusais Road 39
P. O. Box 94141
Dubai ,
Tel. 04 / 2 98 81 51
Fax 2 98 81 41
www.uaeyha.org.ae

▶ **International Youth Hostel Federation (IYHF)**
Trevelyan House Dimple Road, Matlock
Derbyshire, DE4 3YH
Tel. 0 16 29 / 59 26 00, fax 59 27 02
www.yha.org.uk

Arrival · Before the Journey

Travel Options

A variety of airlines offer many daily flights to Abu Dhabi and Dubai from London Heathrow. Direct flights are offered by British Airways (2 flights a day), Virgin Atlantic, Emirates, Royal Brunei, Gulf Air and Etihad Airways, indirect flights by for example Kuwait Airways (via Kuwait), Air France, KLM and others. Qatar Airways flies direct from Gatwick; there are also Emirates flights direct to Dubai from here. Emirates also provides a non-stop service to Dubai from New York as well as from Sydney. The duration of a flight from London Heathrow to Dubai is approximately seven hours.

Entry and Departure Regulations

Travel documents Upon arrival at an airport in the United Arab Emirates – usually Abu Dhabi, Dubai, or Sharjah – UK residents receive a free visa which is valid for 60 days (»visa on arrival«), which can be extended for another 30 days for a fee of 500 dirham. A passport valid for at least another six months, which must not contain any Israeli stamps, is required. A further 33 countries are now treated in the same way as the UK; these include the USA, Canada, Australia, New Zealand and the Republic of Ireland. To enter at a border crossing from Oman, for example during an excursion, a valid visa from the corresponding other country is sufficient for both countries. The UAE departure fee (passenger service charge) of 30 dirham (approx. £4/€6) is usually included in the price of a fight ticket. The return flight must be re-confirmed within 72 hours before departure (except for Gulf Air).

> ## ! Baedeker TIP
>
> ### Stopover in Kuwait
>
> On flights to or from Abu Dhabi or Dubai, Kuwait Airways offers a stopover in Kuwait with an inexpensive overnight stay. The visa is obtained from Kuwait Airways or the hotel, and is also available after arriving at the airport.

Customs regulations Personal items are not subject to any customs regulations when entering the UAE. 2,000 cigarettes, 400 cigars or 2kg/4.4lb tobacco and 2l/3.5pt (4.2 US pints) of spirits as well as 2l/3.5pt (4.2 US pints) of wine can be imported duty free. However, revealing magazine covers can be interpreted as pornography and confiscated.

Returning to the UK Souvenirs up to a total value of approx. €85 are duty free, as well as 500g/18oz coffee or 200g/7oz instant coffee, 100g/3.5oz tea or 40g/1.5oz tea extracts, 50g/1.8oz perfume or 0.25l/9 fl oz eau de toilette for persons over the age of 15, and 200 cigarettes, 100 small cigars,

50 cigars or 250g/9oz tobacco, 2l/3.5pt (4.2 US pints) wine or other beverages containing up to 22% alcohol, as well as 1l/1.7pt (2.1 US pints) of spirits containing over 22% alcohol for persons over the age of 17.

Vaccinations

Vaccinations are not mandatory when entering the UAE, but being protected against polio, tetanus and diphtheria is recommended. Although hygiene standards are very good, a preventive hepatitis A vaccination is recommended, especially for those planning excursions to Oman.

Tour operators

■ Various tour operators offer all-inclusive trips to the United Arab Emirates, often combined with excursions to Oman. Emirates Tours UK (www.emiratestours.co.uk) is one of many offering special deals. Organized excursions within the Emirates and to Oman can also be booked on location.

Travel Insurance

In order to avoid potential financial risk, obtaining private travel health insurance (for a defined period of time) is recommended to cover any costs for doctors and medication.

AIRLINES

▶ **British Airways**
Tel. +44 (0)870 / 850 9850
www.britishairways.com or
www.ba.com

▶ **Emirates Airlines**
Tel. +44 (0)870 / 243 2222
www.emirates.com

▶ **Etihad Airways**
Tel. +44 (0)870 241 7121
www.etihadairways.com

▶ **Gulf Air**
Tel. +44 (0)870 777 1717
www.gulfairco.com/uk

▶ **Kuwait Airways**
Tel. +44 (0)20 741 20006 10
www.kuwait-airways.com

▶ **Qatar Airways**
Tel. +44 (0)870 770 4215
www.qatarairways.com

▶ **Royal Brunei**
Tel. +44 (0)20 7584 6660
www.bruneiair.com

▶ **Virgin Atlantic**
Tel. +44 (0)870 380 2007
www.virgin-atlantic.com

FLIGHT INFORMATION IN THE UAE

▶ **Abu Dhabi**
Tel. 02 / 5 75 76 11

▶ **Dubai**
Tel. 04 / 2 06 66 66

▶ **Sharjah**
Tel. 06 / 5 58 01 00

Beach Holidays

Restful
beach holidays

During the European winter, Dubai and the remaining emirates provide ideal conditions for a restorative beach holiday. Swimming, sailing, water skiing or surfing – Dubai in particular is a luxurious oasis for spoiled holidaymakers.

Beaches

The best-kept beaches – they are cleaned every day in the early morning – are found outside the five-star hotels. Natural beach vegetation is unknown in the UAE, but palms and other tropical plants can be found in the grounds of hotels. On the Gulf of Arabia to the west, most of the beaches are broad, with fine sand. The gently sloping beaches and shallow water are also ideal for children. On the east coast of the UAE, for example in ▶Khor Fakkan and ▶Fujairah, the beaches are not as extensive and sometimes rocky. Here, divers will appreciate the magnificent underwater world.

Jumeirah
Beach

Dubai's flagship beach, Jumeirah Beach, also has its perils. In some places – such as in front of the Meridien Hotel – there are piles of camel manure, and the so-called oil factory next to the Sheraton Hotel provides a free whiff of »supreme« three to four times a day.

Lifeguards keep a constant eye on the beach at the Jumeirah Beach Hotel.

There are also noisy jet-ski drivers everywhere, who increasingly bother swimmers and those who just want to relax. The other beaches in the Emirates are quieter.

Children in Dubai

Native Arabs and Asian foreign workers are very good with children. Children are pleasantly welcomed everywhere.
Also, making special plans for children or even taking along supplies is not required, since everything children need is available in the United Arab Emirates – usually at better prices than at home.

Travelling with children

The large **shopping centres** have play areas for children with free childcare, so parents can concentrate on spending money.

The many **parks** offer mini golf, playgrounds, boating ponds, merry-go-rounds, small trains and other attractions.

Most of the larger **hotels** have a tots' pool (shallow pool reserved for children). Additional beds for children are usually provided. Childcare is normally offered; kids' clubs with attractive leisure programmes are becoming more prevalent.

i Fun for children

- Wild Wadi in Dubai: the attractions in this water park promise lots of fun in the wet.
- Hili Fun City in Al Ain: this large amusement park on the Gulf of Arabia is enjoyed by children large and small from all over the world.
- Al-Nasr Leisureland Dubai: skating in the desert, and much more.
- Sharjah Science Museum: the interactive museum offers attractive activities for children.
- In the Kids' Club of the Royal Mirage Hotel in Dubai, the extremely friendly child minders look after children and teenagers.

Most restaurants have a »family room« where women can dine without a veil and away from the men; thus children are always found here as well. The waiting staff looks after the little ones attentively, bringing a drink and colouring book and often also a small treat.

Family room

Electricity

The voltage in Abu Dhabi is 220 volts, in Dubai 240 volts, 50 Hertz, and in the northern emirates 220/240 volts. For safety plugs, an adapter that can be obtained in electronics stores and supermarkets for a few dirham is required.

Emergency

GENERAL EMERGENCY

► **Police**
Tel. 999

► **Ambulance**
Tel. 998
Only in Abu Dhabi, Al Ain and Fujairah; in the other emirates Tel. 999

► **Red Crescent**
Tel. 998

► **Fire Service**
Tel. 997

BREAKDOWN SERVICES IN UK

► **RAC**
Tel. 08705 722 722
(customer services)
Tel. 0800 82 82 82
(breakdown assistance)

► **AA**
Tel. 0800 88 77 66
(emergency breakdown)
Tel. +44 161 495 8945
(international enquiries)

INTERNATIONAL AIR AMBULANCE SERVICES

► **Cega Air Ambulance (worldwide service)**
Tel. +44(0)1243 621097
Fax +44(0)1243 773169
www.cega-aviation.co.uk

► **US Air Ambulance**
Tel. 800/948-1214
(US; toll-free)
Tel. 001-941-926-2490
(international; collect)
www.usairambulance.net

Entertainment

Evening entertainment   Evening entertainment, at least combined with the consumption of alcohol, can hardly be expected in an Islamic society. As a result, the nightlife in the Emirates is mainly limited to the hotels, although they do have a lot to offer with their cocktail lounges, bars, discos and nightclubs with »theme nights« and theatre nights. However, some locals prefer to visit a Shisha café, where they smoke a water pipe (Shisha) with tobacco that is perfumed if desired. They also play backgammon and chat while enjoying coffee, tea, fruit juice and snacks.

Bars   Usually, any hotel with three or more stars has a bar. The UAE has had British and Irish style bars for quite some time, where the Guinness flows just as it does at home. Over the last few years, jazz bars, karaoke bars, piano bars, wine bars, and even American bars with

! *Baedeker* TIP

Shisha for women

The Apple café and restaurant on the third floor of the Twin Towers is especially pleasant in the evening. Sitting on the balcony, caressed by a soft breeze, the visitor enjoys the magnificent view across the busy Dubai Creek and the occasional puff on the water pipe, which is also offered to women here (Bani Yas Road, tel. 04 / 2 27 44 46).

large television screens showing sports have also sprung up. The latest additions are Australian bars – with the corresponding beer and fast food – and cigar bars.

Discos

Every hotel with four or more stars has its own disco. In addition to hotel guests, the discos cater to younger expatriates and local men. Hot spots such as the »Premiere« in the Hyatt Regency Hotel in Dubai are official members-only clubs, from which undesirable guests are excluded. In the evenings, long queues form outside the better discos which are increasingly hiring well-known foreign DJs.

Nightclubs

Nightclubs are also located in the hotels. They often consist of a restaurant which offers a »floor show« along with dinner, e.g. a Philippine band with two or three singers who perform the latest hits. If an Egyptian belly dancer performs the nightclub is dubbed an »Arabian Nightclub«, even though exposed midriffs and alcohol are not part of UAE culture. A much-advertised draw is also frequently part of the programme. The evening continues with live music and dancing, until at some point the big winners are selected.

Theme nights

These events are held in the garden or pool area of a hotel, on the terrace, or in an air-conditioned restaurant. Often the theme is the cuisine of a certain country (e.g. »Italian Night«), with the national specialities usually being offered in a buffet.

Etiquette and Customs in Dubai

Taboos in the Islamic World

Although at first glance it may not seem that way, in Dubai, the metropolis with international flair, visitors are expected to act in a man-

Bikinis and swimming trunks should only ever be worn on the beach.

ner adapted to the rules of conduct in an Islamic country. This includes the selection of proper clothing: although scantily-clad tourists are increasingly appearing outside the beach hotels, it is better to adapt to Islamic customs and dress correctly in public. Therefore, men should avoid shorts and muscle shirts when strolling through the city; on the other hand, Bermuda shorts that reach the knee and polo shirts are acceptable in Dubai. Women should leave tight skirts and slacks as well as translucent tops or those that expose the midriff or highlight the décolleté at the hotel. Moreover, clothing that covers the body offers better protection from the intense sunlight.

In Islamic countries, wearing your hair open is considered a provocative act – those who have shoulder-length or longer hair should tie it up during excursions outside of Dubai. Couples should also refrain from showing affection in public.

Restraint Regarding Arab Women

Arab women and girls neither want to be photographed nor approached by foreigners, even if it is just to ask for directions. Also, women are greeted without a handshake.

A Drink Anytime?

Drinking alcohol in public is not permitted. The consumption of alcoholic beverages is limited to hotels, licensed restaurants, bars and discos. In the Emirate of Sharjah, alcohol is totally prohibited. Driving under the influence of alcohol is subject to stiff penalties and should therefore be avoided under all circumstances. During the month of fasting, tourists also should not eat, drink or smoke in public.

Photography Prohibited

Some government buildings, port facilities, oil installations and military facilities are »restricted areas« where photography is prohibited. Before photographing the palaces that belong to members of the ruling class, ask permission from the guards. Locals should be asked for permission before their picture is taken.

Private Visits in the Emirates

Should you receive a private invitation to the house of a local – which is unlikely to happen to tourists very often – it is polite to bring a gift for the children but not for the wife; also, it is not done to inquire about the woman of the house. It is customary to remove footwear in private residences. When sitting, ensure that the soles of the feet do not point at another person.

Service Charge and Tipping

On hotel bills, a service charge of 10 to 15% is added in addition to taxes between 8 and 10%; therefore, tipping is not required. However, these fees are not passed on to personnel, so in exceptional cases when extremely good service has been provided a small tip is appropriate. Restaurants are also increasingly following the practice of adding »Service« or »Tip« to the bill amount in addition to taxes. In this case, additional tipping is not required.

Festivals, Holidays and Events

Most of the events and holidays in the United Arab Emirates are based on the lunar Islamic calendar; only a few holidays are based on the Gregorian calendar. The Islamic year is approximately eleven days shorter than the solar year of the Gregorian calendar. Islamic calculation of time begins in the year AD 622, called Hijra, on 15 July 622, the day Mohammed left Mecca; therefore, the year 2008 is the year 1428/1429 AH according to the Islamic calendar (Anno Hijra). Islamic religious holidays and festivals are subject to the sighting of the moon; the exact Gregorian calendar dates of future events can therefore only be estimated.

Expatriate holidays
Easter, Christmas, New Year and other expatriate events and holidays – from St Patrick's Day for the Irish to Thanksgiving for the US Americans – are celebrated at the large hotels.

Events

Theater, concerts
The theatre and concert scene is not highly developed in the UAE; the focus is on sun, fun and shopping. Theatre productions, usually accompanied by dinner, and concerts usually take place in the hotels. Most ensembles come from Great Britain and the productions are in English. The Inter-Continental Hotel in Dubai is the centre of the theatre community (tel. 04 / 2 22 71 71); it also hosts the Indian theatre group »Indian Playhouse«. The amateur ensemble of the Al Ain Amateur Dramatic Society presents its pieces in the Hilton Hotel in Al Ain (Tel. 03 / 7 68 66 66).

Event dates
The monthly magazines *What's On* and *Time Out Dubai* provide information regarding event dates and entertainment programmes for the larger hotels.

▶ HOLIDAYS AND FESTIVALS

ISLAMIC HOLIDAYS

▶ **Weekly day of rest**
Friday is the official weekly day of rest. On this day, banks, government offices and most businesses are closed; believers meet at the mosques for noon prayer.
Some businesses only close during Friday prayers from 11am until approx. 2pm; most government offices are also closed on Thursday.

▶ **Eid al-Adha**
The end of the ten-day Haj period, when Muslim believers embark on their pilgrimage (Haj) to Mecca, is celebrated with the three-day sacrificial feast of Eid al-Adha. Many families butcher a wether on this occasion (dates: 8 December 2008, 28 November 2009, 17 November 2010, 7 November 2011).

▶ **Eid al-Fitr**
Subsequently, the end of the fast after Ramadan is celebrated with three days of opulent meals and the exchange of gifts.
The importance of the feast is often compared to the Christian holiday of Christmas (dates: 1 October 2008, 21 September 2009, 10 September 2010, 21 August 2011).

▶ **Hijra**
First day of the Islamic year (dates:

10 January 2008, 29 December 2008, 18 December 2009, 7 December 2010, 26 November 2011).

► Lailat al-Miraj
Ascension of the prophet Mohammed with his horse Burak from the Dome of the Rock in Jerusalem (dates: 29 July 2008, 19 July 2009, 8 July 2010, 28 June 2011).

► Maulid al-Nabi
Birthday of the prophet Mohammed (dates: 20 March 2008, 9 March 2009, 26 February 2010, 15 February 2011).

► Ramadan
In the holy month of Ramadan, Muslims commemorate the religious revelations of the prophet Mohammed. They do not eat, drink or smoke from sunrise to sunset. Non-Muslims are also expected to forego these pleasures in public. Many businesses and museums have shorter opening hours; restaurants do not open until after sunset (dates: 2 September 2008, 22 August 2009, 12 August 2010, 1 August 2011).

NATIONAL HOLIDAYS

► 1 January
New Year's Day

► 6 August
Accession Day: the day the former president of the UAE, the Emir of Abu Dhabi, Sheikh Zayed Bin-Sultan al-Nayan, took office (1972)

► 2 December
National Day: the day the seven emirates joined together (1971); on this day, a wide variety of cultural events takes place in the UAE.

SPORTING EVENTS

► Dhow regattas
From October to May, there are regular sailing regattas with the traditional Dhows.

Traditional Arabian ships are fast in the water.

► Dubai Desert Classic
The high-class golf tournament takes place annually in March.

► Dubai Rugby Sevens
The main sports event in Dubai: in November or December, the best rugby teams in the world compete for trophies and cups.

► Dubai Tennis Open
The famous tennis tournament takes place every year in February or March.

► Dubai World Cup
The horse race with the most generous prize money in the world, at over six million US dollars, takes place at the Dubai Racing Club in March of each year.

► Camel races
Camel races take place during the winter months, from November to March, every Thursday and Friday

starting at 8am, even on the national holiday (2 Dec). In the emirate of Dubai, the Nad al-Shiba racetrack is located south of the city.

▶ Horse races
Horse races offering large prizes are organized in Dubai under the patronage of the ruling family, whose members themselves own many race horses. Between November and April, six races take place two days a week starting at 7pm.

▶ Powerboat races
High-powered racing boats zoom across the water in October and November, for example at the »Emirates Grand Prix« or the »Dubai Duty Free Grand Prix«.

▶ Rallies
At the »UAE Marlboro Desert Challenge« or the »Dubai International Rally« that take place in November and December, both drivers and spectators have to eat a lot of desert dust.

▶ Sailing regattas
The famous sailing regatta from Dubai to Muscat takes place every year in March.
The Maktoum Cup – the traditional rowing regatta on the Dubai Creek – takes place every year in April.

FOLKLORE EVENTS

▶ Dubai Summer Surprises
Every year, numerous folklore events take place in the Heritage Village from May to September.

Food and Drink

Changes in eating habits After the discovery of oil, the traditional eating habits of the population underwent rapid changes; among other factors, this was caused by the large number of migrant workers who came to the country and enriched the local cuisine with the culinary traditions of their native countries. In addition to Arab cuisine, which is now offered in several variations (Lebanese, Syrian, Egyptian), there are also Indian, Philippine and Pakistani restaurants. Since the hygiene standards are excellent across the UAE, tourists can eat and drink everything without concern even in simple tearooms. Most of the large hotels have speciality restaurants with international cuisine.

Gastronomic culture During a traditional Arab meal, diners sit on the floor which is covered in rugs and cushions. Culinary delights are then served: the main course usually consists of meat and fish, often cooked in a rich sauce. This is served with rice or Muaddas – a mixture of rice and lentils – salad, various vegetables, bowls of yogurt, pickled vegetables, and fresh-baked flatbread.

Today, cutlery is also increasingly used: the times when everyone helped themselves from a common platter using their fingers are pretty much in the past. However, this tradition is frequently revived

The hotel buffets are also a feast for the eye.

during picnics or in Bedouin tents, and in this case the right hand is used for eating since the left is regarded as unclean, and the flatbread used to scoop up rice, fish or meat serves as »disposable cutlery«.

The host serves the guest first, with the largest and best pieces; food is eaten quickly, with little conversation. After the abrupt end of the meal, everyone goes to an adjacent room to drink coffee.

When drinking coffee, the following rules apply: refusing a cup of coffee is an insult to the host. If you do not indicate that you have had enough after the first cup, it will be refilled a second and third time. The coffee is served in small cups without handles, which are only filled to one-third.

Buffets

For many tourists, the highlight of a trip to the United Arab Emirates is a buffet set up in the sand dunes, for example during a desert safari. The selection of oriental specialities is savoured sitting on comfortable rugs or soft cushions.

The **theme nights** organized several times a week by many hotels are popular with tourists as well as locals. They have buffets matching a certain motto – for example »Seafood Night« or »Italian Night«. Since the nightlife outside the hotels is rather meagre, the events organized by the hotels – frequently accompanied by a musical or cultural programme – are greatly appreciated by the guests.

! *Baedeker* TIP

Dinner cruises

The dinner cruises offered in Dubai are a special experience: while sitting on the top deck of a traditional dhow gliding across the creek, diners look out onto the beautifully illuminated nighttime metropolis and later enjoy the meal. Such dhows can be found at Quay 1, Dhow Warfage (tel. 04/39 39 860; www.creekcruises.com), on the bank of the creek on the Deira side between the InterContinental and Sheraton hotels, and in the Al-Boom Tourist Village (tel. 04/32 43 000).

Breakfast   The Arab breakfast is very rich. The locals prefer humus, chick pea porridge dressed with sesame oil and some garlic, ragouts cooked with white beans, tomatoes, and meat, as well as flatbread and tea. The tourist hotels have conventional breakfast buffets, but humus and bean dishes are also served.

Lunch   At noon, the hotels have sumptuous lunch buffets: after the appetizers consisting of tomatoes, cucumbers, fennel and spicy salads, meat and fish dishes follow as the main course. A large selection of vegetables, potato dishes and rice round out the meal.

A certain amount of restraint is advised, considering the **desserts**: mousse au chocolat, Italian panna cotta, crème caramel and delicious sorbet, accompanied by fresh fruit and the full range of Arab sweets: puff pastries dripping with honey and filled with pistachios and walnuts, as well as candied figs and oranges.

Supper   Supper at the hotels is usually extraordinarily beautiful; in some cases, it is served outside by candlelight. The hotel guests help themselves from the buffet which is attractively presented with tropical flowers and fine table linens, or they make their selection à la carte. If hotel management has organized an accompanying musical programme, dinner can extend from sunset until midnight. In high-end hotels, the food meets the highest culinary standards; however, it is also very good in the mid-range establishments.

Food

Meat   Residents of the UAE like meat cooked on a spit. Lamb, beef and goat meat dishes are very popular. Pork and products made from pork are forbidden under the Qur'an, which is why they are not offered; importing pork is not permitted.

Fish and seafood   The waters of the Gulf of Arabia are very rich in fish and shellfish. Cooking over hot coals as well as roasting, baking and steaming are popular. Fish dishes are also served in a spicy, rich sauce along with vegetables. The most popular type of fish which is on every menu in the UAE is hammour, a type of perch prepared in a thousand and one different ways. It is usually served with khoubiz or chubs, warm flatbread broken into small pieces and used instead of a fork and spoon.

i   **Marriageable**

■ Although nobody will actually count, the opinion in the Emirates remains that a woman is only marriageable once she knows at least 50 recipes for eggplant.

Fruit and vegetables   Fruit and vegetables are very important in Arab cuisine. The most popular vegetables include cucumbers, green beans, eggplant, white turnips, carrots, chard, fennel, cauliflower and chick peas, either cooked or steamed, or pickled in a vinegar marinade. Grilled and roasted meat dishes are traditional-ly served in a sauce with vegetables. In Arab culture, eggplant has long been given almost magical importance.

i Pricing Categories

- Expensive = from 99 AED (£13 / US$26 / €20)
- Moderate = 39.5 AED (£5.40 / US$10.75 / €8) – 99 AED (£13 / US$26 / €20)
- Inexpensive = up to 39.5 AED (£5.40 / US$10.75 / €8)

Baked goods and **sweets**, served after every meal on a separate table or even in another room, are extraordinarily popular. Most recipes include pistachios, honey, almonds, rose water and syrup. Delicious but high-calorie puddings are prepared using coconut milk and cream. However, the classic dessert still consists of dates, which are served pitted and filled with almonds, marzipan or chocolate.

Spices

Every Arab meal is accompanied by the exotic fragrance of spices and herbs. The use of many versatile spices is typical for cuisine in the United Arab Emirates. Every local housewife values cardamom, coriander, cumin, cinnamon, chilli powder, ginger, turmeric and saffron. Arab cuisine is frequently seasoned with Baharat, a mixture of ground pepper, coriander, cinnamon, cloves, cumin, nutmeg and paprika. It is traditional to soak saffron strands in rose water and drip this mixture over the dish near the end of its cooking time, in order to provide some additional colour and flavour.
Dried limes, which are used whole or in powder form, are also popular for extra flavour. Sesame seeds, which are used to make oils and pasta and also roasted and added to dishes, are an important traditional food said to have many healthy characteristics.

Beverages

The most common beverage is mineral water which is bottled in the Emirates of Fujairah and Ras al-Khaimah, but is also imported. A large bottle of water (1.5l/2.6pt) is usually automatically served with each meal. Fresh juice made from tropical fruits and vegetables (mangoes, oranges, papaya, pomegranates, carrots) is available everywhere; it is more expensive when it is made from imported fruits.

In addition to tea, the national Arab drink is coffee. Both are served in small cups or glasses without handles; the coffee is unsweetened and usually spiced with cardamom, while the tea is very sweet. It is not

A cup of coffee in elegant surroundings...

polite to refuse tea or coffee offered by acquaintances or business partners, in shops, or in government offices. Refills are offered until you express thanks, wiggle the cup, or swing it back and forth.

Restaurants

Naturally, the multiculturalism of the UAE is also reflected in its restaurants. In addition to Arab establishments with Lebanese, Syrian, or Egyptian cuisine, there are also restaurants with international specialities as well as expatriate restaurants with Indian, Pakistani, Ceylonese, or Philippine cuisine.

Since the residents of the United Arab Emirates come from all over the world, the eating habits of the country have been subject to numerous influences. Thus the time periods during which meals are held are also quite long: breakfast between 6am and 10am, lunch between noon and 3pm, supper between 7pm and 11pm.

Food courts Visitors to a simple Arab restaurant where food is consumed without the use of cutlery – but with the aid of flatbread – should use the right hand only and leave the left hand under the table. A food court, which can be found in most shopping malls, is also suitable for a quick bite to eat. Just make a selection from one of the several different self-service restaurants and get a table in the large seating area.

Health

Medical Assistance

Medical care In the United Arab Emirates, the supply of hospitals and clinics is excellent; the doctors usually speak English. In emergencies, tourists also receive free treatment in state-run hospitals. When visiting a clinic, a consultation including initial treatment costs about 100 to 200 AED.

Pharmacies

Pharmacies or chemist's are found in commercial areas and shopping centres. Almost all medications are available, many without a prescription and quite inexpensive; however, they are often sold under other names, so regular medication should be taken along on the trip.

HOSPITALS

ABU DHABI

▶ **Central Hospital**
Tel. 02 / 6 21 46 66

▶ **Mafraq Hospital**
Tel. 02 / 51 23 10 00

▶ **Salam Clinic**
(Outpatient centre and dentist)
Tel. 02 / 6 72 43 24

DUBAI

▶ **Al-Wasl Hospital**
Tel. 04 / 3 24 11 11

▶ **Al-Maktoum Hospital**
Al-Maktoum Hospital Road
Tel. 04 / 2 22 12 11
(24 hours)

▶ **Rashid Hospital**
Tel. 04 / 3 37 40 00

Pharmacies are usually open from 8am or 9am until 8pm, with a lunch break of approximately two hours between 1pm and 5pm. To find out which pharmacies offer services at night, on Fridays and during holidays, call tel. 04 / 2 23 22 32. *Opening hours*

Preventive Healthcare

Sufficient protection from the sun is essential. At temperatures as high as those in the UAE during the day, it is important to drink plenty of liquids in order to compensate for the body's water loss. *Protection from the sun*

Almost all public buildings, hotels and restaurants in the United Arab Emirates are kept quite cool by air conditioning systems. Since there is a significant temperature difference – often more than 15 °C – compared to outside, one can easily catch a cold. Therefore tourists are advised to always bring a light jacket or sweater along on excursions and sightseeing tours. *Risk of colds*

Information

The Government of Dubai has a Department of Tourism & Commerce Marketing (DTCM) whose mission is »to position Dubai as the leading tourism destination and commercial hub in the world«. The London office is located at 125 Pall Mall, full details below. Information is also available from travel agencies – both at home and in the sheikdoms – and from airlines such as Emirates and Gulf Air as well as the press offices of the embassies.

USEFUL ADDRESSES

TOURIST INFORMATION

▶ **Government of Dubai Department of Tourism and Commerce Marketing**
First floor
125 Pall Mall
London SW1Y 5EA
Tel. +44 (0)20 7839 0580
Fax +44 (0)20 7839 0582
www.dubaitourism.ae

▶ **Abu Dhabi Tourism Authority**
No. 1 Knightsbridge
London SW1X 7LY
Tel: +44 (0)207 201 6400
Fax: +44 (0)207 201 6426
www.exploreabudhabi.ae

EMBASSIES

▶ **Embassy of the United Arab Emirates, UK**
30 Princes Gate
London SW7 1PT
Tel: 020 7581 1281
Fax: 020 7581 9616
www.uaeembassyuk.net

▶ **Consulate of the United Arab Emirates, UK / Visa Section**
48 Princes Gate
London SW7
Tel: 0870 005 6984

▶ **Embassy of the United Arab Emirates, Republic of Ireland**
(accredited in London)
30 Princes Gate
London SW7 1PT
Tel: +44 20 7581 1281
Fax: +44 20 7581 9616
www.uaeembassyuk.net

▶ **Embassy of the United Arab Emirates, USA**
3522 International Court, NW
Suite #400
Washington, DC 20008
Tel: 202 243 2400
Fax: 202 243 2432
www.uae-embassy.org

▶ **Embassy of the United Arab Emirates, Canada**
45 O'Connor Street
Suite 1800, World Exchange Plaza
Ottawa, Ontario
Tel: 613-565-7272
Fax: 613-565-8007
www.uae-embassy.com

▶ **Embassy of the United Arab Emirates, Australia**
36 Culgoa Circuit
O'Malley ACT 2606
Tel: 61-2-6286 8802
Fax: 61-2-6286 8804

EMBASSIES IN THE UAE

▶ **British Embassy, Dubai**
P.O. Box 65
Dubai
Tel. 04 309 4444
Fax 04 309 4257 (Consular)
www.britishembassy.gov.uk/uae

▶ **British Embassy, Abu Dhabi**
P.O. Box 248
Abu Dhabi
Tel. 02 6101100
Fax 02 6101586 (Consular)
www.britishembassy.gov.uk/uae

▶ **Embassy of the United States, Abu Dhabi**
P.O. Box 4009
Abu Dhabi
Tel. 02 414 2200
http://uae.usembassy.gov

► **The Embassy of Canada to the United Arab Emirates**
9th & 10th Floor, West Tower
Abu Dhabi Trade Towers
(Abu Dhabi Mall)
P.O. Box 6970
Abu Dhabi
Tel. 02 694 0300
Fax 02 694 0399
Email: abdbi@international.gc.ca

► **Australian Embassy in the United Arab Emirates**
14th floor, Al Muhairy Centre
Sheikh Zayed the First Street
P.O. Box 32711
Abu Dhabi
Tel. 02 634 6100
Fax 02 639 3525
www.uae.embassy.gov.au

► **Irish Embassy, Riyadh, Saudi Arabia (also responsible for UAE)**
P.O. Box 94349
Riyadh 11693
Saudi Arabia
Tel. +966 (0)1 488 2300
Fax +966 (0)1 488 0927
www.embassyofireland-riyadh.com

INTERNET

► **www.alfujairah.com**
The homepage of the Emirate of Fujairah with information about the country and its people.

► **www.arabianwildlife.com**
Belongs to the magazine of the same name, and offers videos, images and information regarding flora and fauna and, in particular, bird-watching tips.

► **www.dubaitourism.ae**
Supplies well-organized information regarding the Emirate of Dubai. It is also possible to book hotel rooms here.

► **www.sharjah-welcome.com**
This well-designed website is primarily directed at tourists and visitors to the emirate.

► **www.uaeinteract.com**
The website of the Ministry of Information and Culture offers current news and a lot of mainly tourism-related information regarding the United Arab Emirates.

► **www.dubaicityguide.com**
Colourful site overflowing with information and tips on restaurants, hotels, nightclubs and sightseeing.

Language

The official language in the UAE is Arabic, but due to the British influence on the Emirates in the past and the especially close relationship with Great Britain, most locals also understand English – at least in Abu Dhabi and Dubai. English has also established itself as the language of commerce. Most street and building signage is bilingual, in Arabic and English.

Official language

Language of the Prophet

Arabic is the language of the prophet, so it is said with self-confidence on the Arabian peninsula. The Arabic language spread to the entire peninsula during the 7th century in parallel with the spread of Islam. Numerous regional languages with various dialects that differ from classic high Arabic developed over subsequent centuries. In general, the following applies: the closer the respective language area is to Mecca and Medina, the centre of Islam, the more prevalent high Arabic is.

Family of languages

The Arab language is a member of the Semitic group of languages. It is based on the ancient Semitic consonant script of the Nabataeans and is comprised of 28 characters that are based on just 17 different shapes. These are further differentiated by one or more dots above or below the letters. It is written from right to left. Arab numbers are an exception, since they are read from left to right. There are two different styles of lettering: an angular monumental script that was common into the 12th century and the round cursive style used today. Currently, Arab lettering is the second most used in the world after Latin.

Arab names

The names on the Arabian peninsula are unusual for visitors from the West; they are always comprised of several components. In addition to the given name and surname, a full name also includes the name of the father (and often the grandfather), and sometimes even the name of the tribe. These elements are joined by »Bin...« , »son of...«, or »Bint...«, »daughter of...«. Thus women keep their name even after marriage.

For the rulers of the emirates, the name of the tribe is also part of their full name: Sheikh Zayed Bin-Sultan Bin-Khalifa Bin-Zayed al-Nahyan al-Bu Falah means: Sheikh Zayed, son of the sultan, son of Khalifa, son of Zayed from the Nahyan family of the tribe of Bu Falah.

Pronunciation

Below, the Arab words are shown in simple phonetics (centre column).

ARAB PHRASE BOOK

At a glance

Yes	na'am	نعم
No	la/kalla	كلا/لا
Please	'afwan	عفوا
Thank you!	shukran	شكرا
Sorry	'udhran	عذرا
Excuse me?	na'am?	نعم؟
Good day	as-salamu 'alaikum	السلام عليكم!

Good evening!	masā' l-chair	مساء الخير!
Hi / hello!	marhaban	مرحبا!
Goodbye	ila l-liqā' / ma' a s-slama	إلى القاء / مع السلامة!
Can you	hal tastai' musa'adati	هل تستطيع مساعدتي
help me please?	min fadlika	من فضلك؟
I would like ...	urīd	أريد ...
What does it cost?	mādha jukallif	ماذا يكلف؟
What time is it?	kam is-sa'a	كم الساعة؟

Places

Bus station	markaz intilaq otobisat	مركز إنطلاق أوتوبيسات
Airport	matar	مطار
Ladies' toilet	mirhad as-sayidāt	مرحاض السيدات
Gents' toilet	mirhad irridjāl	مرحاض للرجال
Post office	maktab al-barīd	مكتب البريد
Taxi	udjra / taksi	أجرة / تكسي
Tourist information	marakiz ista'lamat assiyaha	مركز إستعلمات السياحة
Square	sāhat`	ساحة
Street	shari`	شارع
Market	sūq	سوق
Restaurant	mat`am	مطعم
Hotel	funduq	فندق
Castle / fortress	qal`at	قلعة
Palace	qasr	قصر
Valley	wadī	وادي
Mosque	djami`	جامع
Museum	mathaf	متحف
Monastery	deir	دير
Mountain	djabal	جبل
Friday mosque	djami`	جامع

Out and about

left / right	jasāran / jaminjan	يسارا / يمينا
straight ahead	ila l-amām	إلى الأمام
near / far	qarib / ba`īd	قريب
Excuse me please, where is ...?	min fadlak aina	من فضلك أين
How far is that?	kam il masāfa	كم المسافة

I would like ... litres	`urid ... litran	أريد ... لترا
normal petrol.	min al-banżin al-`ādī	من البنزين العادي
super petrol.	min al-banżin al-mumtaż	من البنزين الممتاز
diesel.	min id-dīżil	من الديزل

Fill her up please.	imla´ il-khażżan min fadlika	إملأ الخزان من فضلك
My car has broken down.	ta`atalat sayyarati	تعطلت سيارتي
Would you tow my car	hal tastati` sahb sayyarati	هل تستطيع سحب سيارتي
to the next	ila aqrab warsha	إلى أقرب ورشة؟
service station?		
Where is the nearest	`aina tudjad aqrab warsha	أين توجد أقرب ورشة؟
garage?		
Help!	al-nadjda	النجدة
Can you please quickly call	utlub (f -bi) bi sur`a	أطلب بسرعة
	min fadlak	من فضلك ...
an ambulance.	sayyarat ´is`āf	سيارة إسعاف
the police.	ash-shurta	الشرطة
It was my / your fault.	ana / anta (f ti) l-mas´ul	أنا / أنت المسؤل
	`an wuqu` hadha l-hadith	عن وقوع هذا الحادث

Doctor

Can you recommend a good	hal tastati` an tushir li	هل تستطيع أن تشير
doctor?	bi tabib?	بطبيب
I have pain here.	´ashùru bi-ālām huna	أشعر بآلام هنا

Bank

Where can I find a bank?	aiyna yudjad masraf huna?	أين يوجد مصرف هنا؟
I would like to exchange	´urid an uhauwil	أريد أن أحول
... Euros	min al-yuro	من اليورو
... Swiss Franks	nim al frank as-swisri	من الفرنك السويسري
for	ila	إلى

Overnight stays

Could you please	hal yumkinuka an	هل يمكنك أن ترشدني إلى
... recommend	turshidni ila	
... a good hotel	ila funduq djayid	إلى فندق جيد؟
... a bed and breakfast	nuzul / bansiyon	نزول / بنسيون
Do you have any rooms avai-lable?	hal ladaykum ghurfa?	هل لديكم غرفة ...
a single room	ghurfa li-schakhs wahid	غرفة لشخص واحد
a double room	ghurfa li-shakhsain	غرفة لشخصين
with bathroom	fiha hammam	فيها حمام
for one night	li-layla wahida	لليلة واحدة
for one week	li-´usbu`	لأسبوع
How much is the room with ...	kam tukallif al-ghurfa?	كم تكلف الغرفة

breakfast	ma` l-futur	مع الفطور؟
half board	ma` wadjbatein	مع وجبتين؟

Food and drink

Where can I find a good restaurant?	aina yudjad huna mat`am djayied	هل يوجد هنا مطعم جيد؟
a reasonably priced restaurant?	mat`am mu`tadil	مطعم معتدل
Where can I find a café/ a tearoom?	hal tudjad huna maqha	هل توجد هنا مقهى؟
Please make a reservation for tonight. a table for four	ihdjiz lana min fadlika tāwila li araba`a `ashkāhs hadha l-masā´	إحجز لنا من فضلك طاولة لأربعة أشخاص هذا المساء
To your health!	fī sahatak (f -ik)	في صحتك
I would like the bill please.	al-hisāb min fadlak	الحساب من فضلك
How was it?	hal kana at-ta`ām djayied	هل كان الطعام جيد
The meal was excellent.	kana it-ta`ām mumtāż	كان الطعام ممتازا

Breakfast

Flatbread	raghif	رغيف
Bread	khubż	خبز
Toast	tost / kubz muqammar	توست / خبز مقمر
Soft-boiled egg	baida nisf masluqa	بيضة نصف مسلوقة
Hard-boiled egg	baida maslūqa	بيضة مسلوقة
Fried egg	baid maqli	بيض مقلي
Butter	żubda	زبدة
Cheese	djubn	جبن
Feta cheese	djubn min laban il-ghanam	جين من لبن الغنم
Goat's cheese	djubn min laban il-ma`iż	جين من لبن الماعز
Soft cheese	djubn tarrii	جين طري
Sausage	sudjuq	سجق
Honey	`asal	عسل
Marmelade	murabba	مربى
Yogurt	laban żabadi	لبن زبادي
Omelette	ùdjdja	عجة

Snack

Falafel	falāfil	فلافل
Liver sandwich	sandawish kibda	سندويش كبدة
Kabab	kabāb	كباب
Sausages	naqniq	نقنيق

Main Meal

Meze (various appetizers)	mażża munawa`a	مزة منوعة
Grilled shrimp	djambari mashwi	جمبري مشوي
Roasted meat	lahm muhammar	لحم مجمر
Grilled meat	lahm mashwi	لحم مشوي
Grilled fish	samak mashwi	سمك مشوي
Meatballs	kifta	كفتى
Grilled chicken	dadjadj fi-l-furn	دجاج في الفرن
Pasta casserole	ma`karuna fi-l-furn	مغكرونة في الفرن
Rice	rużż	رز
Potatoes	Batāta	بطاطا
Pasta	Ma`karuna	مغكرونة
Vegetable soup	shurbar khudar	شوربة خضر
Fish chowder	shurbat samak	شوربة سمك
Garden salad	salata khadra	سلطة خضرة
Tomato salad	Salata Tamātim	سلطة طماطم

Fruit and Sweets

Oranges	burtuqāl	برتقال
Apples	tuffāh	تفاح
Pears	idjās	إجاص
Pomegranates	rummān	رمان
Figs	tīn	تين
Prickly pears	tīn shauki	تين شوكي
Peaches	khaukh / Durraq	خوخ / دراق
Apricots	mishmish	مشمش
Mango	mango	منقو
Fresh dates	balah	بلح
Dried dates	tamr	تمر
Grapes	`inab	عنب
Melons	battikh	بطيخ
Quince	sfardjal	سفرجل
Bananas	mawz	موز
Baklava	baqlāwa	بقلاوة
Pastry	ka`k	كعك

Beverages

Tea with milk / with lemon	shai bi-l-halīb / bil-l-laimūn	شاي بالحليب / بالليمون
Black coffee	qahwa bila halīb	قهوة بلا حليب
Coffee with milk	qahwa bil halīb	قهوة بالحليب
Arab coffee	qahwa `arabiya	قهوة عربية

with caradamon	bi-l-hāl	بالحال
Cold / warm milk	halīb barid / sākhin	حليب بارد / ساخن
Lemonade	laymoūnada	ليمونادة
Mineral water	Ma´ madaniya	ماء معدنية
Orange juice	`asīr burtuqāl	عصير برتقال
Carrot juice	`asīr djassar	عصير جزر
Mango juice	`asīr Mangha	عصير منجة
Wine	khamr / nabīdh	نبيذ
Rosé wine	nabīdh rose	نبيذ روزيه
White wine	nabīdh abiyad	نبيذ أبيض
Beer	bīra	بيرة

Numbers

0	sifr	٠	صفر
1	wāhid	١	واحد
2	´ithnain	٢	إثنين
3	thlātha	٣	ثلاثة
4	´arba`a	٤	أربعة
5	khamsa	٥	خمسة
6	sitta	٦	ستة
7	saba`a	٧	سبعة
8	thamāniya	٨	ثمانية
9	tis`a	٩	تسعة
10	`ashara	١٠	عشرة
11	´ahada `ashara	١١	أحد عشر
12	´ithnā `ashara	١٢	إثنا عشر
13	thalāthata `ashara	١٣	ثلاثة عشر
14	´arba`ata `ashara	١٤	أربعة عشر
15	khamsata `ashara	١٥	خمسة عشر
16	sittata `ashara	١٦	ستة عشر
17	sab`ata `ashara	١٧	سبعة عشر
18	thamāniyata `ashara	١٨	ثمانية عشر
19	tis`ata `ashara	١٩	تسعة عشر
20	`ishrūn	٢٠	عشرون
30	thalāthūn	٣٠	ثلاثون
40	´arba`ūn	٤٠	أربعون
50	khamsūn	٥٠	خمسون
60	sittūn	٦٠	ستون
70	sab`ūn	٧٠	سبعون
80	thamānūn	٨٠	ثمانون
90	tis`ūn	٩٠	تسعون
100	miyya	١٠٠	مئة
1000	´alf	١٠٠٠	ألف
10 000	`asharat ´alāf	١٠٠٠٠	عشرة الاف

Literature

Fiction   *The Arabian Nights*; Everyman's Library (1992).
The stories in this volume, which are over 700 years old, were translated by Husain Huddawy from the oldest Arabian manuscript by Muhsin Mahdi. The translator has produced a clear, fluent and readable version.

Jelaluddin Rumi: *The Essential Rumi: Selected Poems.* Penguin Books Ltd; New Ed edition (24 Jun 2004).
Coleman Barks has produced exquisite translations of the 13th-century Persian mystic's words.

History   **Fatima Mernissi:** *Islam and Democracy: Fear of the Modern World*; Perand politics   seus Books, US (1994).
For those wishing to acquire understanding of the Muslim heart and mind, this is essential – and provocative – reading.

Albert Hourani: *A History of the Arab Peoples*; Faber and Faber (2005).
In this hefty tome, Hourani relates the definitive history of the Arab peoples from the seventh century, when the new religion of Islam began to spread from the Arabian Peninsula westwards, to the present day.

Islam,   **Fazlur Rahman:** *Islam*; University of Chicago Press (1979).
Cultural History   A rather academic but comprehensive history and analysis of Islam. Rahman has been widely praised as one of the world's most incisive scholars in this field.

Walter M. Weiss: *Islam (Crash Course Series)*; Barron's Educational Series (2000).
A crash course in Islam: the author describes 13 centuries of Islamic history, art, and culture on less than 200 easily comprehensible pages with just as many photos.

Edward W. Said: *Orientalism*; Vintage Books (1979).
A provocative critique of Western attitudes about the Orient which has become a modern classic.

Keith Critchlow: *Islamic Patterns: An Analytical and Cosmological Approach*; Inner Traditions (1999).
The geometry and underlying cosmological principles of Islamic patterns explained.

Attilio Petruccioli (Editor), Khalil K. Pirani (Editor): *Understanding Islamic Architecture*; RoutledgeCurzon (2000).

Architects and academics discuss how it is possible to build in the spirit of Islam.

Wiebke Walther: *Women in Islam*; Wiener (Markus) Publishing Inc., US (1995).
Stories from the classical period to the present day of Muslim warriors, poets, slaves and dancers – all of whom are women.

Images of Dubai and the UAE (Photography Book); Explorer Publishing (2006).
Stunning prize-winning views of the Emirates, city and country, ancient and modern.

Ross E. Dunn: *The Adventures of Ibn Battuta: A Muslim Traveler of the Fourteenth Century*; University of California Press (2004).
Ibn Battuta, the »Arab Marco Polo«, jurist, pilgrim, adventurer, and diplomat, travelled as far as India and China on his journeys that lasted 27 years. Dunn's classic retelling of his accounts makes the legendary traveller's story accessible to a wide audience.

Wilfred Thesiger: *Arabian Sands*; Penguin Books Ltd (1984).
This report by Wilfred Thesiger is a great work of travel literature: from 1947 to 1950, the British researcher and world traveller crossed the desert of Rub al-Khali, the »empty quarter« of the Arab peninsula, with a group of Bedouin.

Lutz Jakel: *Dubai New Arabian Cuisine*; Parkway Publishing (2007).   Arab cuisine
A well-illustrated cookery book whose combination of traditional Arab ingredients with elements of European cuisine represents a mix of cultures typical of Dubai.

Road Maps and City Plans

Maps and plans from geological projects and from Fairey/Falcon are available for the individual sheikdoms in branches of Family Bookshop, the bookshops in the luxury hotels, and in some specialized bookstores.
Since new roads and highways are always being built, it is very important to ensure maps are current.

The best books on Arabia

- Sultan Bin Muhammad Al-Qasimi (ed.): *The Gulf in Historic Maps 1493 – 1931* Leicester, UK, Haley Sharpe (1996). A unique collection of historic maps of the Emir of Sharjah (available only in bookshops in the UAE).
- Walter M. Weiss (author), Kurt-Michael Westermann (photographer): *The Bazaar: Markets and Merchants of the Islamic World* Thames & Hudson (2001).
- Stefano Bianca: *Urban Form in the Arab World* Verlag der Fachvereine Hochschulverlag AG an der ETH Zurich (1994). Palaces and gardens between desert and oasis.
- Walter M. Weiss (author), Kurt-Michael Westermann (photographer): *The United Arab Emirates and Oman: Two Pearls of Arabia* Art Books Intl Ltd (2000).

Media

Radio

There are numerous English language radio stations in the UAE, including Channel 4FM 104.8 (music, news, sport and competitions), Dubai 92 (the Gulf's longest established radio station playing hits of today and the past; 92.0FM), Dubai Eye 103.8FM (the official broadcaster for the Arabian travel market; news, business, talk, music), Emirates Radio 1FM (contemporary dance and R&B music) and Emirates Radio 2 (caters for a more mature audience with musical tastes from the 1960s onwards). The BBC World Service (Dubai: 87.9FM; Abu Dhabi 90.3FM) offers news as well as cultural and entertainment programmes.

Television

Abu Dhabi, Dubai, Sharjah and Ajman have their own television stations with various programmes, including some in English. Satellite TV is very common, and most hotels offer a large selection of television programmes.

Newspapers • Magazines

The magazines *Time Out Dubai* and *What's On* appear monthly and provide information about all events in the UAE, including the entertainment programmes offered by the larger hotels.
The quarterly brochure *Sharjah What Where* contains information regarding attractions, hotels, restaurants and events in the Emirate of Sharjah.

The English-language newspapers *Gulf News*, *Khaleej Times*, and *Emirates News* are available at most hotels. Foreign daily newspapers and magazines can be found in hotel bookshops and supermarkets, with a day's delay.

Money

National
currency

The national currency is the dirham (AED, also Dh), divided into 100 Fils. Coins in 1, 5, 10, 25, and 50 Fils as well as 1 AED denominations and notes in 5, 10, 50, 100, 200, and 500 AED denominations are in circulation. The dirham is fixed to the US currency at 3.67 AED per 1 US$. Money can be changed at banks, in hotels and at bureaux de change. Cash can be obtained at over 300 automated cash machines, by debit or credit card.

Credit cards are the most common form of payment in the UAE. Some small stores add a surcharge of 3 to 5% for credit card payments as opposed to cash.

In case of loss or other credit card problems in Dubai (area code: 04), contact: American Express tel. 3 36 50 00; Diners tel. 3 49 82 00; Master Card Tel. 3 32 29 56; or Visa tel. 2 23 68 88.

i Rates of exchange

- 1 AED = £0.14
  £1 = 7.33 AED
- 1 AED = €0.20
  €1 = 4.94 AED
- 1 AED = US$0.27
  US$1 =3.67 AED
  Current exchange rates at www.oanda.com/convert/classic

Most banks are open Sat–Thu 8am–noon/1pm; some banks are also open from 4pm–5.30pm.   Opening hours
The money exchanges are open 9am–1pm and 4pm–8pm daily.

Nature Reserves

The UAE is increasingly making efforts to conserve nature and protect wildlife; therefore, some desert and lagoon areas have been declared nature reserves.

Numerous bird sanctuaries have been established in the Sheikdoms.

ABU DHABI

► **Al-Wathba Lake**
A bird sanctuary covering 5 sq km/ 2 sq mi located 40km/25mi south-east of Abu Dhabi; approximately 200 species of bird live and nest here.

► **Sir Bani Yas**
Private island off the coast of Abu Dhabi. Nature reserve for Oryx antelopes and other Arabian and African animals. Only accessible for school classes and scientists (contact P.O. Box 77 in Abu Dhabi).

DUBAI

► **Al-Maha Desert Resort**
The luxury eco-hotel is located 65km/40mi south-east of Dubai in a 25 sq km/10 sq mi nature reserve (►Baedeker Special, p.201).

► **Khor Dubai Wildlife Sanctuary**
Tel. 04 / 3 47 22 77
This bird sanctuary is located at the end of the creek, approximately 8km/5mi from Dubai.

FUJAIRAH

► **Khor Kalba Mangrove Reserve**
Khor Kalba
Swamp and mangrove landscape with bird sanctuary located south of Kalba.

SHARJAH

► **Sharjah Desert Park**
Sharjah Airport Road
Junction No. 8
Dhaid Highway
Nature reserve located halfway between Sharjah and Al-Dhaid.

Personal Safety

The United Arab Emirates are among the safest countries in the world. Pickpocketing or carjacking, fraud at restaurants or while shopping and in particular theft and violence are practically unheard of, either in the Emirates or for that matter on the entire Arabian peninsula. Visitors can move around freely anywhere around the clock without cause for nervousness; this also applies to women travelling alone. In case of complaints or doubts, the Tourist Security Department of the Municipality of Dubai is available at tel. 800 4438.

Post · Communications

Post

Postage   A postcard to Europe costs 2.50 AED, an airmail letter 3.25 AED; mailing time to Europe is 5 to 7 days. Stamps are also available in hotels and shops.

► MAIN POST OFFICES AND AREA CODES

► **Abu Dhabi**
East Road (between Al-Falah and
Zayed 2nd Street)
Tel. 02 / 6 21 54 15

► **Dubai**
Zabeel Road
Umm Hureir
Tel. 04 / 3 96 12 43

► **Country codes**
From UK and Republic of
Ireland ...
... to the UAE: 00 971
From USA, Canada and
Australia...
... to the UAE: 0011 971
The 0 that precedes the subse-
quent local area code is omitted.

From the UAE ...
... to the UK: 00 44

... to the Republic of
Ireland: 00 353
... to the USA/Canada: 00 1
... to Australia: 00 61
The 0 that precedes the subsequent local area code is omitted.

► **Local area codes**
Abu Dhabi: 02
Ajman: 06
Al Ain: 03
Dubai 04
Fujairah: 09
Ras al-Kaimah: 07
Sharjah: 06
Umm al-Quwain: 06

► **Directory inquiries**
180 (no charge)

Post offices are open Sat–Wed 8am–1pm and 4pm–7pm, main post
offices until 10pm.

Opening hours

Telephone Calls

Almost every street corner has a public telephone that accepts phone
and credit cards. Phone cards for 30, 50 and 100 AED are available
in many shops.

Public telephones

The mobile phones common in western Europe work in the United
Arab Emirates without any problems.

◄ *Mobile phones*

Prices · Discounts

During the summer, the hotels reduce their prices significantly and
frequently even offer »special rates or packages« with half or full
board. Due to the very low ticket and admission prices (1 to 5 AED;
14 to 70 pence), public transport and museums do not offer any special discounts.

▶ WHAT DOES IT COST?

Three-course meal
99 AED / £13.50 / €20

Simple meal
35 AED / £4.70 / €7

Cup of coffee
4.90-7.40 AED /
£0.67-£1 / €1-1.50

Glass of fruit juice
4.90-7.40 AED /
£0.67-£1 / €1-1.50

Double room
approx. 494 AED /
£67 / €100

1l/0.22gal petrol
1.73-1.98 AED /
£0.24-£0.27 / €0.35-0

Shopping

Due to the low tariffs levied by customs and the prevalent lack of taxes, many international brand name items – especially clothing, electronics and cosmetics – are often significantly less expensive than in Europe. In addition, beautiful handicrafts can be found in the United Arab Emirates, though these usually come from neighbouring countries.

Shops are usually open Sat–Thu 8am–1pm and 4pm–8pm, souks often until 10pm.

Abu Dhabi, Dubai, Al Ain and Sharjah have numerous **shopping malls** that follow the US model and are also known as commercial centres; Dubai alone has 32 of these modern shopping complexes. Various types of stores are housed on several levels; there is usually a central food court where different self-service restaurants offer fast food.

! *Baedeker* TIP

Dubai Shopping Festival

Around three million visitors travel from all over the world every year in order to hunt for bargains during the Shopping Festival in Dubai from mid-January to mid-February. Over 2,000 stores reduce their prices by up to 50%, generating sales of over one billion US dollars. Fashion items, jewellery, electronics, and cars are among the articles offered. Those who would like to participate in the festival should book their flight and hotel room early (information at www.mydsf.com).

Duty-free shops   The duty-free shops at the airports in Abu Dhabi, Dubai and Sharjah offer a large selection of products, some at very reasonable prices, and are also open to transit travellers to and from the far east. The

A lively atmosphere at Dubai's traditional spice souk

duty-free shop at the Dubai airport is a regular shopping paradise when it comes to product selection. Before and after the flight, brand-name items can be purchased at favourable prices on over 9,000 sq m/96,875 sq ft of retail space.

Souks

Souks, the symbol of shopping in the orient, are shopping districts consisting of several bazaars; the shops are arranged according to the type of products they offer, so that similar items are available in multiple adjacent stores within a certain alley or section. The Gold Souk in Dubai is especially well known. The Spice Souk in the emirate has a lively atmosphere. The souk in the Heritage Village in Dubai's historic Shindaga quarter was beautifully constructed in the traditional style. The Souk Al-Arsah in Sharjah was also newly rebuilt. The Blue Souk in Sharjah and the New Souk in Khor Fakkan are also elaborately designed.

Antiques

Most of the antiques offered for sale in the United Arab Emirates come from foreign countries, usually Iran, Syria and India. Items that were actually made in the United Arab Emirates are very rare, while those from Oman and Yemen are commonly found. The old wooden chests called sanduks, which are beautifully carved and decorated, are very attractive.

Bedouin jewellery

Most of the silver, wood and leather Bedouin jewellery offered in the UAE comes from Oman and Yemen. Therefore, the best selection and prices can be found in Buraimi near Al Ain.

TEARS OF THE GODS

As an old Arabian saying has it, »the scent of incense reaches heaven like no other«. For thousands of years, frankincense from Southern Arabia was one of the most precious goods in the world.

Pliny the Elder described how the Roman Emperor Nero burnt a year's worth of frankincense at the funeral of his wife Poppea. Inside the tomb of the Egyptian pharaoh Tutankhamen a small amount of frankincense was found, which at that time was a precious ingredient for embalming bodies. That incense was once nearly as valuable as gold is also illustrated in the legend of the Three Kings who set out to Bethlehem with gold, frankincense and myrrh.

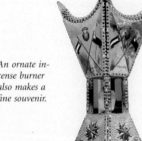

An ornate incense burner also makes a fine souvenir.

World of smells and scents

In the UAE, scents are still tremendously important. Souk alleys carry the smell of frankincense and incense sticks. A mixture of sandalwood, myrrh, musk and frankincense is decocted in rosewater and sugar to produce a lump which, when cold,

creates a hard incense resin. This resin is then used to scent rooms and clothes. Frankincense is also one of the most commonly used ingredients in the traditional Gulf trade of perfume making.

Expensive cure-all

Frankincense, the resin of the only two to three metre (6.6-9.9ft) high Boswellia tree, has been known in the Arab world for thousands of years. In Arabic it is called »luban«, which means white or milky. It was used to heal diseases and cover unpleasant smells. It was also employed for the production of cosmetics. Frankincense had only one major disadvantage: it was expensive. In antiquity, this resin, also called »tears of the Gods«, was on a par with gold. Harvesting this much-desired fragrance involved numerous rituals, a practice reserved only for members of a certain caste.

Incense Road

One of the most significant caravan routes for frankincense led from Sheba (Yemen) to Marib (Yemen), then parallel to the coast of the Red Sea via Petra (Jordan), the centre of the Nabateans, to the Mediterranean harbour town of Gaza (Palestine).

The most valuable resin came from the area of what is now Southern Oman. The trees that grow here produce a resin that is gleaming white and particularly aromatic. The trees are harvested between March and May by means of cuts into the bark; the tapped resin is then stored for several months. Price and quality are determined by colour, and lighter resin is usually more expensive. The resin is burnt in specially-manufactured burners, mostly made of clay or metal. Across the entire UAE and Oman, guests are welcomed with clouds of incense.

Books   English-language books, mainly about the UAE, and travel guides as well as illustrated books are available in the better hotels and Family Bookshops.

Designer knockoffs   Many stores in the United Arab Emirates offer (illegal) knockoffs and forgeries of designer goods and brand-name products – watches, jewellery, bags and clothing – with the logos and tags of the originals. Dubai has an entire shopping district, the Karama Bazaar, with shops that offer imitation designer items which are almost indistinguishable from the originals (Gucci, Dolce & Gabbana, Prada, Calvin Klein, Tommy Hilfiger, DKNY) for a song. Back home, even the local watchmaker will be fooled by the Cartier watch for £17; however, you have to ask for it, since it is only shown in a back room where you are shown a case containing Rolex, Dior, Hermès and so on. The latest Breitling model is a little more expensive at £33 – battery included. However, importing such forgeries into the EU is not permitted.

ℹ The best shopping locations

- Abu Dhabi Mall: elegant stores, cafés and restaurants
- Sharjah Book Mall: unbeatable selection and atmosphere
- Blue Souk: the top floor of the Sharjah Souk offers the most beautiful antiques and old handicrafts
- Majlis Gallery: Dubai's number 1 store for handicrafts
- Bur Juman Centre: the most exclusive of Dubai's many shopping malls, with 175 boutiques on four levels

Arab daggers   Arab daggers are available in every conceivable variation, from plastic imitations to silver works of art. Most of them are produced in Yemen and Oman, where they are called Djambia or Khanjar.

Spices   All souks have their section for oriental and Asian spices, which are sold from bulk bags or pre-packaged at excellent prices. The best selection can be found at the Spice Souk in the Sikat al-Khalil Street in Dubai, between the Gold Souk and the creek.

Gold   In Abu Dhabi and Sharjah, the souks and shopping complexes have separate departments for gold jewellery. The Gold Souk in Dubai is comprised of approximately 200 shops; arm bands, chains, rings and brooches glitter in more than 600 display windows. Gold is sold by weight, regardless of the style and design; the price for a gramme of 22-carat gold is around 40 AED or £5.45.

Coffeepots   An Arab coffeepot (dallah) made of sheet metal or steel with the typical beak-shaped spout makes a charming souvenir and is available everywhere.

Ceramics   Most crockery in the UAE comes from Ras al-Khaimah, where it is still made from local clay and fired in traditional kilns even today.

SHOPPING ADDRESSES

ANTIQUES

In the Al-Nasr Street in Abu
Dhabi, some stores also carry
silver items from Yemen and
Oman in addition to antiques.
In the Emirate of Sharjah,
antiques are mainly sold on the
top floor of the Blue Souk.

► Orient Art Gallery
Bur Juman Centre
Corner of Bank Road and
Khalid Bin-Walid Road
Dubai
Local handicrafts are also offered
on the ground floor of the shop-
ping centre, in addition to
antiques.

► Hunar Gallery
Rashidiya
Dubai
Drawings and watercolours, rugs
and books can be found here in
addition to Persian oil paintings.

BOOKS

All five-star hotels in the United
Arab Emirates run their own
bookshops, where popular illustrated books, travel books, off-
road guides and maps are available. The Book Mall in Sharjah
carries the largest selection of
books about the sheikdoms.

► The Book Mall
Behind the Expo Centre
Sharjah

GOLD

► Dubai
Gold Souk
Naif Road

► Sharjah
Gold Centre
Al-Wahda Street
(Corner of Al-Qasimia Road)
Al-Yarmook

CERAMICS

► Abu Dhabi
Abu Dhabi Pottery
Al-Rumarthy Building
Khalidiya Park Street

► Dubai
The Courtyard
Sheikh Zayed Road
In addition to beautifully decora-
ted ceramics, antiques and leaded
glass are also offered here.

ART • HANDICRAFTS

► Abu Dhabi
Cultural Foundation
Sheikh Zayed 1st Street
(Corner of Old Airport Road)

► Dubai
Arts & Crafts, Shop 19
Markaz al-Jumeirah
Jumeirah Beach Road
In addition to select handicrafts,
rugs, occasional furniture and
exquisite textiles are also available.

Majlis Gallery
Al-Fahidi Roundabout
Bastakiya, Bur Dubai
Regional art and handicrafts from
the Gulf of Arabia are sold here.

SHOPPING MALLS

► Abu Dhabi
There are several modern shopping complexes in Hamdan Street.
The Liwa Centre presents itself in
the post-modern style, with three
levels in green granite and lots of

Dubai is brightly lit during the »Shopping Festival«.

glass. The food court is located on the third floor; the »Café Moka« is a popular hangout, and Japanese cuisine is available in the »Fujiyama«.

The She Zone
Khalidiya Street
The shopping centre includes 33 shops, a movie theatre, restaurant and health centre. It is staffed exclusively by women, and the complex is also entirely reserved for women, who can take off their veil and shawl here. The otherwise common security cameras are not present here.

▶ **Dubai**
Al-Guhrair Centre
Umer Ibn Al-Khattab Street
(Corner of Al-Riqqa Road)
Bur Deira

Bur Juman Centre
Bank Road
(Corner of Khalid Bin-Walid Road)
Bur Dubai

Deira City Centre
Tariq Bin-Ziad Road
Bur Deira

Lamcy
Karama Street
Bur Dubai
With a replica of the London Tower Bridge; opposite, a waterfall plunges through an artificial cliff landscape from a height of 20m/ 66ft – inside the building.

Wafi Mall
Zabeel Road
Bur Dubai
The huge shopping complex is home to about 140 stores plus Pyramids Restaurant, Cleopatra's Health Spa and Planet Hollywood. Those who want to take a virtual tour of the shopping complex can do so at www.waficity. com.

▶ **Sharjah**
Al-Fardan Centre
Khalid Lagoon Corniche
With large food court

Sharjah in particular is home to a lively arts scene that promotes local artists; it is centred around the Sharjah Arts Area with the Sharjah Arts Museum and galleries.

Art, Handicrafts

Traditional silver jewellery is imported from Yemen and Oman, and is therefore more expensive than in the originating countries. The melted silver from the Maria-Theresia taler, which reached Yemen as payment for coffee in the 18th and 19th centuries, was turned into finely engraved silver jewellery. Incense (luban) and other tree resins as well as potpourri (bokhur) mainly come from Oman, but are also prepared in the United Arab Emirates. The incense burners, called mubkhar, are available in antique and art shops. Dates and oriental spices make tasty souvenirs.

Souvenirs

Dubai, Abu Dhabi, Al Ain and Sharjah have many shops offering rugs and fabrics, most of which come from Iran, Pakistan and central Asia. The best selection can be found at the Iranian Market near the port of Abu Dhabi.

Rugs, fabrics

Sport and Outdoors

Sporting Fun

Both coasts of the UAE provide all types of water sports, including windsurfing, water skiing, jet skiing and sailing. Many beach hotels offer taster courses in snorkelling and diving. Advanced divers prefer the underwater world of the east coast. Four and five-star hotels are equipped with tennis and squash courts as well as modern fitness centres. Dubai has four golf courses, three of which are world class. Dubai's most exotic sport is dune skiing on mono-skis, also called sand skiing. And for those who prefer a real winter atmosphere, there are several ice skating rinks.

▶ SPORT OFFERS

ICE SKATING RINKS

▶ **Abu Dhabi Ice Rink**
Airport Road
Abu Dhabi
Tel. 02 / 4 44 84 58
Daily 10am–10pm
Admission: 5 AED (2 hrs)

▶ **Al Ain Ice Rink**
Mohammed Bin-Khalifa Street

Al Ain
Tel. 03 / 7 84 55 42
Open Sun–Thu 4pm–10pm, Fri from 9am, Wed women only
Admission: 5–10 AED (2 hrs)

▶ **Galleria Ice Rink**
Galleria Shopping Centre
Hyatt Regency Hotel
Dubai

Tel. 04 / 2 09 65 51
Open daily 10am–9.30pm
Admission 25 AED (2.5 hrs)

Locals in particular are enthusiastic ice skaters.

FITNESS CENTRES

▶ **Tourist Club**
Sheikh Hamdan Street
Abu Dhabi
Tel. 02 / 6 72 34 00
Open Sat–Thu 8am until midnight
Offers all types of water sports as well as bowling, badminton, ice skating, tennis and squash.

▶ **Al-Nasr Fitness Centre**
Al-Nasr Leisureland
Umm Hureir, Bur Dubai
Dubai
Tel. 04 / 3 37 12 34
Open daily 9am–10pm
Large amusement park with numerous sports facilities, including squash courts, bowling alleys, go-kart tracks and ice skating rinks

▶ **Le Mirage Health & Leisure Club**
Le Meridien Jumeirah Beach Hotel
Al-Mina al-Siyahi Street
Dubai
Tel. 04 / 3 99 55 55
Open Sat–Thu 8am–10pm
Including a pool with children's pool, minigolf, squash, tennis, water sports.
Admission 80 AED

▶ **Hotel Holiday International**
Khalid Lagoon (Buheira)
Corniche, Al-Majaz
Sharjah
Tel. 06 / 5 73 66 66
Open daily 8am–10pm
Includes pool, tennis court and sauna. Admission 40 AED

▶ **Flamingo Beach Resort**
UAQ Tourist Club
Umm al-Quwain
Tel. 06 / 7 65 11 85
Leisure centre and water sports club

GOLF

▶ **Dubai Golf Office**
P.O. Box 2 40 40
Dubai
Tel. 04 / 3 99 52 05
Fax 3 99 53 77
www.dubaigolf.com
Central booking service for Dubai golf courses

▶ **Emirates Golf Club**
Sheikh Zayed Road (Street to Jebel Ali)
Dubai
Tel. 04 / 3 47 32 22
The golf club is situated 25km/15mi south of the city and is easily recognizable by its seven enor-

18-hole course includes several ponds, three saltwater obstacles and sophisticated bunkers. There is also another 9-hole course. The club has four restaurants, including the »Boardwalk« with terrace dining (tel. 04 / 2 95 60 61) and the »Aquarium« (tel. 04 / 2 82 57 77), an exquisite fish restaurant. Green fees: 330 AED

► **Abu Dhabi Airport Golf Club (Al Ghazal Golf Club)**
Channel Road
(situated behind the new airport on the road to Umm Al-Nar)
Abu Dhabi
Tel. 02 / 5 75 80 40, www.addf.ae
The 18-hole course, which comprises 125ha/309ac, is irrigated underground by an artificial lake of desalinated seawater.

MARATHON

The Dubai Marathon takes place every year in the middle of January, and has grown into an international event. For information and registration: tel. 04 / 3 36 93 21.

HORSE RIDING

Emirates Golf Club: one of the Emirates' most exclusive sports facilities.

mous Bedouin tents made of concrete and glass. An eighth tent, located slightly to the side, is reserved for the owner of the golf course, Muhammad Bin-Rashid al-Maktoum, Crown Prince of Dubai. Two 18-hole courses are in operation, three additional courts are in planning. Green fees: 365 AED.

► **Dubai Creek Golf & Yacht Club**
Deira Creek Side
Dubai
Tel. 04 / 2 95 60 00
The club is visible from a distance thanks to its sail-shaped roof. The

► **Abu Dhabi Equestrian Club**
Saeed Bin-Thanoun Street
Mushrif, Abu Dhabi
Tel. 02 / 4 45 55 00
60 school and rental horses, from 50 AED per hour.

► **Ajman Equestrian Club**
City Centre Road
(situated behind the city centre)
Ajman
Tel. 06 / 7 43 31 23
Riding lessons and outings on horseback through the desert take place between 8am and 12pm and from 4pm to 7pm.

▶ **Inter-Continental
Riding Stables**
Inter-Continental Hotel
Al-Salam Street
Al Ain
Tel. 03 / 7 68 66 86
Lessons and outings on horseback
between September and May.

▶ **Dubai Polo Club & Horseriding**
Hatta Road
Dubai
Tel. 04 / 3 33 11 88
The club offers horse riding and
polo lessons daily between 6am
and 8pm, starting from 60 AED
per hour. Spectators are welcome
to attend the polo games – between November and April.

▶ **Sharjah Equestrian Centre**
Dhaid Road km 17
(On the corner of New Dubai
Road)
P.O. Box 19 91
Sharjah
Tel. 06 / 5 31 11 55
The club operates a horse riding
school and a race track.

▶ **UAQ Marine Club &
Riding Centre**
UAQ Lagoon
Umm al-Quwain
Tel. 06 / 7 66 54 46
Riding lessons from Tue–Sun be-
tween 7am–7pm. Beach, night and
desert rides also offered.

SAND SKIING

Sand dune skiing is becoming
increasingly popular. Many travel
agencies in the UAE organize tours
and rent out equipment.

Water Sports

The beach hotels and clubs on the east and west coasts of the United
Arab Emirates offer their guests an extensive range of water sports:
sea angling, diving and snorkelling are more popular and worthwhile
on the east coast of the United Arab Emirates, particularly in Khor
Fakkan and Fujairah; here an offshore coral reef and numerous small
rocky islands create an ideal environment for a rich underwater
world.

▶ WATER SPORTS

SEA ANGLING

Sea angling tours are offered by
numerous charter firms; alterna-
tively it is possible to rent a boat
and choose your own destination.
Bounty Charters in Dubai offers a
12m/39ft boat for up to six people
as well as angling tours (half days
1,300 AED, full days 2,000 AED)
to the east coast and up to Oman.

▶ **Bounty Charters**
Dubai, tel. 04 / 3 48 30 42

SAILING

In Dubai, the hotels Jebel Ali,
Hilton, Jumeirah Beach, Meridien,
Oasis, Royal Mirage and Dubai
Marine own their own sailing
boats, and they also offer sailing
lessons.

DIVING

Only the east coast of the UAE is good for diving, while the west coast is too shallow and sandy and doesn't offer divers much in terms of a spectacular underwater world.

► **Maku-Divecenter**
Holiday Beach Motel
(south of Dibba)
P.O. Box 14 33, Fujairah
Tel. / fax 09 / 2 44 57 47
This diving centre offers equipment, (PADI) training courses and tours to the 15km/9.3mi dive coast. The dive locations are 6–20m/20–66ft deep, the visibility is between 10–30m/10–33yd.

► **Sandy Beach Diving Centre**
Sandy Beach Motel
Dibba – Khor Fakkan Highway
P.O. Box 659
Fujairah
Tel. 09 / 2 44 50 50
www.sandybm.com
The centre is situated on the beach of Al-Aqqa, halfway between Dibba and Khor Fakkan. It also offers PADI training courses.

WATER PARKS

The Wild Wadi Aqua Park is unique in its architectural and technical design, which also explains the high admission and the masses of visitors. A good alternative is the aqua park in Umm al-Quwain, which is more relaxed and inexpensive and mainly visited by expatriates.

► **Wild Wadi Aqua Park**
Jumeirah Beach Road
Dubai, tel. 04 / 3 48 44 44
www.wildwadi.com
Open daily 11am–7pm
Admission: 99 AED, children 80

AED, Thu and Fri 120 / 100 AED
From 4pm 65 / 50 AED
The water park close to the Burj al-Arab impresses with a high-speed water slide, surfer pool and artificial rain storms.

► **Dreamland Aqua Park**
Umm al-Quwain
Tel. 06 / 7 68 18 88
Open Sat–Thu 10am–8pm, Fri from 2pm (families only)
Admission:
30 AED, children 20 AED
The water park is situated 14km/8.6mi north of the UAQ roundabout, on the road to Ras al-Khaimah.

WATERSKIING

The large beach hotels usually offer their guests an opportunity for waterskiing, for example at the Al Boom Marine Water Sports in the Royal Mirage Hotel, tel. 04 / 2 89 48 58, daily 9am–6pm.

► **Dubai Water Sports Association**
P.O. Box 1 34 13, Dubai
Tel. 04 / 3 24 10 31
Fax 3 24 10 83
The clubhouse of the Dubai Water Sports Association is located in Al-Jaddaf (Garhoud), at the top end of the creek where the estuary becomes shallower and smoother. Here, even non-members are allowed to water ski (10 minutes for 50 AED), though hotels often have better offers.

WIND SURFING

Nearly all larger beach hotels offer wind surfing, for example at the Al Boom Marine Water Sports in the Royal Mirage Hotel in Dubai, tel. 04 / 2 89 48 58, daily 9am–6pm.

Birdwatching

Mainly in early spring and autumn, the estuaries and lagoons of the Emirates of Dubai, Sharjah, Ajman, Ras al-Khaimah as well as the mangrove swamps of Umm al-Quwain make ideal places for bird-watching. Tours are organized by the Birds Records Committee in Dubai (tel. 348 52 77).

Desert Driving

Driving in the desert Self-organized desert tours are always risky. Absolutely never drive off-road in a car without four-wheel drive! But even in a four-by-four, the chances of getting stuck in the soft sand are relatively high. The general rule is, the darker the ground, the harder the surface. For those who choose to leave the paved roads, remember to let some air out of the tyres: on hard, rocky ground the tyre pressure should be around 75% of the recommended air pressure, in soft desert sand a maximum of 50%, so the tyre has better grip. Driving with decreased tyre pressure, however, requires great caution. Always go on the road with at least two fully-tanked vehicles. Also bring a spare fuel canister, water supply, a spare tyre, a tow rope, tools, a plank to jack the vehicle, sand shovels and a large piece of sheet metal to put under the tyres if the car gets stuck in the sand. To prevent the car from overturning, sand dunes should be approached straight on, not diagonally.

Driving courses ▶ Plenty of organizers offer »desert driving courses«. An all-day course costs between 250– 300 AED.

Time

The United Arab Emirates is four hours ahead of Greenwich Mean Time, and in summer only three hours ahead of British Summer Time (there is no adjustment for daylight saving in the UAE).

Transport

Road Traffic

Road network The road network in the UAE is in excellent condition. The city motorways and highways have four to six lanes, and signposting is generally in English.

Traffic regulations The UAE has right-hand traffic. Seat belts must be worn when driving; children under the age of ten are required to sit in the back

Exclusive vehicles can be found on the sheikdoms' streets.

seat. Traffic coming from the right has right-of-way unless signposted otherwise. Typically, there are numerous roundabouts (R/A) rather than traffic lights in the UAE: here the circling traffic has right of way. Driving while under the influence of alcohol is severely punished, as is speeding. Tourists are usually required to pay the fine straight away.

Maximum speed for passenger cars: 25–38mph/40–60kmh within city limits, 44–56mph/70–90kmh on country roads, 75mph/120kmh on motorways. Cars (even rental cars) driving faster than 75mph/120kmh have a warning signal to warn the driver that the speed limit has been exceeded.

Car Rental

The minimum age for renting a car is 21 (for four-by-fours 25). Although it is a requirement to carry an international driver's licence, a national driver's licence is often enough as car rental companies can issue a temporary local driver's licence for a fee of 10 AED. A small car with air-conditioning costs between 100 and 150 AED per day. Since larger hotels pick up their guests at the airport and usually provide a car rental service, it is normally not necessary to rent a car at the airport.

Breakdown Service

In the event of a car accident the police should be immediately informed (tel. 999). The vehicle must not be moved until the accident has been recorded. Also, a vehicle may not be repaired without a police accident report. What to do in the event of an accident with a rental car is explained in the documents for the rental car. In the event of a breakdown, it usually only takes a few minutes before a police car stops to organize assistance.

Taxis

In Abu Dhabi In Abu Dhabi, all taxis run on a taximeter. The basic fee is 3 AED including 3km/2mi; each additional kilometre (0.6mi) costs 0.75 AED. A trip from the airport to the city centre costs about 70 AED. In Abu Dhabi and Al Ain, it is best to use the Al-Ghazal taxis with the gazelle logo; their drivers usually speak English (tel. 4 44 93 00).

In Dubai In Dubai, there are taxis with and without a meter. The beige-coloured taxis of the Dubai Transport Corporation (tel. 2 08 08 08) cost 3 AED basic fee and 1.20 AED per kilometre (0.6mi); night fares are slightly higher. Expect to pay between 35 and 40 AED for a trip from the airport to the city centre.

In the other emirates In all other emirates, the fare must be negotiated beforehand. Prices are low, but it is best to ask your hotel for a benchmark. A trip within the city limits usually costs just under 10 AED. The drivers are mostly Asian and often don't speak English. It helps to name a prominent building (e.g. a hotel) close to the desired destination.

Share taxis Share taxis or service taxis (sometimes called collective taxis) are vehicles for four to six people. Parked at specific locations in the cities, they only leave with a full load, which means a bit of waiting around

Abras are a quick and inexpensive way to cross the creek.

BUS STATIONS • LANDING STAGES

BUS STATIONS
► **Abu Dhabi**
Hazza Bin-Zayed Road

► **Dubai**
Al-Khor Street
Al-Ras
(between the Hyatt Hotel and
Gold Souk)
Al-Sabkha Road (Bur Deira)

SERVICE TAXIS
► **Dubai**
Al-Ghurair Shopping Complex

ABRAS LANDING STAGES
► **Ajman**
Khor Ajman

► **Dubai**
Bandar Talib Station on the Al-
Khor-Corniche in Bur Deira;
Abra Docks in the Bastakiya dis-
trict in Bur Dubai

► **Ras al-Khaimah**
Al-Khor, between the western part
of the old town and the eastern
part of the Nakheel district

at first. The taxi is crowded when full, but in return a trip to another emirate costs next to nothing. From the service taxi stations in Dubai a trip to the northern emirates on the west coast costs between 5 and 15 AED per person, 25 AED to the east coast, 60 AED to Abu Dhabi or Al Ain.

Public Transport

Abu Dhabi and Dubai are the only emirates with a regular public bus service. The destinations of the buses are not always signposted in English. The Transport Department in Dubai (tel. 8 85 94 01) operates about 20 routes from 6am to 11pm every day. A single ticket costs on average between 1 and 4 AED; it is 5 AED to Jebel Ali (40km/15mi) and 12 AED for a 100km/62mi bus ride to Hatta. Tickets are available from the driver.

In Abu Dhabi there are fewer public buses however, they run around the clock. One trip on the island of Abu Dhabi costs between 2 and 5 AED, and 15 AED to Al Ain.

The other emirates are served by minibuses of the Dubai Transport Corporation (tel. 2 27 38 40).

◄ buses
Dubai

◄ Abu Dhabi

◄ Emirates

Travellers with Disabilities

Overall, the United Arab Emirates – particularly the sheikdoms of Dubai, Abu Dhabi and Sharjah – are quite easily accessible for those

Access for
individuals with
disabilities

▶ ORGANIZATIONS FOR THE DISABLED

▶ **RADAR (UK)**
12 City Forum
250 City Road
London EC1V 8AF
Tel. 020 7250 3222
Fax: 020 7250 0212
www.radar.org.uk

▶ **Mobility International USA**
132 E. Broadway, Suite 343
Eugene, Oregon USA 97401
Tel. Tel: (541) 343-1284
Fax: (541) 343-6812
www.miusa.org

▶ **MossRehab ResourceNet**
MossRehab Hospital
1200 West Tabor Road
Philadelphia, PA USA

Tel. 215 456 9900
www.mossresourcenet.org

▶ **Accessible Travel (UK)**
Avionics House
Naas Lane
Quedgeley
Gloucester GL2 2SN
Tel. 01452 729 739
Fax 01452 729853
www.accessibletravel.co.uk

▶ **UAE Handicapped Guardians Association**
P.O. Box 25800
Sharjah, UAE
Tel. 009 71 / 6 / 5 56 42 22
Fax 5 56 44 99
www.hga-uae.org.ae

with disabilities. In public buildings, airports, shopping malls and hotels in the four and five-star category, special parking spaces, ramps, wide doors, lifts with low-mounted buttons and toilets for the disabled can be found. The cruise ship harbour in Dubai is also properly equipped for the needs of disabled individuals. The museums are a different matter; with the exception of the Dubai Museum, they are usually not wheelchair accessible.

Organizations | There are various institutions that organize group trips; trained travel agents arrange individual trips and provide assistance.

Weights, Measures, Temperatures

Linear measures	1 inch (in;) = 2.54 cm	1 mm = 0.03937 in
	1 foot (ft;) = 12 in = 30.48 cm	1 cm = 0.033 ft
	1 yard (yd;) = 3 ft = 91.44 cm	1 m = 1.09 yd
	1 mile (mi;) = 1.61 km	1 km = 0.62 mi
Square measures	1 square inch (in²) = 6.45 cm²	1 cm² = 0.155 in²
	1 square foot (ft²) = 9.288 dm²	1 dm² = 0.108 ft²
	1 square yard (yd²) = 0.836 m²	1 m² = 1.196 yd²

1 square mile (mi²) = 2.589 km²	1 km² = 0.386 mi²
1 acre = 0.405 ha	1 ha = 2.471 acres

Cubic measures

1 cubic inch (in³) = 16.386 cm³	1 cm³ = 0.061 in³
1 cubic foot (ft³) = 28.32 dm³	1 dm³ = 0.035 ft³
1 cubic yard (yd³) = 0.765 m³	1 m³ = 1.308 yd³

Liquid measure

1 gill = 0.118 l	1 l = 8.747 gills
1 pint (pt) = 4 gills = 0.473 l	1 l = 2.114 pt
1 quart (qt) = 2 pt = 0.946 l	1 l = 1.057 qt
1 gallon (gal) = 4 qt = 3.787 l	1 l = 0.264 gal

Weights

1 ounce (oz;) = 28.365 g	100 g = 2.527 oz
1 pound (lb;) = 453.59 g	1 kg = 2.206 lb
1 cental (cwt;.) = 45.359 kg	100 kg = 2.205 cwt

Temperature

Fahrenheit:	0	10	20	32	50	68	89	95
Celsius:	-18	-12	-6.5	0	10	20	30	35

Conversion:

$$\text{Fahrenheit} = 1.8 \times \text{Celsius} + 32 \qquad \text{Celsius} = \frac{5\,(\text{Fahrenheit} - 32)}{9}$$

Clothing sizes

Men's clothing

For men's suits, coats and shirts measurements are identical in the UK and the USA.

Men's shoes:

UK	7	8	9	10	11
US	8	9	10	11	12

Women's clothing:

UK	8	10	12	14	16	18
US	6	8	10	12	14	16

Women's shoes:

UK	3	4	5	6	7	8
US	5.5	6.5	7.5	8.5	9.5	10.5

Children's sizes:

UK	3-4 yrs	4-5 yrs	5-6 yrs	6-7 yrs	7-8 yrs
US	3	4	5	6	6X

When To Go

Winter travel destination

With a relatively short flight of approximately 7 hours from London and the pleasant temperatures between October and April, the UAE is an ideal winter travel destination. The months of November through to March are the best time to travel, but Christmas, Easter, and in Dubai also the »Shopping Festival« taking place from mid-January to mid-February are regarded as the peak seasons when the hotels are largely booked out.

Many locals leave the Emirates during the hot summer months, and hotels lower their prices starting in May. But since temperatures rise as high as 50°C, visiting the UAE during these months is not recommended.

Ramadan, the month of fasting (▶ Festivals, Holidays and Events) when rules of conduct are very strictly interpreted, is also unsuitable for a visit. During these four weeks, restaurants do not open until after dusk, and business and public life is reduced to a minimum. In Dubai however, the restrictions related to Ramadan are less pronounced.

Climate

The climate of the UAE is arid year-round. Rain usually falls only during the winter months. The average amount of annual precipitation is less than 100mm/4in. Temperatures seldom fall below 20°C.

During the **summer months** between May and August, the thermometer climbs above 40°C; sometimes, it even goes as high as 50°C in the shade. The average amount of daily sunshine is eleven hours (eight hours during winter). Relative humidity is low; in the interior of the country, where it sometimes does not rain for years, it is around 20%. Therefore, the streets are practically deserted on a typical summer day; the locals fly to cooler regions during this time.

During the **winter months**, daytime temperatures decrease to values between 20° and 30°C. During this time of »increased rain«, relative humidity is often considerable and can even reach 90% on some days.

A luxurious holiday residence: the Burj al-Arab

The notorious wind known as **Shimal** (»north«) which blows from the north-west between May and June can be accompanied by sandstorms and occasionally by rain.

The Shimal causes severe discomfort for sensitive individuals, causing headaches and sometimes breathing problems.

The **sea** is warm enough for swimming all year. The water temperature reaches 20°C even in January and February. During the following months, the water temperature increases gradually and reaches an average of 31°C in August.

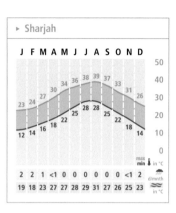

▸ Sharjah

Tours

YOU DON'T KNOW WHERE
YOU WANT TO GO YET?
OUR TOUR SUGGESTIONS
HELP YOU – WITH TIPS
FOR THE BEST ROUTES AND
SUGGESTIONS FOR THE BEST
ACCOMMODATIONS.

TRAVELLING IN THE UNITED ARAB EMIRATES

The Emirates have plenty to offer besides beaches and shopping malls. It is therefore highly recommended to venture outside the tourist centres of Dubai, Sha and Abu Dhabi and take a closer look at the many beautiful features of country. Al Ain and Muscat can be reached by bus, the northern emirates by lective taxi. All other destinations can be visited in the ubiquitous organi tours. Renting a car is the easiest option – the streets are safe and in excel condition.

▬▬ TOUR 1   **Dubai to Al Ain**
Palm trees, bougainvilleas, golden-red desert sand and grazing camels along the desert highways to Al Ain. The date palms and clay houses a characteristic of the Buraimi oasis in Oman. ► **page 124**

▬▬ TOUR 2   **Abu Dhabi to the oases of Liwa**
Oil fields and recovery plants along the salt desert near the coast; the green oases of Liwa emerge behind the sand dunes, on the edge of the Rub al-Khali, the Great Arabian Desert. ► **page 126**

▬▬ TOUR 3   **Sharjah to the east coast**
Neo-Islamic architecture, oriental gardens and a palm tree grove; lunch the beach restaurant. The Hajar Mountains offer numerous vantage po with great views into steep, rocky ravines. ► **page 127**

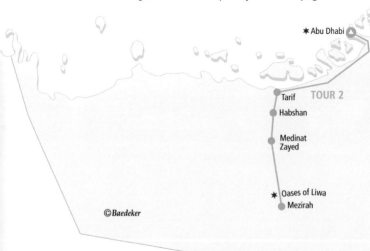

★ Abu Dhabi

Tarif   TOUR 2
Habshan
Medinat Zayed
★ Oases of Liwa
Mezirah

©Baedeker

S A U D I   A R A B I A

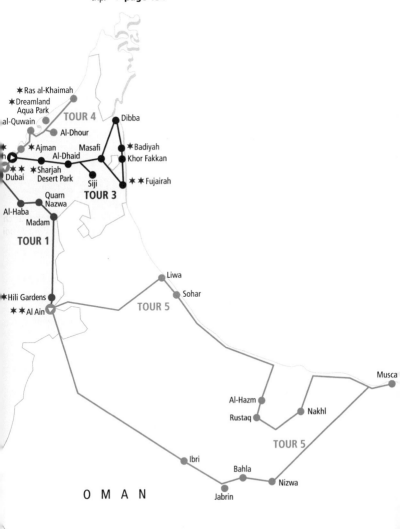

Through Deserts, Wadis and Mountains

Preparations for your trip

Within the space of just a few years, Dubai has become a synonym for luxury vacations. The region is unrivalled among medium-distance destinations: Sunshine almost around the clock, well-kept beaches, and a tourist infrastructure that amazes even spoiled jet setters. For a long weekend or the two-week family vacation – Dubai and the Emirates are ideal travel destinations for the **winter months**: Exotic, free of health risks, and almost one hundred percent safe. The beach hotels along Jumeirah Beach and the elegant city hotels are ideal starting points for an eventful stay. And all types of water sports are offered, from jet skiing to diving courses.

Visiting the Emirates

Those interested in architecture can find pre-Islamic and Islamic guard towers and forts, mosques from the entire Islamic era all the way to grand neo-Islamic mosques, Portuguese forts and the most modern residential and office buildings.

! **Baedeker** TIP

Finding your own accommodation
If you're planning to find a hotel yourself, either from home before the trip or when you get there, then the following applies: hotels at the beach are more expensive than those in the city. The further from Dubai, the lower the prices, and in the Emirates of Fujairah, Khor-Fakkan and Ras al-Khaimah three and four-star accommodation of comparable comfort to that in Dubai is available for half the price. The clientele in two star hotels consists almost exclusively of Asian visitors. »Funduks«, rooms and dormitories for male guests only, are not recommended.

In Dubai and Sharjah, old Souks were reconstructed in detail and historical villages and downtown areas were restored or recreated as »Heritage Villages« – outdoor museums. They offer **insight into traditional Arabic life** before the oil boom and a tranquil change to the modern Emirate cities.

In addition to visiting oriental bazaars and hyper-modern shopping complexes or touring the most famous construction projects currently being completed in the region, **excursions into the desert** woo the traveller. These can be easily organized on site. For example, any hotel rents (off-road) vehicles. The roads are in excellent condition and make travelling a real joy. Now the mountains and desert no longer loom in the distance but can be seen close up.

Desert Safaris and Dinner Cruises

A stay in Dubai and the Emirates requires a **desert safari**, which is offered by several organizers (half days approximately 250 Dh): They will pick you up at your hotel in the afternoon. Soon thereafter, the off-road vehicle leaves the pavement and drives through the desert. Meter-high sand dunes are climbed at a rapid pace. After sunset, the party reaches a »**Bedouin camp**« where a buffet is set up. After an extensive meal, various musical performances, belly dancing and camel rides, one is brought back to the hotel. Really special desert experiences are offered by a multi-day stay in the **Al-Maha luxury resort** at the edge of the Hajar mountains (▶Baedeker Special, page 201). Finally, **boat tours** along the coast or in the lagoons show the country from a new, unfamiliar perspective. Whether it is a three-hour dinner cruise or full-day fishing trip, exciting diversions are always assured.

!   Baedeker TIP

Coffee or tea?

Although coffee comes from Arabia and mocha from the Yemeni port city of the same name, tea is still the most popular drink amongst the locals. »Chai« (tea) is available everywhere, often with milk and lots of sugar. But coffee lovers need not fear: recently, many cafés have been opening in Dubai which will also serve up a cappuccino or a latte macchiato.

Excursions ...

Since the distances between the seven emirates are not great and the roads are excellent, Dubai is handy as a fixed base; from there, one can undertake day trips and excursions comfortably. However, one can plan for an overnight stay on an outing to Muscat in Oman, and for tours of Al Ain or Liwa this is recommended.

... with shared taxis and rental cars

Public transportation is scarce, but there is a bus line from Dubai to Abu Dhabi, Al Ain and Muscat and also from Abu Dhabi to Al Ain. Fast and inexpensive shared taxis travel between the capital cities of the emirates. However, your trip will not start until the vehicle has collected its full complement of 7 or 8 passengers, and then things get very crowded. The inexpensive and numerous taxis are suitable for shorter distances in the areas around Dubai, Sharjah and Ajman. The best solution is a rental car: They are inexpensive, gas is cheap, the roads are excellent and signage is extremely good. The major rental companies are well represented, which is useful in case of an emergency, but smaller local firms also give good deals and are very helpful.

A trip to the desert is a quintessential Emirates experience.

Tour 1 From Dubai to Al Ain

Length of the tour: 180km/112mi   **Tour duration:** 1 day

The outing to the oasis settlement of Al Ain, which is part of the emirate of Abu Dhabi, leads to a wealthy city which nevertheless has a significant traditional character. The oasis is also extremely important from a cultural history point of view: Al Ain has graves which are thousands of years old and prove that the site was already inhabited around 2000 BC.

One leaves ❶ ✳ ✳ **Dubai** at its south-eastern edge between the end of the Creek and the camel racetrack of Nad Al-Shiba. From there, do not take the Al Ain Road at the Bu Kidra / Country Club Roundabout, which leads directly to Al Ain, but rather the four-lane Ras Al-Khor Road towards **Hatta**. This soon turns into the Hatta Road and crosses a scenically charming area of high sand dunes with a reddish shimmer. The metropolis of Dubai keeps spreading further into the desert. One finally leaves the last houses and settlements behind, and the rubble and sand desert extends to the right and left of the road. Wire mesh fences prevent free-ranging camels from crossing the road.

After 30 km/19mi, one reaches the settlement of **②Al-Haba**. At the Haba Roundabout, the road from Dubai meets a freeway that runs from Jebel Ali to Hatta. Eight kilometres / five miles further on, is the hamlet of **③Quarn Nazwa** where a road crosses the Hatta Road in a north-south direction. Here, a hill looms above the red sand where the remains of shells, starfish and other sea creatures can be found, indicating that this region used to be under water.

After another seven kilometres / four miles, the desert to both sides of the road forms hills of sand. Here there is a gap in the wire mesh fence that protects the road against stray camels. Those travelling with off-road vehicles usually drive to the top of one of the up to 150 m/492ft high hills of the Hatta Road Sand Dunes. On the weekends, one can see many glide down the dunes with the Monoski; dune bashing, where one tears across the dunes in daring manoeuvres, is also popular.

15 km/9mi after Qarn Nazwa, one comes to the **④Al-Madam** roundabout and exits right onto the road to Al Ain. One first crosses the southern part of the Al-Madam plains, a flat rubble desert where several wadis of the surrounding mountains end. The rest of the route is dominated by flat sand and rubble desert occasionally enlivened by bush.

As one gets close to Al Ain, dunes reappear to the left and right of the road; huge mountains of sand

shimmer in brown and red, and are then interrupted and finally replaced by oasis fields. Date palms and vegetable fields now dominate the scenery. The approximately 200 wells and watering holes in this region form the basis for a rich agricultural community that supplies the emirate of Abu Dhabi.

The **⑤✱ Hili Gardens** archaeological site with an approximately 4700 year old restored circular grave is located approximately 10km/6mi before Al Ain to the east of the road. Subsequently, the road to Al Ain – called Dubai Road here – crosses part of the Oman oasis of Buraimi, before it reaches the centre of the »Garden City« of **⑥✱✱ Al Ain**. The climate here is hotter than it is on the coast, but it is more bearable since the humidity is significantly lower.

While Al Ain embodies the ideal of a modern oasis, the neighbouring **Buraimi** of Oman still has traditional mud houses and date groves irrigated using the ancient system of canals (►Baedeker Special, page 214).

Tour 2 From Abu Dhabi to the Oases of Liwa

Length of the tour: 270km/168mi   **Tour duration:** 1 – 2 days

A road trip from Abu Dhabi to the southern oases of Liwa is a trip into the past, into a time when petroleum dollars did not yet shape the appearance of towns and cities. The ancestors of today's rulers of Abu Dhabi, who founded a settlement on the coast in 1793, came from here. Although the houses of the oases of Liwa were not built until the 1970s and 1980s and are not made from mud, the atmosphere here is much less modern and western.

After leaving ❶ ✱ **Abu Dhabi City** on the four-lane freeway, one follows the road to the south and, at the town of **Mafraq**, exits onto the highway that runs close to the coast towards **Tarif** and **Ruwais**. The well-built road passes numerous offshore islands and oil fields, and runs through the grey salt desert of Sabkha, a barren landscape devoid of life.

The Liwa Oases are on the edge of an uninhabited, sandy desert.

Shortly after the industrial settlement of ❷ **Tarif**, which also has a gas station and several stores, one heads inland towards the oases of Liwa and Saudi Arabia.

28km/17mi after Tarif, past several oil fields and refineries, comes ❸ **Habshan**, where a road branches off to the **Bu Hasa oil field**. After another 30 km/19mi, one reaches ❹ **Medinat Zayed**, a Bedouin settlement with a large park founded by Sheikh Zayed. After that, the road leads straight through the sand dunes for 80km/50mi; seeing the gantries and towers of the oil production facilities are part of the scenery.

Finally, one reaches ❺ **Mezirah**, the commercial centre of the ✳ **oases of Liwa**, 15 small towns that stretch along the edge of the Rub al-Khali, a sand desert devoid of human life. They form the largest continuous oasis district of the UAE. The population mainly sustains itself through agriculture. Tomatoes, cabbage and potatoes are the main crops grown in the fields. From Mezirah, the road leads east and west. The remaining oases are strung along this approximately 50km/31mi road, which is paved initially but eventually gives way to a rubble and sand track. Golden and brownish shimmering sand dunes up to 150m/492ft high can be found between the settlements. There are reforestation projects, date palm groves and vegetable fields, all nicely fenced in to protect them against the ever-present hungry goats. There are also palm frond fences here and there to protect against sanding. Most of the houses in the settlements are more recent, but there are also occasional Bedouin tent encampments.

✳ Abu Dhabi ①

Tarif ②

132 km/ 82 mi

28 km/ 17 mi

Habshan ③

30 km/ 19 mi

Medinat Zayed ④

80 km/ 50 mi

✳ Oases of Liwa

Mezirah ⑤

Tour 3 From Sharjah to the East Coast

Length of the tour: 320km/200mi   **Tour duration:** 2 – 3 days

The scenic high point of this trip to the east coast of the UAE is crossing the majestic Hajar mountains. Those who have enough time should plan for an overnight stay, so they can explore the beauty of this still largely natural region more extensively. There are several hotels in charming locations next to the ocean, for example in Khor Fakkan, a beautiful port city and Sharjah exclave on the east coast.

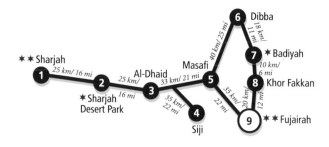

From **❶ ✳ ✳ Sharjah City**, one follows the freeway towards Al-Dhaid. The Sharjah International Airport, which appears after only ten kilometres / six miles, is worth a side trip. With its three domes, tower and multiple decorations, the airport building looks more like a neo-Islamic mosque then a modern functional building. The airport was built at the end of the 70s in the 20th century, at a time when Sharjah was the first emirate to open itself to tourism. Sheikh Sultan made a significant contribution to the design; the Emir, who studied in a foreign country and has written several scientific books, is regarded as an intellectual among all the government leaders of the UAE.

 DON'T MISS

- Looking for shells on Fossil Rock
- A trip to the waterfall of Wurayah
- The mosque of Badiyah, the oldest sacred structure in the country
- The fort and museum in Fujairah City
- A look at the fort of Bithnah

15 km/9mi farther on is the **❷ ✳ Sharjah Desert Park** with a game reserve, a natural history museum and a herbarium. After another 25 km/16mi through sand and rubble desert, sand dunes tower outside **❸ Al-Dhaid** and one reaches the agricultural town, a modern and economically prosperous trade centre. New, beautifully decorated residences, an elaborately constructed mosque and a modern Souk bear witness to Al-Dhaid's prosperity. Shops and restaurants line the streets. Gardens with fragrant lemon and orange trees, date palms, vegetable fields and sand dunes surround the settlement. In Milheiha, 12km/7mi from here, the bare »**Fossil Rock**« rises above the desert. Here one can discover fossils that are more than 100 million years old (however, taking them with you is a punishable offence!).

From Al-Dhaid, another 33km/21mi over well-built roads takes you to Masafi. 13km/8mi after Al-Dhaid, a road leads to the village of **❹ Siji** next to the reservoir of the same name, surrounded by a copse of palms; it is a popular destination for an excursion, especially on weekends. Finally, after reaching the foothills of the Hajar Mountains, one comes to the long street village of **❺ Masafi**.

This is a great place to take a break and saunter through the open-air market, which is among the largest and most colourful markets in the region: Farmers sell vegetables, fruit and firewood; Bedouin women squat on the ground hawking essential oils, henna powder, and woven baskets. Goats bleat loudly in the background, and potential buyers inspect carpets and pottery in a leisurely manner.

Masafi is the beginning of the most beautiful landscapes along the route – past canyons that rise steeply, appearing hostile and barren, bathed in glistening light by the sun, with wonderful vistas of green valleys lying far below. One can choose between the northern mountain route that leads to Dibba and the southern route to Fujairah. The best choice is to take one road on the way there, and the other on the way back.

On the northern route, one first passes a bottling factory for mineral water and then reaches the pass after 10 km/6mi; just 30 km/19mi further on, one reaches the picturesque fishing village of ❻ **Dibba**, located on the Gulf of Oman on the northern end of the UAE. At the time of prophet Mohammed, Dibba was the capital of Oman; today, the city is split into three

The harbour at the three-zone city of Dibba

parts: The sections belong to Sharjah, Fujairah and Oman; however, there are no borders and the difference between the Omani part and the areas belonging to the UAE can only be recognized by the more Arabic architectural style in the Omani district.

The trip continues southward along the coastal road. One first passes the town of **Dhadnah** which was designed on the drawing board with dozens of identical white row houses: Public housing in modern Arabia. 15km/9mi further on, comes the charming fishing village of **Al-Aqqa**.

Just a few kilometres south of Al-Aqqa lies ❼ ✳ **Badiyah**. Two guard towers, the remains of a Portuguese fort, rise above the oldest mosque in the UAE; two nearby cemeteries date back to Islamization

! *Baedeker* TIP

Sandy Beach

A stopover in Al-Aqqa, 15km/9mi south of Dibba, is well worth it. The beautiful beach and alluring shimmering ocean invite you for a swim. And the sympathetic Sandy Beach Motel with its good, inexpensive terrace restaurant is ideal for taking an extended break, especially for divers (P. O. Box 659, Al-Aqqa, Fujairah, tel. 09/ 2 44 55 55, www.sandybm.com).

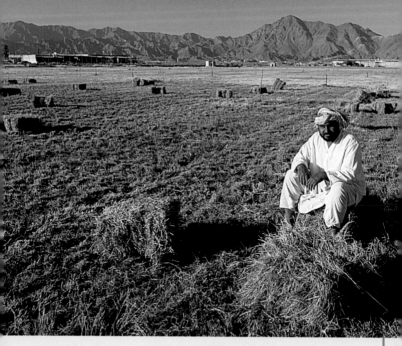

The plentiful springs and profitable agriculture at Khor Fakkan are thanks to the Hajar Mountains.

in the 7th century and the conquest by the Portuguese in the 16th century.

Another side trip leads to the **waterfall of Wurayah**. About five kilometres / 3 miles before Khor Fakkan, a road branches off to the only waterfall in the UAE that has water all year; it is a very popular destination for outings, as people come here to picnic and to bathe in the waterfall's small basin.

Finally, one reaches the port city of ❽ **Khor Fakkan**, crowned by a palace on top of a hill owned by the family of the Emir of Sharjah. A tree-lined beachfront street, a Souk modelled after the one in Sharjah, many water sports activities, and the beautiful Oceanic Hotel invite travellers to take a break.

Another 20km/12mi take you from Khor Fakkan to ❾ ✳ ✳ **Fujairah**. With its fantastic location between the Hajar Mountains and the ocean as well as its well-kept green spaces, the capital of the emirate with the same name is drawing ever more visitors. South of the city lies ✳ **Khor Kalba** with a nature reserve that extends to the border of Oman.

Tour 4 From Dubai to Ras al-Khaimah

Length of the tour: 100km/62mi   **Tour duration:** At least 1 day

For the trip along the west coast of the UAE, a rental car is not essential. One can also take one of the affordable shared taxis from one emirate to the next; they wait in specified locations and do not leave until they are full. However, the tour cannot be completed in a day in this case. Not that this is recommended anyway, since there is a lot to see in the smaller emirates of Ajman, Umm al-Quwain and Ras al-Khaimah which have remained more pristine due to their lack of oil reserves. Umm al-Quwain and Ras al-Khaimah have several hotels that are recommended for an overnight stay.

With ❶ ✱ ✱ **Dubai**, one leaves the richest and most modern of the seven emirates. Thanks to its industry, the only 15km/9mi distant sheikhdom of Sharjah is quite wealthy and was able to extensively renovate its historical buildings. The main road between Dubai and Sharjah, the Al-Ittihad Road, turns into the Al-Wahda Road, the main commercial street of the city which runs to the south of the two lagoons. ❷ ✱ ✱ **Sharjah City** has many attractions and outstanding museums – especially in the restored Old City – which one should plan to tour for at least an entire day.

Eight kilometres / five miles to the north, ❸ ✱ **Ajman**, the capital of the smallest sheikhdom in the UAE which bears the same name, lies on a peninsula. The community used to live off fishing and a dhow shipyard; today, industrial districts, a large shipyard and a television station have been added. The fort erected at the end of the 18th century, which protected the emirate in conjunction with the guard towers by the shore and which served as the seat of the ruling family for 150 years, was converted into a museum which is well worth a visit.

Ajman, capital of the smallest of the seven Emirates

In Ajman, one can already feel the transition from the wealthy emirates like Dubai and Sharjah with a large proportion of foreigners to the poorer emirates, where the locals are still in the majority. Life is quieter here, the restaurants are simpler, the locals are more friendly and the buildings are made from coral and adobe instead of concrete and marble. Also noticeable are the forts, which are carefully restored in the northern emirates and thus probably come closer to their original appearance than the perfectly reconstructed forts in Dubai and Sharjah, which sometimes appear sterile.

The trip north leads 30km/19mi to the emirate of ❹ ✳ **Umm al-Quwain**. The small sheikdom with its 20km/12mi of coastline leads a traditional fishing and agricultural existence. The capital, which has the same name as the emirate, extends along a peninsula which is ten kilometres / six miles long and only one kilometre/0.6mi wide, formed by a long estuary. The Old City, protected by three guard towers and a fort, is located at the northern end. A museum has been established in the renovated fort. The old port and traditional fish market – which is still very busy – are located on the east side of the Old City. The large lagoon is ideal for a few hours of bathing.

 DON'T MISS

- The Heritage Area with the old Souk in Sharjah
- The Old City of Umm al-Quwain
- A visit to the old fort of Ajman
- Water fun in the Dreamland Aqua Park

Outside the city, two other attractions can be found: At the southern end of the peninsula, a side road leads to the ❺ **Al-Dhour** archaeological site, and on the coast, about half-way to the emirate of Ras al-Khaimah, the huge ❻ ✱ **Dreamland Aqua Park** invites visitors for a day of water fun.

45km/28mi north of Umm al-Quwain, ❼ ✱ **Ras al-Khaimah** is reached. The capital city of the emirate with the same name also lies on a peninsula formed by the gulf and a lagoon. In the Old City erected on the northern tip of the peninsula in the 16th century, many decayed houses are made from coral limestone using traditional construction techniques. The fort from the 19th century, topped by a splendid wind tower, now houses a museum with archaeological finds, ancient documents, rare coins and a shell collection; the museum is well worth seeing. The busy fish market and the Irani Souk are located nearby. A bridge leads across to the modern district if Nakheel, which extends to the foothills of the Hajar Mountains.

Baedeker TIP

Medieval Arabia

Julfar, which used to be a booming port of trade in pre-Islamic times, is located about one kilometre/0.6mi north of Ras al-Khaimah. The »Palace of the Queen of Saba« – which was not built until the 16th century – is located a few kilometres further on at the top of a hill.

The old fort at Ras al-Khaimah houses a museum.

Sinbad the Sailor is said to have once lived in the port town of Sohar.

Tour 5 From Al Ain to Muscat in Oman

Length of the tour: 365km/200mi   **Tour duration:** At least 3 days

Up until the 70s of the 20th century, a trip to Oman was a time-consuming and risky affair. Travelling from the west to the east coast meant crossing the Hajar Mountains. Fields of rubble, occasional Bedouin attacks and a lack of water during the summer months made for a difficult journey. Today, two major highways join the emirates to the east coast. It is still a route of unrivalled scenery: The jagged flanks of the Hajar Mountains gleam majestic and bleak in the sunlight; in some cases, the cliffs rise vertically next to the road. One repeatedly passes deep valleys where date palms thrive.

i **Cleared to Enter**

■ Visitors to the United Arab Emirates who have a visa or entry permit for the UAE in their passport can also visit Oman without an additional visa (this also applies in the opposite direction).

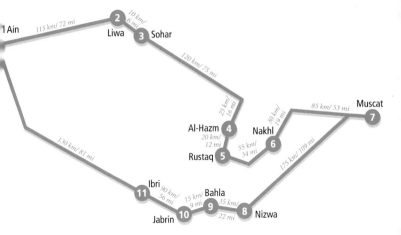

The sultanate of Oman has 500 forts and palaces, many of which have been reconstructed, restored and returned to their former glory. Life here is less hurried than in the neighbouring sheikdoms, and also more »Arabic« due to the comparatively lower proportion of foreigners. However **Muscat**, the capital of Oman, is a city with a surrounding »Capital Area« that resembles the metropolises of the United Arab Emirates.

From ❶ ✳ ✳ **Al Ain** the journey continues into the neighbouring **Buraimi** and then follows Highway 07 via **Hail** towards Sohar. After almost 120km/75mi, one comes to ❷**Liwa** on the coastal road between Fujairah and Sohar; the trip continues south along this road for ten kilometres / six miles to the port city of ❸**Sohar**. This city is always related to Sinbad the sailor, who is said to have lived here in the 8th century. A large white fortress from the 14th century is located at the city centre and provides a panorama view of the city and the ocean. Some of the rooms were converted into a museum regarding the marine history of the city. A stroll along the new corniche to the busy fish market is also enjoyable.

From Sohar, the coastal road continues through the **plains of Batinah**, a fertile area that supplies the north of Oman with fruits and vegetables. After approximately 120 km/75mi, the journey heads inland between **As-Suwaiq** and **Al-Musanah** to tour three Omani forts in the midst of beautiful oases on a 130 km/81mi excursion that returns to the coastal road.

25 km/16mi after leaving the coastal road, one reaches ❹**Al-Hazm**, an impressive restored fortress with a working Falaj system (►Baedeker Special, page 214) as a special attraction. 20 km/12mi further on

Baedeker TIP

Push and Win

On the way to Muscat, one passes the coastal village of Barka. Every Friday, it hosts a traditional Omani style bullfight in the bullring; two strong, snorting, stomping bulls push each other around with their heads until one of them has had enough. The bull – and its owner – have then lost the match. This type of bullfight is a bloodless spectacle received by the population with great enthusiasm.

is the fort of ❺**Rustaq** towering on a hill above the Old City. The fortress, which originates in the 7th century and goes back to the 18th century in its present form, has now been perfectly restored. The hot **spring of Ain Al-Kafsah** with its bath houses and the new mosque donated by the sultan also make a visit to this settlement at the foot of the **Jebel Akhdar** (»Green Mountain«) worthwhile.

After another 55 km/34mi, the monumental fortress of ❻**Nakhl** towers on a cliff. The hot **spring of Thowarah** in the vicinity of the fort irrigates a green valley, where there are always local families out for a picnic. From here it is only about 30km/19mi before one returns to the coastal road.

Via **Barka**, the journey continues to **Seeb** where the international airport of the capital is located; the so-called Capital Area that stretches for 45 km/28mi all the way to ❼**Muscat** begins soon thereafter. The Old City of Muscat has two Portuguese forts that line a small bay with the sultan's Alam Palace. The ethnological museum of Bait Al-Zubair, which shows beautiful traditional crafts among other exhibits, is worth a visit. One of the most beautiful hotels on the Arabic peninsula is located south of the city: The Hotel Al-Bustan Palace.

The souk at Nizwa, the »silver capital« of Oman

The Al-Mirani Castle rises picturesquely over Muscat.

For the return to Al Ain, an alternate route is recommended. The first stop is **Nizwa**, the former capital of Oman, 175 km/109mi south of Muscat, which has a monumental fort with a tower that provides an enchanting view of the blue and gold Great Mosque. At the foot of the fort is a Souk with old Omani silver decorations.

Approximately 35 km/22mi west of Nizwa, one comes to ⑨ **Bahla**, the centre of Omani pottery, with a twelve kilometre / seven mile long clay city wall. Although the fortress from the 17th century located within the wall is a UNESCO World Heritage Site, it is in a deplorable condition.

The palace of ⑩ **Jabrin** located 15 km/9mi from Bahla, also from the 17th century, has been extensively restored and illustrates the artistic sense of an imam who had the stately rooms equipped and decorated with the finest.

In ⑪ **Ibri**, located 140 km/87mi from Nizwa – the trip leads along a wadi – there is another historical fort with a Souk. Al Ain is reached after another 130km/81mi.

✓ **DON'T MISS**

■ An excursion to the Falaj Canals of Al-Hazm and the Fortress of Nakhl

■ A stroll along the corniche and through the fish market of Sohar

■ A visit to the marine museum in the Fort of Sohar

Sights from A to Z

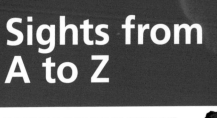

DESPITE RAPID DEVELOPMENT AND NUMEROUS BUILDING PROJECTS, THE SEVEN EMIRATES' OLD ARABIAN DISTRICTS, TRADITIONAL SOUKS AND MAGNIFICENT LANDSCAPES HAVE LOST NONE OF THEIR CHARM.

ABU DHABI

Area: 67,340 sq km/26,000 sq mi
(excluding the islands)
Emir: Sheikh Khalifa Bin-Zayed
al-Nahyan (since 2004)

Population: 1,850,230

Enormous revenues from oil sales have allowed the sheikhdom to create a modern infrastructure with new roads, covered with greenery on each side, high-rise buildings and motorways traversing the desert. And yet Abu Dhabi, the richest of all seven emirates, was once far less interested in tourism than the others.

At more than 67,000 sq km/25,900 sq mi the Emirate of Abu Dhabi, the largest of the federation's seven emirates, covers more than four fifths of the entire UAE. It extends over 400km/249mi from the Qatar Peninsula and the Saudi Arabian border in the west, along the coastline of the Arabian Gulf to ► Dubai in the north-east. The coastal region is mainly comprised of salt flats (sabkhas). The emirate is divided into three regions: the Abu Dhabi Region, the Western Region and the Eastern Region. The majority of the population lives in the city of Abu Dhabi; the city is the capital of the UAE, the Abu Dhabi Emirate

The Gulf's wealthiest emirate

and the **Abu Dhabi Region**, which consists of Abu Dhabi island and the mainland. The **Eastern Region** is blessed with extensive groundwater resources and about 200 springs, making it the sheikhdom's most fertile region. Its capital city, ► Al Ain, situated on the border to Oman, is home to the emirate's university. In the **Western Region** there are numerous oil fields and refineries, the largest of which is located in Ruwais. The district is administered by the city of Beda Zayed, located on the road from Tarif to Madinat Zayed.
Among the many off-shore sand islands, which often barely rise above the surface as shallow sand banks, Das, Mubarraz, Zirku and Arzanah are the most prominent because oil is extracted there.

One key factor of the Emirate's economic development is **diversification**, i.e. the development of additional industries and sources of revenue. The government and private enterprise have been investing in the expansion of the agricultural sector and in the development of a fishing fleet. The sheikhdom's economic focus is on trade and an efficient telecommunications network throughout the entire UAE.

Economy

← *The view over the Corniche, Abu Dhabi's hallmark*

Tourism In recent years, the emirate has become more engaged in the tourism industry. Although, with few exceptions, there are hardly any historical buildings, visitors have a choice of several worthwhile destinations and popular **recreational activities**. The sheikhdom is host to a number of luxurious hotel resorts, which also attract business people from the Arabian Peninsula. Several five-star hotels line the Corniche Road in Abu Dhabi, with spectacular views of the ocean and the city's skyline. Inexpensive accommodation can be found in the city centre.

✶ Abu Dhabi

E 4

Population:: 1,850,000

On a peninsula surrounded by the ocean, high-rise buildings shine in the sun. The densely built-up city centre is criss-crossed by wide highways lined with palm trees and flowers; a pleasant and revitalizing contrast is provided by two dozen parks and gardens. But though the city of Abu Dhabi may look like a western metropolis, it is still largely dominated by conservative tradition.

The sheikhdom's eponymous capital was built on a shallow sand island and is connected to the mainland by two bridges. It is surrounded by sand banks such as Lulu Island or Sadiyat, which have been incorporated into the development of the city. While Sadiyat is primarily used for agriculture, Lulu Island provides a leisure and entertainment park as well as beach facilities.

Highlights Abu Dhabi

Emirates Palace
A seaside palace hotel, which will transport you into the Tales of the Arabian Nights.
► page 149

Bateen Dhow Harbour
Bizarre-looking cargo ships still built according to tradition.
► page 151

Heritage Village
An insight into the Emirate's past before the oil boom.
► page 154

Corniche
Six kilometres (3.7 miles) of parks and splendour along the coast, illuminated at night.
► page 147

Al-Hosn Fort
The first settlement on the peninsula, also called the »White Fort«.
► page 151

Iranian Souk
Romantic bazaar shopping with romantic lighting at sunset.
► page 155

History

3000 BC	First settlement of Umm al-Nar
1761	The al-Nahyan family settles in Abu Dhabi.
1955	Abu Dhabi's population grows to 5,000
1962	First oil is extracted
1971	Abu Dhabi is made capital of the newly founded United Arab Emirates

Even if the first impression is that of a young city, Abu Dhabi can look back on thousands of years of history. Archaeological finds confirm that the region's first settlement dates back 5,000 years. In the 1950s, Danish archaeologists discovered the ruins of a large settlement on the small island of Umm al-Nar, situated 15km/9.3mi south of the city centre. The people of the so-called **Umm al-Nar culture** most likely lived from fishing and hunting. Based on the remains of large fish found only in the open sea, it is argued that the inhabitants were also able to build large vessels and go deep-sea fishing; ship-building appears to have been a highly advanced skill. Besides numerous fragments of foundation wall, the excavations also uncovered circular, once tower-shaped tombs. These **tomb towers** reached heights of up to 8m/26ft with a diameter of up to 15m/49ft.

Gold and silver jewellery, pearls and drinking vessels made of soft soapstone found in the surroundings of the settlement are proof of the early settlers' advanced cultural development, and are also an indication of early Arab trade. Red ceramic vessels decorated with black geometrical motifs that were found everywhere in Umm al-Nar bear a striking resemblance to equally old jars discovered in Mesopotamia. From this, archaeologists concluded that there must have been trade relations between the settlers of Umm al-Nar and the land between the Euphrates and Tigris rivers.

The history of Abu Dhabi's second colonization, however, began much later. The **Bedouin tribe of the Bani Yas**, to which today's ruling families of Abu Dhabi and Dubai also belong, has produced the region's most powerful families since the mid-18th century. Largely as a result of their unity, the attacks of the orthodox Wahhabi, from the area of what is now Saudi Arabia, were successfully averted. In 1761, members of the **Bedouin family al-Nahyan** from the Bani Yasi tribe, who lived in the ►Liwa Oases, found a freshwater spring on a shallow sand island on the Arabian Gulf coast and settled there. At that time, numerous gazelle herds still roamed the island. When the Bedouins saw a gazelle drinking from a water hole, today the site of the Al-Hosn Fort, the newly founded settlement was called Abu Dhabi, »Father of the Gazelle«. In 1793, other members of the Nahyan family left Liwa to settle in both ►Al Ain and Abu Dhabi.

First settlement

◄Umm al-Nar culture

◄Trade with Mesopotamia

Second colonization in the 18th century

Abu Dhabi Plan

Arabian
Gulf

AR RAS
AL-AKHDAR

Al-Dana
Ladies' Beach

③

① ②

Breakwater
Island

The Breakwater

New Presidential
Diwan

Hilton
Hotel

Corniche Road

Khubeirah
Street

AL-KHUBEIRAH

High
Court

Children's
Garden

Post
Office

AL-KHALIDIYAH

Al-Khalidiyah

Water
Tower

Khalidiyah
Park

Zayed t

Ministries

Zayed Street

Pa

AL-BATEEN

Al-Bateen
Municipal
Centre

Khaleej Al-Arabi Street

Bamunah Street

Sultan Bin

Al-Manhal
Street

Stre

Bus Station
Municipal
Market

Al

Khalifa Bin Shakhbut

Post
Office

Bateen

Street

Sultan Bin-Zayed Street

Palace

Khor Al-Bateen

Hideriyyat

Al-Khaleej Al-Arabi Street

Dalma Street

Bateen
Palace

N

0,25 mi

©*Baedeker*

Palace

Mohammed Bin-Khalifa Street

Sultan Bin- Zayed
Street

Al-Khaleej
Al-Arabi Street

Palace

Heritage Village

Re
Tr

Where to stay
① Al Ain Palace Hotel ③ Emirates Palace ⑤ Dana Hotel
② Federal Hotel ④ Mina Hotel

Lulu Island

Mina Hurr/ Free Port

Fish Market

Dhow Harbour

Customs Department

Iranian Souk

Slaughter House

Clock Tower

Corniche Road

Ittihad

Istiqlal St.

Square

Corniche Road

Post Office

Mina Road

Sheikh Khalifa Bin-Zayed

ALMARK AZIYAH

Post Office

Sheikh Hamdan Bin-Mohammed Street

Fort Al-Hosn

Cultural Foundation

Grand Mosque

Etisalat

Zayed the Second Street

As Salam Street

Post Office

Tourist Club

Post Office

Grand Souk

East Road

MEDINA

Bani Yas Street

ZAYED

Bus Station

Manhal Street

Al-Falah Street

Sudani Social and Cultural Club

Post Office

AL-DHAFRAH

Hazaa Bin-Zayed Street

Al-Wahdah Sports and Cultural Club

Bus Terminal

AL-WAHDAH

AL-TABBIYAH

AL-KARAMAH

Maktoum Street

Defence Street

MUSSALA EL EID

Prayer Yard

Sheikh Rashid Bin-Saeed Al-

Khalifa Street

Al-Mushairif Garden

Women's Association

National Theatre

East Road

As Salam Street

Sea Palace Road

Eastern Ring Road

Sea Palace

Sea Palace

Where to eat

1. Havanna Café
2. Restaurant Al-Safina
3. Restaurant Abu Sharka
4. Restaurant La Fayette
5. City Palace
6. Mandarin Chinese Restaurant

Lush, green spaces characterize this city.

Even in the 1950s, the settlement was still inhabited by only around 5,000 people. At that time, Abu Dhabi was comprised only of the **Al-Hosn Fort** and a few surrounding mud houses and palm huts. The sheikhdom's population lived primarily from **agriculture** (Al Ain), **fishing**, and **pearl diving** (▶Baedeker Special p.242). The latter lost its significance in the 1930s with the emergence of artificial pearl farming. Up until the mid-20th century, Abu Dhabi could only be reached on foot during low tide, and was hardly more than a poor settlement, with no electricity or sewage system and with an illiteracy rate of more than 70%.

i Women's Association

■ On the initiative of the President's wife, Sheikha Fatima Bint-Mubarak, a women's association has been created in the southern part of the Peninsula, on Sheikh Rashid Bin-Saeed Al-Maktoum Street (Airport Road). The Handicraft Centre presents the traditional techniques of rug weaving and pottery. Without prior arrangement, visitors can stroll through the centre and observe the women at work. On request (by women), taking the occasional photograph is allowed. This is also a great opportunity to learn more about and acquire Arabic objects of daily use such as incense burners and perfume oils (Open: Sat–Wed 8am–12.30pm, free admission).

By the end of the 1930s, after the decline of a once thriving pearl industry, the former ruler Sheikh Shakhbout, gave concessions to British companies to dig for and produce petroleum. From 1962, the off-shore and desert oil reserves of the Emirate of Abu Dhabi were tapped by foreign firms, which led to enormous wealth within twenty years. Abu Dhabi owns an estimated ten percent of the world's oil reserves, which means that at an average production volume of two million barrels per day, the emirate could supply oil for another 100 years.

Abu Dhabi is one of the richest cities in the world. Magnificent buildings – modern, often only recently built constructions with futuristic designs – shape the cityscape. While many buildings are built in neo-Islamic style, i.e. reminiscent of the traditional Arabic architecture with arches and turrets, not much remains to suggest the origins of the old Arab settlements. Abu Dhabi, with its wide, long, straight roads, bears far more resemblance to cities of the western world.

Wealthy metropolis

Like many countries on the Arabian Peninsula, Abu Dhabi cherishes its monuments and memorials, which are erected all along the Corniche and at roundabouts. The many enormously sized coffee cups and coffee pots are **symbols of Arabian hospitality**. Besides the portrayals of deer or falcons, imitations of European cultural heritage and famous sites are also popular.

Monuments and memorials

Residential areas have been extended southward and beyond the island. Ever more land is reclaimed from the desert for cultivation. While many Indian and Pakistani workers live in older and simpler high-rise buildings close to the city centre, the suburbs are filled with spacious villas surrounded by lush gardens. Following the American role model, the people here prefer to drive down the wide boulevards rather than walk. The side streets of the northern city centre offer plenty of simple restaurants run by Indians, Lebanese, Pakistanis or Chinese.

 Environmental sins

■ It is noticeable to visitors that the city is extraordinarily clean. However, this cleanliness is to some extent »bought« with a large number of waste bins and strict fines. The fine for throwing a cigarette butt or a paper tissue on the ground is 200 AED (£27). Car littering is fined 500 AED (£68); illegal waste disposal around 3,000 AED (£408). Uniformed and plainclothes inspectors ensure these provisions are enforced.

What to See in Abu Dhabi

Abu Dhabi's landmark is the 6km/3.7mi **waterfront**. Bordered by the two luxury hotels Sheraton to the east and Hilton to the west, and flanked by street lanterns shaped like traditional fortified towers, it is the ideal place to take a stroll while citizens of the more than one hundred nations living in Abu Dhabi meet here after their day's work.
Colossal artificial cliffs, at night illuminated in all the colours of the rainbow, the image of the late leader in the form of a mosaic – the modes of artistic expression are many and varied. Fountains, symbols of life in the desert, adorn not only many of the roundabouts on the numerous highways through the town, but also feature as highlights of the newly designed Corniche, for which more land has been reclaimed from the gulf since 2003.

★ ★
Corniche

● VISITING ABU DHABI

INFORMATION
Abu Dhabi Tourism Authority
P.O. Box 94 000
Abu Dhabi
Tel. +971 (0)2 444 04 44
Fax +971 (0)2 444 04 00
www.abudhabitourism.ae
Email: info@adta.ae

SHOPPING
Abu Dhabi Mall
Tourist Club Area
Open: daily 10am–10pm,
Fri from 3.30pm

INTERNET CAFÉ
Cyber Café
Sahara Residence Hotel
Zayed 2nd Street
P.O. Box 7 14 53
Abu Dhabi
Tel. 31 90 00
www.saharahotelapartments.com/
cyber.htm

WHERE TO EAT
► **Expensive**
Abu Tafesh
Bateen Dhow Harbour
Tel. 6 66 63 31
This floating restaurant offers a wide
range of fish specialities.

► **Moderate**
② *Al-Safina*
Breakwater
Tel. 6 81 60 85
Previously an emir's dhow, now
turned into a traditional restaurant.
Located on the long breakwater
stretch off the northern coast of the
city.

④ *La Fayette*
Corniche
This coffee house and restaurant is
located in a semi-open, two-floor
rotunda with a large terrace and
ocean view.

Baedeker-recommendation

► **Moderate**
① *Havanna Café*
Breakwater
Tel. 6 72 44 00
Modern and stylish hotspot for the y[
Arab hipster crowd situated at the we
of the Corniche. The large outdoor te
offers a spectacular view of the Abu [
skyline.

⑥ *Mandarin Chinese Restaurant*
Al Ain Palace Hotel
Umm Al-Nar Street
Tel. 6 79 52 88
The »Mandarin« has the best reputa-
tion of all Chinese restaurants in
town.

► **Inexpensive**
③ *Abu Sharka*
Istiqlal Street
Tel. 6 31 34 00
Arab snack bar with delicious humus
(chickpea paste).

City Palace
Khalifa Street
Tel. 6 26 27 62
At this two-floor restaurant not far from the Corniche, fast and attentive waiters serve excellent value Arabian cuisine.

WHERE TO STAY

► Luxury

③ *Emirates Palace*
Corniche West
Tel. 690 90 00
Reservations:
Tel. 690 88 88
Fax 960 99 99
www.emiratespalace.com
320 rooms and 92 suites
Resembling a palace from an oriental fairy tale from the outside, with marble and gold leaf contributing to the exquisite splendour inside. A large troop of staff tends to your every need in the huge hotel and its extensive grounds.

► Mid-range

① *Al Ain Palace Hotel*
Umm Al-Nar Street
P.O. Box 33
Tel. 6 79 47 77
www.alainpalacehotel.com; 120 rooms
Traditional hotel with large inner courtyard, pool, good restaurants and diverse evening entertainment.

► Budget

⑤ *Dana Hotel*
Tourist Club Area
(across from the Abu Dhabi Cooperative Society)
P.O. Box 4 73 00
Tel. 6 45 60 00
www.aldiarhotels.com; 112 rooms
All rooms include a small kitchenette, which makes this hotel ideal for self-caterers. With coffee shop, Pizza

Corner, Wild West Club and a rooftop restaurant on the 16th floor.

② *Federal Hotel*
Khalifa Street
(on the corner of Umm Al-Nar Street)
P.O. Box 4 30 67
Tel. 6 78 90 00
www.aldiarhotels.com
53 rooms and suites
All rooms are equipped with a kitchenette. The hotel includes a pizzeria and an English pub. Hotel parking.

④ *Mina Hotel*
Mina Road
(on the corner of Salam Street)
P.O. Box 4 44 21
Tel. 6 78 10 00
www.aldiarhotels.com
106 rooms
Situated close to the Corniche, all rooms of this city hotel are equipped with a small kitchenette. Includes a business centre and beach club.

Parks   Abu Dhabi is proud of its 20 gardens and parks, equipped with fountains, trails and often with a playground for children. Besides the large parks along the Corniche there are small oases all over town. Located next to the Women's Higher College of Technology on 32nd street, the Khalidiya Children's Garden is only accessible to women and children.

Those who don't have access to a hotel beach or beach club will appreciate the facilities of the **Al-Raha Beach** (Channel Road). The beach located on the road from Abu Dhabi to Dubai provides sun loungers, sun shades and a cafeteria.

Breakwater   One of Abu Dhabi's most attractive places is the Breakwater close to Lulu Island, rising out of the water at the west end of the Corniche. The many tall palm trees along the peninsula, which is artificially made from white sand and the debris of demolished buildings, create a **tropical beach atmosphere**. A wide boulevard leads through an arcade, displaying portraits of the rulers from the individual sheikhdoms, out to the spit where the Havana Café, dhow restaurants and the Heritage Village can be found.

Emirates Palace   With an entrance like an old Arab drawbridge, and fountains and flights of steps like in a French palace, the huge palace hotel an astounding 800m/2,625ft long is crowned by 114 domes, the largest with a diameter of 42m/138ft. Opened in 2005, the Emirates Palace located at the west end of the Corniche impresses through its incredible size and opulence and represents Abu Dhabi's glittering entry into first-class tourism. After finding a parking space in the underground car park, perhaps alongside the hotel's own fleet of white Rolls Royces, guests take the lift to the foyer and eventually wander through halls adorned with marble and gold leaf. A 1.3km/1430yd-long beach belongs to the hotel estate.

Fairytale-like luxury hotel:
Emirates Palace

Slightly further west the **Ittihad Square**, or Federation Square, splits from Corniche Road and leads southward into Sheikh Rashid Bin-Saeed Al-Maktoum Street, also called Airport Road. South of the square, the New Souk is on the left-hand side. On the other side of the bridge, crossing Khalifa Street, the Old Souk stretches from here all the way to Hamdan Street. Both souks still have something of an old oriental bazaar atmosphere.

Built in 1793, the first **fort of the Nahyan family** was the ruling dynasty's seat of government and residence for almost two hundred years. The enormous building on Khalid Bin Al-Waleed Street was erected at the spot where once the legendary freshwater spring was discovered. Eventually the mud-built fort was torn down as a result of the oil boom. In 1982, however, the new interest in architectural heritage led to the palace's reconstruction. Although it was rebuilt exactly according to the original plans, the straight walls and gleaming white paint make it seem rather new. This is also what earned the palace, which is surrounded by high-rise buildings, its name: »White Fort«. The fort can also be visited, as some of the rooms have been turned into a museum. The

Al-Hosn Fort

> ## ! Baedeker TIP
>
> ### Spectacular views
> The best view of the Abu Dhabi skyline can be enjoyed from the terrace of the Havana café and restaurant. This modern and stylishly designed café, located directly at the front of the Breakwater peninsula, is the place to be for the young and hip Abu Dhabi crowd. It gets really busy on Thursday and Friday mornings, when local families meet here for breakfast.

other rooms store parts of the state archive. The inner courtyard and the exterior grounds are extensively covered with greenery and laid out with walkways.

During restoration, a **cultural centre** was added to the fort, which contains a **library**, exhibition rooms and a cultural institute hosting frequent musical and folklore events. Besides Arabic books, the library also holds 100,000 English titles and 900 English magazines. The Emirate's antique books and Qu'ran collections are also exhibited here, including a 700-year old papyrus manuscript. A free brochure with information on all current events is available in the city centre. (Zayed 1st Street/Airport Road, tel. 6 21 53 00; Open: Sat–Wed 8am–1.30pm, Thu until 12pm).

Across from the Cultural Foundation, at the crossroads of Sheikh Rashid Bin-Saeed Al-Maktoum Street (Airport Road) and Sheikh Zayed the First Street, rises the enormous neo-Islamic **Grand Mosque**, with its numerous elaborately decorated domes. The building does not allow admission to non-Muslims. Sheikh Zayed comes to the Grand Mosque during Ramadan and occasionally for Friday prayer.

Grand Mosque

Beyond the area of government departments in the west end of the city lies the harbour of Al-Bateen. The traditional Arab dhows are still built here, although they are now powered by diesel engines. A

Al-Bateen

Even in wealthy Dubai, not anyone can afford a well-schooled hunting falcon.

Heraldic animal and hunting companion

FALCONS

The falcon is the national emblem of the United Arab Emirates. Alongside the camel and the horse, the proud bird of prey is one of the favourite animals of the traditional Arabs.

These hunting birds were already being bred on the Arabian Peninsula in the millennium before Christ; today it is mainly the originally European peregrine falcon that is trained for hunting from a very young age.

Falconry

Hunting with trained falcons, something which the European aristocracy have also practiced since the Middle Ages, is in fact a great art, and is furthermore a very exclusive hobby: up to 200,000 AED (approx. £27,000) is the price for talented, female young birds – as they are better hunters than the males.

The **elaborate training** of the animal takes several months, with the ultimate goal being to teach the bird to hunt in the wild and to bring its prey (steppe birds, sometimes even a desert hare) back to the owner.

The **first step** of the training is for the bird and owner to trust one another. The falcon spends weeks and months in the constant vicinity of its new owner and trainer. It is hand-fed by the owner. A black leather cap, the burqa, is put over the bird's head as soon as the animal becomes agitated. Eventually the birds are taught to lift off from the owner's arm to catch dummy prey on command. Every time the animal returns the dummy to its owner, it is given a reward.

It takes many months to train a falcon to hunt.

Training in the desert

The next step is flying in the wild, where the falcon is trained to catch lure pigeons.

The **training is successful** if the falcon spots and catches prey in the desert and brings it back. If an animal floats in the air for too long without spotting any prey, the owner simply around a campfire to drink tea and tell stories.

Those **who can afford it** don't drive to the hunting grounds in a four-by-four – they fly in a private jet. In fact, the rulers of the emirates host regular hunting excursions to especially game-rich areas in Pakistan or India.

Falcon hunting is an exclusive hobby: a talented but untrained young bird costs up to £27,000.

waves some easily-visible dummy prey. The bird of prey returns to receive its reward of food.

The **animal's head** is covered with the burqa and then placed on a 50cm/20in-high perch (wakir) which is artistically upholstered with cloth. A foot chain tethers the animal in its place.

Hunting societies

In the United Arab Emirates, groups of men venture out into the desert in hunting societies. After a successful day of falcon hunting, the men sit

Falcon clinic

Parasites, broken wings, lung diseases – even falcons can fall ill. In Dubai there is a special falcon hospital that treats these precious animals. Treatments at the clinic, which was established by Sheikh Hamdan bin Rashid al Maktoum and has been run by an American veterinarian for two decades, are free for locals. Examinations, x-rays and operations take place around the clock, as the people running this clinic have by now realized that »if there's one thing that Arabs can't stand, it's a closed falcon clinic.«

Fort Al-Hosn is home to the town archives and a museum.

visit to the dhow yard allows a peek at the boat builders at work. Some older boats, in need of restoration, are grounded on the beach, while others bob about on the water. This area also has a number of restaurants, some of which are converted dhows. It is a great place to enjoy the view of old Abu Dhabi and watch the hustle and bustle of the harbour.

Heritage Village
The **open-air museum** is situated behind the National Exhibition Centre on Musafah Road, easily recognized from the two large towers at the entrance. The coral limestone and mud houses of the old town were all demolished as a result of the steady flow of petrodollars; at Heritage Village, the citizens of Abu Dhabi pay tribute to their past. Visitors can wander through a reconstruction of a Bedouin village, a portrayal of the traditional way of life from the time before the oil boom. The boat on the small manmade lake was once used for pearl diving. It is shown how the Bedouin huts of the past, built from palm leaves and mud, can also be furnished and equipped in a modern style. Exhibitions provide information about traditional boat and camel races, while courageous visitors can take a horse or camel ride. On Friday afternoons, the **arts and crafts market** at the Heritage Village sells baskets made of date tree leaves, ceramics and camel-hair rugs. The afternoon highlight is the **falconry** demonstration (open: daily 9am–10pm, free admission).

Friday market ▶

⊕

Today, dhows are built by immigrant workers.

Grand Souk

The Grand Souk is situated in Medinat Zayed between Zayed the Second Street (Electra Street) and Al-Falah Street (Passport Street). The large complex was meant to combine the many small souks that are spread all over the city. However, many of the small booths in the Grand Souk are still empty, leaving a somewhat sterile impression. This state of affairs should change soon: increased efforts are being made to attract merchants and expand the range of meat and fish, vegetables, spices, rice, household goods from the Far East and synthetic and silk fabrics from India and China.

Iranian Souk

Persian souks exist in every emirate. Here, the Iranian market can be found at the Free Port (Mina Hurr) where dhows bring in the goods from Iran. A long row of small – and very small – shops sell inexpensive rugs, souvenirs and handicrafts. Visit the Iranian Souk at sunset, when lanterns create a romantic bazaar atmosphere.

> **! Baedeker TIP**
>
> **Fresh from the sea**
> The fish market behind the Iranian Souk is best visited before noon, when it is at its busiest. A nearby building complex houses several restaurants, some with outdoor seating under palm roofs.

The **Tourist Club** is situated in a park-like area on the east end of Sheikh Hamdan Bin Mohammed Street. It provides numerous leisure and water sport facilities, including a public pool, tennis and squash courts, bowling alleys and restaurants. The club also offers boat trips to the off-shore island **Sadiyat**, which is used as a beach club. The club (tel. 7 72 34 00) is only open to members, though tourists can acquire a limited membership.

Maqta Tower

The Maqta Tower on a small island in the shallow water is visible when leaving the main island over the Al-Maqta Bridge. The three-

Locals doing their daily shopping at the fruit and vegetable souk

storey **defence tower** was erected in the 19th century on the ruins of a Portuguese watchtower. It was used to guard the island and its settlement, which at that time could only be reached from the mainland by walking across a ford during low tide.

Umm al-Nar From the highway, a 4km/2.5mi bridge leads to the large island of Umm al-Nar, where an **archaeological excavation site** (Bronze Age circular tombs) is located. Unfortunately, the island does not allow access to tourists due to the presence of a large refinery plant.

✶ ✶ Al Ain

F 4

Population: 422,000

The »garden city« of Al Ain, 160km/99mi east of Abu Dhabi, is situated in the middle of the desert at the foot of the Hajar Mountains. This 200 sq km/77 sq mi oasis region includes around 200 springs and fountains. During the course of the oil boom a city has developed which not only supplies the emirate with agricultural goods but is also a cultural centre with the country's largest university.

Green city Al Ain and Abu Dhabi are connected by one nearly continuous, multi-lane road, the sides of which have been covered with greenery. As the **birthplace of Sheikh Zayed**, Al Ain is held in high esteem by the entire UAE. The city has an international airport with direct flights to other Gulf States and has developed extensive import and export industries. About 15km/9.3mi south of the city, the Jebel Hafeet rises 1,350m/4,429ft above the flat, rocky landscape.

The green city is traversed by endless wide streets which are lit at night and lined with palm trees and oleander bushes. Every square and inner courtyard is planted with grass, flowers or shrubbery. The large administrative buildings in modern Islamic style are surrounded by gardens and parks; futuristic-looking mosques are a display of the city's wealth. Road signs are in both Arabic and English, which makes route finding easy.

History

3000 BC	First settlement of Hili and the Jebel Hafeet
18th century	The al-Nahyan family occupies Al Ain.
1966	Drawing up of the border between Al Ain and Buraimi (Oman)

The area of what is today the border region between Oman, Saudi Arabia and the United Arab Emirates has been settled for 5,000 years. Hundreds of stone tombs from 3000 to 2700 BC have been discovered in **Qarn Bint-Saud**, 15km/9.3mi north of Al Ain on the slopes of Hafeet Mountain, a foothill of the Hajar Mountains. The grave findings suggest trade relations with Mesopotamia.

First settlement

In Hili, 10km/6.2mi north of Al Ain, tourists can visit the reconstructed foundation walls of a 3,000 year old settlement. Due to its generous water resources, the settlement was used as a hub for caravans for many centuries.

Hili

Most of Al Ain's history is unknown. At the end of the 18th century, the **al-Nahyan family**, which at that time still lived in the Liwa Oasis further south, occupied parts of the oasis in the Al Ain region. In the 19th century, the Nahyan shared the oases with the Sultan of Oman. In 1866, the Wahhabi conquered the **Buraimi Oasis**, but lost it again to the Sultan of Oman three years later.

19th century

In 1949, Saudi Arabia raised a claim to the Buraimi Oasis and eventually re-conquered it in 1952, with support from Omani fundamentalists who wanted to overthrow Oman's Sultan Taimur for bringing a non-Islamic oil company from overseas into the country. Three years later, the sultan re-conquered the oasis region with support from British troops.

20th century

Until 1966, Sheikh Zayed, who before his death in 2004 held the offices of Emir of Abu Dhabi and President of the United Arab Emirates, was Governor of the Al Ain Province. In 1966, the Sultanates of Oman and Abu Dhabi agreed upon the border between Al Ain and Buraimi. In 1974, Saudi Arabia finally renounced its claims and ac-

► VISITING AL AIN

INFORMATION

The Al Ain Museum and the Hilton Hotel provide tourist information.

AL AIN INTERNET CAFÉ

Al Ain International Centre
Tel. 8 63 02 22
Fax 8 62 43 33
www.alain-icafe.co.ae

WHERE TO EAT

► Expensive

② *Fishmarket*
Hotel Inter-Continental
Al Salam Street
Tel. 7 68 66 86
The speciality of this hotel restaurant is a particularly varied Far East fish buffet.

► Inexpensive

① *Golden Gate*
Al Ain Street
(across from the Clock Tower)
Tel. 7 66 24 67
Fast-food restaurant with mostly Filipino and Chinese dishes, and an extra take-away menu.

WHERE TO STAY

► Luxury

② *Hilton*
Zayed Bin-Sultan Street
(on the corner of Khaled Bin-Sultan Street)
P.O. Box 13 33
Tel. 7 68 66 66
Fax 7 68 68 88
220 rooms
Guests are accommodated in the modern main building or in particularly beautiful chalets and small villas in the spacious hotel park. The hotel grounds feature tennis and squash courts, as well as a 9-hole golf course.

③ *Inter-Continental*
Al Salam Street
(at the east end of Khaled Bin-Sultan Street)
P.O. Box 1 60 31
Tel. 7 68 66 86
Fax 7 68 67 66
www.interconti.com
200 rooms
This hotel is ideal for sports lovers as it includes two pools, floodlit tennis courts, two squash halls, a horse stable and a golf driving range with a simulator. Guests needn't go far to enjoy some very fine cuisine: the hotel restaurant »Fishmarket« offers a delicious fish buffet.

Baedeker-recommendation

► Mid-range

① *Al-Buraimi*
P.O. Box 330
Al-Buraimi PC 512
Oman
Tel. 0 09 68 / 65 20 10
From the UAE:
Tel. 050 / 47 49 54
Fax 0 09 68 / 65 20 11
40 rooms and 20 »villas«
You don't need a visa to stay at this hotel situated in the Omani city of Buraimi. Th villas, simple small bungalows, are arrange around a pool. Creature comforts and entertainment are provided by the renowned restaurant and the Tropicana nightclub.

The green city of Al Ain is surrounded by palm groves.

cepted the border south of the oasis. In 2000, the line of the border was protected by a treaty. Today Buraimi belongs to Oman, and the neighbouring Al Ain to the United Arab Emirates.

What to See in Al Ain

The fort, also called »Al Ain Fort« and »Al-Hosn« can be found on Zayed Ibn-Sultan Street. The enormous fortification was built in the beginning of the 20th century by **Sheikh Sultan Bin-Zayed al-Nahyan**, grandfather of the current emir.

The Al Ain Museum is situated in one of the side buildings. Opened in 1971, it is one of the oldest museums of this young state. The ethnographical section depicts life in the desert before the beginning of the »Oil Age«. Life-size puppets are used to reconstruct the everyday life of Bedouins, pearl divers and fishermen. The archaeological section exhibits Bronze and Iron Age finds from Hili and Jebel Hafeet. Most visitors are particularly interested in the presents given to Sheikh Zayed by foreign state visitors, including an elephant tusk and several stuffed animals (open: Sun–Thu 8am–1pm and 2pm–5pm).

✳
Al-Sharki Fort

🕐

The Jahili Fort, with thick mud brick walls and three round towers, is located next to the public gardens on Mohammed Bin-Khalifa Street and was built at the end of the 19th century by the grandfather of the current president. The building and **former emir's residence** is a complete reconstruction using only traditional building materi-

Jahili Fort

Al Ain Plan

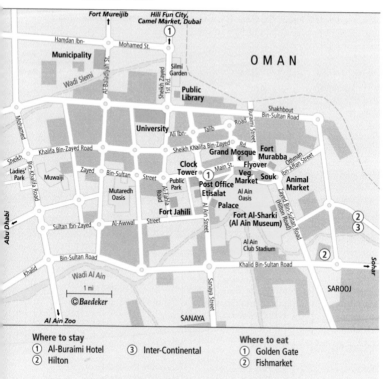

Where to stay
① Al-Buraimi Hotel   ③ Inter-Continental
② Hilton

Where to eat
① Golden Gate
② Fishmarket

als. The mud bricks are made by hand, air-dried and plastered with a mixture of mud and straw, creating an authentic impression. (open: daily except Fri 9am–6pm).

Camel Market   The camel market, where merchants sell single-humped Arabian dromedaries, is located south of the Hili Gardens. On Thursdays and Fridays, when the choice of dromedaries is particularly large, locals from Abu Dhabi and other emirates drive here in their pickup trucks to examine the animals closely in a relaxed and friendly market atmosphere. The prices are comparatively low; there are no high-class racing camels or breeding mares here, just animals that are valued for their milk and meat supply (market hours: daily 7am–12pm).

Souk   On the other side of Zayed Bin-Sultan Street stretches the historic souk of the oasis city, a mix of oriental colours and Asian scents. This very modern market has sections for meat, fish and vegetables, as well as household goods.

South of the city centre, the historic oasis of Al Ain is now a public park, the **Central Public Gardens**. It contains several fountains and a large playground for children. Part of the old irrigation system has been restored.

Al Ain Oasis

On Al-Jimi Street in the Qattarah district – close to the crossroads of Khalid Bin Al-Waleed Street and Al-Baladiya Street, north-west of the city centre – stands the city's oldest fort, built in 1830 by Sheikh Shakhbout Bin-Diab al-Nahyan. Except for the old foundation walls, the fort is a complete replica. The fortified roof and surrounding walls are crowned with battlements (open: daily 7am–10pm, from 4pm for women only).

✶
Mureijib Fort

⊙

Men and boys from the age of 10 upwards are not welcome in one of the most popular relaxation parks of Al Ain. The Ladies' Park, also known as Basra Park (Mohammed Bin-Khalifa Road/Sheikh Khalifa Bin-Zayed Road) gives women (and their children) a chance for a relaxed picnic in the park where they can chat with friends while the offspring is happily entertained at the playground.

Ladies' Park

Silmi Garden, situated north-west of the city centre on Sheikh Zayed the First Road, is popular with local families going for an evening stroll. Like all parks in the Emirate of Abu Dhabi, this garden is impeccably clean and planted with the most beautiful tropical trees and flowers. Kitsch meets romance when the park walls are illuminated with colourful, fluorescent lights after dark.

! Baedeker TIP

Photo opportunities

The livestock market (or cattle market) across from the Al-Sharki Fort presents great opportunities for a snapshot: goats, sheep, chickens, sometimes even calves are brought here early in the morning and kept in pens made of rope, where they wait patiently for their new owners (market hours: daily 7am–12pm).

Around Al Ain

Abu Dhabi's most prominent excavation site is located in the middle of a big park. In the 1960s, Danish archaeologists discovered numerous remains of settlements and overground **circular tombs**, which confirmed the theory that this region was already inhabited more than 5,000 years ago. The Hili Archaeological Gardens can be accessed from Ardh Al-Jaw Street near the Dubai Highway, through a large iron gate decorated with flowers. The Great Hili Tomb is the most significant find. Made of smooth stone blocks the tomb has a diameter of 8m/26ft and is 2.5m/8ft high. Its date of origin is estimated at 2500 BC.
Remarkable are the two tomb entrances with the architect's engravings above. They display the shapes of humans and Oryx antelopes, which can be clearly identified by their two long horns.

✶ ✶
Hili Archaeological Gardens

Hili Archaeological Gardens, the Emirates' most notable excavations site

Based on the burial objects, some of which are exhibited at the Museum of Al Ain, the tomb is attributed to the **Umm al-Nar culture** between 3000 and 2000 BC.

After visiting the circular tombs, allow time for a stroll through the park. It is particularly lively on Thursdays and Fridays, when numerous local families come here to host picnics on the extensive lawns. A restaurant offers simple meals and refreshments (open: Sat–Thu 4pm–11pm, Fri from 10am).

Hili Fun City The 85ha/210ac amusement park Hili Fun City, often referred to as the »**Disneyland of the Middle East**«, on Ardh Al-Jaw Street (in the direction of Dubai), provides year-round fun for the entire family, including a fun fair with a rollercoaster, botanical garden and boat rides as well as cafés and restaurants (open: Sat–Thu 4pm–10pm, Fri 9am–10pm, Tue and Wed for women and children only).

Al Ain Ice Rink ▶ Directly next to Hili Fun City is the **Al Ain Ice Rink**, which is very popular among both locals and expatriates (open: see Hili Fun City).

Al Ain Zoo The Al Ain Zoo is situated south of the city, at the end of Zayed Al-Awal Street. A thousand mammals from Arabia, Africa and India live here on 400ha/988ac. Founded in 1969 under the emir's aegis, the zoo is dedicated to the **breeding of rare species**, a role in which it has been successful in the cases of the endangered Arabian Oryx an-

Entrance to the ice skating rink at Hili Fun City in Al Ain

telope, the desert leopard and a rare fox species which have all been saved from extinction. Furthermore, the zoo houses reptiles and almost 2,000 birds, while the aquarium gives insight into the diversity of fish in the Arabian Gulf. Numerous playgrounds and a miniature train that rides from enclosure to enclosure provide extra entertainment for children (open: daily except Sat and Wed 8am–6pm).

Al Ain's camel race track is located at the west end of the city, on the road to Abu Dhabi. During the racing season – between October and March – the camel races on Thursdays and Fridays are heavily frequented by the local population; admission is free.

Camel race track

The Omani town of Buraimi can be visited without visa formalities. In fact, entering **Oman** from Al Ain often goes entirely unnoticed. The first Omani frontier post is located 40km/25mi away from the city, in the direction of Sohar. A stroll through the old oasis with its vegetable gardens, palm tree groves, water channels and mud houses is particularly pleasant.

Buraimi

The historical Al-Khandaq Fort, situated in the centre of Buraimi, was built in around 1780 by the local tribe of Al-Bu Shami. The restored compound is bordered by four defence towers and a wide moat (open: Sat–Thu 8am–6pm, Fri 8am–1pm and 4pm–6pm, admission free).

◄ **Al-Khandaq Fort**

Idyllic palm grove in Buraimi

Archaeological sites in the Hafeet Mountains
During archaeological excavation work on the island of Umm al-Nar the former Governor of Al Ain, Sheikh Zayed, noticed a resemblance to hills in Jebel Hafeet. Examinations of so far approximately **100 tombs** have brought to light objects from the end of the third millennium BC. The sites cannot be visited, but numerous finds, including fine copper works, are exhibited at the museum of Al Ain.

Ain Al-Faydah
Both Arabs and expatriates enjoy coming to the natural hot spring of Ain Al-Faydah (beneficial spring) for a relaxing weekend. Located on Haza Bin-Sultan Street at the foot of the Hafeet Mountain, the locals also call the spring Ain Abu Sukhna, »Father of Warmth«. A few decades ago, the area around the lake was turned into a spa region with hotels, bungalows and playgrounds, as well as sports and leisure facilities. Unfortunately, the once picturesque lake has lost some of its charm as it is now bordered by a large concrete basin.

✳ Fossil Valley
Several travel organizations in Dubai and Abu Dhabi offer trips to Fossil Valley, some 15km/9.3mi north-east of Al Ain, on the road to the Omani city of Mahdah near Jebel Qatar. The valley is surrounded by a rocky plain and was covered with water millions of years ago, as the numerous **fossils** of shells and starfish that can be discovered during a stroll here prove.

Mahdah
Mahdah, situated in Oman around 30km/18.6mi from Al Ain, is an **oasis town** with a fortress-like mosque – date of origin unknown. Today, there is not much to remind visitors of Mahdah's past as an important caravan hub. The ancient houses made of mud and palm leaves are in ruins, and so are the two forts in the historic town centre.
The citizens of Mahdah were moved to new houses; according to **Sultan Qaboos'** ambitious plans, every citizen of Oman should live in a modern house with running water and electricity.

Liwa Oases

D 5

Population: 30,000

There have been Bedouin settlements along this 50km/31mi stretch of oases surrounded by date trees and high sand dunes for about 300 years. Today, the largest of the total of 15 towns, which are arranged in a wide circle, is the newly founded town of Mezirah. The rich supply of groundwater makes it possible to maintain numerous gardens and fields.

The Liwa oases, one of the **largest oasis systems** on the Arabian Peninsula, are located on the edge of the Rub al-Khali desert, known as the »Empty Quarter«. During the heat of summer, it is mainly the locals who leave the coastal region to enjoy the less humid and climatically more pleasant town of Liwa.

On the edge of the »Empty Quarter«

The Liwa settlements often don't fit the common idea of a traditional oasis town. New, simply constructed houses are lined along the sandy trails; barbed wire keeps the free-roaming goats from grazing

◄ Settlements

The Liwa Oases are characterized by modern settlements and green plantations.

⏵ VISITING THE LIWA OASES

DAY TRIPS
Many hotels in Abu Dhabi offer day trips to Liwa in four-by-four like vehicles, including a trip to the sandy desert.
(approx. 400 AED/£54 per person).

WHERE TO EAT

▶ Expensive
Mezoon
in the Liwa Hotel
Tel. 8 82 20 00
International and Arab cuisine; a view onto sand dunes and gardens.

▶ Moderate
Al Rawaq
in the Liwa Hotel
Tel. 8 82 20 00
The coffee shop offers lunch and dinner buffets as well as simple meals à la carte.

▶ Inexpensive
Liwa Resthouse
Mezirah
behind the police station
Tel. 8 82 20 75
The restaurant of this small hotel serves simple Arabic dishes.

WHERE TO STAY

▶ Luxury
Liwa Hotel
Mezirah City
Tel. 8 82 20 00
Fax 8 82 28 30
www.ncth.ae
Luxury accommodation in the sandy desert: this hotel (66 rooms including three 3-bedroom villas) is located on a hill surrounded by green parks; includes a large pool and tennis courts

▶ Budget
Liwa Resthouse
Mezirah
on the hill behind the police station
Tel. 82 20 75
19 rooms, 2 suites
This simple hotel includes a pool and offers multiple sports facilities, including sand skiing.

Medinat Zayed Guesthouse
Medinat Zayed
Tel. 8 84 62 81
38 rooms
This guesthouse is pleasantly comfortable; at weekends it is popular with Arab families.

their way through the laboriously tended oasis region. Small shops sell food and textiles while restaurants, which seem more like snack bars, offer basic meals.

History   The founding fathers of Abu Dhabi and Dubai came from the Liwa oases, which were colonized by the Bedouin tribe, the **Bani Yas**, in the early 18th century. They lived in simple Barasti huts made of palm leaves. The – initially only temporary – settlement was associated with political differences among tribe members. In 1793, the **Al Nahyan family** left the tribe to settle in the coastal region further north which led to the foundation of Abu Dhabi. In 1833, another branch of the Bani Yas, under the leadership of **Sheikh Maktoum**, left the oases and founded another settlement north of Abu Dhabi: Dubai. For Europeans, the region south of the pirate coast was unknown territory for a long time. In 1948, British colonial officer **Wilfred Thesiger** (►Famous People) was the first European to reach the oases with his camel caravan.

Medinat Zayed consists of newly built houses that were made available to the Bedouins. The settlement has a number of cafés and restaurants which are worth stopping at. Eventually, you pass 150m/164yd-high sand dunes to the left and right of the street. Every now and again, free-roaming camels walk up to the fence which keeps them from wandering down the street.

Medinat Zayed

The **main oasis town** is Mezirah, from which a paved road leads east and west, interconnecting the individual villages; other trails in some villages also lead north and south. Due to the lack of signposts however, visitors are advised not to go on desert tours alone.

Mezirah

AJMAN

Area: 260 sq km/100 sq mi
Emir: Sheikh Humaid Bin-Rashid al-Nuaimi (since 1981)

Population: 235,000

Tourism is still in its infancy in Ajman. With a new luxury hotel resort, however, the emirate is now trying to catch up. After all, the sheikhdom's wide, sandy Ajman beach is one of the UAE's most beautiful coastal stretches.

The smallest of the seven emirates, situated between Sharjah and Umm al-Quwain on an inlet of the Arabian Gulf, is completely surrounded by Sharjah. Ajman has two exclaves used for agriculture: Masfut, located in the Hajar Mountains close to the border with Oman, which is also known for its marble quarries; and the oasis settlement of Manama, approximately 60km/37mi east of Ajman. The emirate has now also begun to exploit its **copper and iron resources**.

Emirate surrounded by Sharjah

As no oil has yet been found in Ajman, it is one of the poorest regions in the UAE, and has largely depended on Abu Dhabi for the last three decades. With the emirate's financial support, Ajman has managed to build a thriving shipyard, a large photo laboratory and a steelworks, the Arab Heavy Industries Company. Living expenses in Ajman are among the lowest in the UAE, which is why more and more foreign workers decide to live in Ajman and commute to the other sheikhdoms.

Part of the population still lives on fishing, e.g. sardines, which are dried and sold as fertilizer to agricultural businesses.

◄ Fishing

Ajman's history is identical to that of ►Sharjah. Under **Sheikh Rashid Bin-Humaid al-Nuaimi**, the first ruler of Ajman, who reigned between 1820 and 1838, the emirate separated from Sharjah in 1820. In the same year, Sheikh Rashid was one of the seven emirs to sign the first General Treaty with the British making it a protectorate. In 1892 it signed an Exclusive Agreement with the British government, which placed its foreign affairs solely in their hands, and which was meant to stop Turkish and French expansion on the coast.

History

← *A magnificent fountain defines the city centre of Ajman.*

* # Ajman

F 3

Population: 189,000

While there are still some old buildings in the northern part of the peninsula, the modern and largely characterless buildings beyond the lagoon and in the southern fringe areas of Ajman characterize a fast-growing 21st-century Arabic city.

Ajman, the **capital of the emirate** of the same name, is situated on a peninsula between the Arabian Gulf and the Khor Ajman estuary which cuts inland in the north. Small shops line the streets of the city centre, as well as several banks, bureaux de change and simple restaurants serving Arabic cuisine. A stroll through the Old Souk is a great way of becoming familiar with the hustle and bustle of everyday life; here, the haggling over prices lasts from early morning until long after dark. Except during lunchtime that is, when the city streets seem entirely deserted.

▶ VISITING AJMAN

INFORMATION

The Ajman Tourist Centre on Arabian Gulf Street provides tourist information and also functions as a hotel, restaurant and beach club.

SOUKS

The Old Souk on the east side of the marina mainly sells foods such as meat, fish, spices, fruit and vegetables.

Oriental spices: an ideal culinary gift

The separate fish souk has a particularly varied selection. At the Iranian Souk near the marina, merchants offer imported household goods, especially plastic goods in all shapes, sizes and colours. The Gold Souk on Omar al-Khatab Street, somewhat oversized for Ajman, primarily attracts a more local crowd. The modern souk, the Ajman City Centre, with numerous shops and several restaurants, is located outside the city on the road to Ras al-Khaimah.

BEACHES

The wide and sandy beach between Sharjah and Ajman is little frequented, but also lacks proper infrastructure. The beach on the west coast of the peninsula is less appealing and often quite dirty; it is only cleaned at Coral Beach and in front of the Ajman Beach Hotel. Note: the tide at the Ajman beaches can be dangerous.

What to See in Ajman

The city's most prominent site is situated on the east side of the Central Square: the Ajman Museum. Housed in an 18th-century fort, it is the oldest monument of the city. The building, parts of which were erected in 1775, once served as **residence to Sheikh Rashid al-Nuaimi**, the current ruler's father, who died in 1981. Two watchtowers secured the coast and the Khor Ajman; wind towers provided cooler conditions during hot summer days (►p.246).

★
Ajman Museum

WHERE TO EAT
► Expensive
① *Hai Tao*
at the Kempinski Hotel, tel. 7 45 15 55
Fine Szechuan and Cantonese cuisine.

► Moderate
② *Falcon*
Ajman Marina, Tel. 7 42 33 44
Enjoy Arabic specialities in a pleasant atmosphere.

► Inexpensive
③ *Ajman City Centre*
Tel. 7 43 14 31
The food court of the Ajman City Centre is ideal for a quick snack in between exploring the sights.

Al-Diwan
Ajman Immigration Road
Tel. 7 44 22 81
A busy, simple restaurant serving Arabic cuisine.

Chinese Home Restaurant
Ajman Corniche, tel. 7 42 22 02
Inexpensive Chinese restaurant

WHERE TO STAY
► Luxury
③ *Ajman Kempinski Hotel & Resort*
Ajman Corniche
P.O. Box 30 25
Tel. 7 45 15 55

www.ajmankempinski.com
189 rooms and suites
Directly located on a beautiful, wide private beach, the Ajman Kempinski offers plenty of sports facilities, including water sports, tennis and squash. Ideal for families (mini club). All rooms and suites come with an ocean view. The hotel houses eleven restaurants and bars.

► Mid-range
② *Ajman Beach Hotel*
Al-Khaleej Road
(Ajman Corniche)
P.O. Box 874
Tel. 7 42 33 33
www.bhatia.com/abh.html
65 rooms
The hotel is situated approx. 20km/12.4mi from Dubai airport. The rooms are comfortable; the beach is covered with bright, white sand. Daily shuttle bus service to Dubai.

► Budget
① *Al-Waha*
Main Road
(near Kuwaiti Hospital)
P.O. Box 28 69
Tel. 7 42 43 33
233 rooms
Simple hotel, centrally located. All rooms equipped with bathroom and air-conditioning.

Ajman Plan

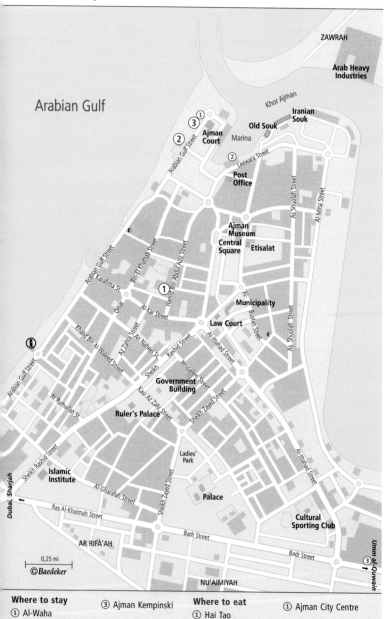

ZAWRAH

Arab Heavy Industries

Arabian Gulf

Khor Ajman

Iranian Souk

Old Souk

③ ①
② Ajman Court
Marina
② Leewara Street

Post Office

As Shuolah Street
Al-Mina Street

Ajman Museum
Central Square
Etisalat

Arabian Gulf Street
Karahma St.
Bin-El-Khattab Street
Hamid Bin-Abdul Aziz Street

① Omar
Al-Kar Street
Az Zahra Street
An Nakheel St.

Municipality
Al-Bustan Street
Law Court
As Shuolah Street

Khalid Bin Al-Waleed Street
Rashid Street
Al-Ittahad Street

Sheikh
Jerusalem Street
Government Building
Kasr Az Zahi Street
Sheikh Zayed Street

Ar Rumailah St.
Ruler's Palace

Dubai, Sharjah
Sheikh Rashid Street

Ladies' Park

Islamic Institute
Al-Gharafah Street
Sheikh Zayed Street
Palace

Ras Al-Khaimah Street
Cultural Sporting Club
Al-Ittahad Street

AR RIFA'AH
Badr Street
Umm al-Quwain ③

0,25 mi
©Baedeker
Badr Street

NU'AIMIYAH

Where to stay
① Al-Waha
② Ajman Beach Hotel
③ Ajman Kempinski

Where to eat
① Hai Tao
② Falcon
① Ajman City Centre

Since 1991, this perfectly restored monument has been home to an interesting museum of **archaeological exhibits**; among them are Bronze Age burial objects and a replica of a 5,000-year old burial site. The finds in the emirate confirm that Ajman was also colonized at a very early stage. As at the museum in Dubai, life-size figures portray everyday scenes from the past. On the ground floor the exhibition rooms, arranged all around the large inner courtyard, include a traditional bakery, a tailor, a barber and a herbal healer, as well as a replica of an old Arab coffee house. A Qur'an school and an old police station are exhibited on the first floor, which is also an ideal place to take a closer look at the **wind towers** and the simple, yet effective, construction of the traditional air-conditioning system, which Persian merchants introduced in the 19th century (open: Sat–Thu 9am–1pm and 4pm–7pm, Fri 4pm to 7pm).

The old fort now serves as a museum.

Ruler's palace

The former palace of **Sheikh Humaid Bin-Rashid al-Nuaimi** on Sheikh Rashid Street, where the Emir resided long after his inauguration in 1981, is not open to visitors. Sheikh Humaid now lives in a new palace on the northern Arabian Gulf Street across from the Ajman Beach Hotel. The palace, built in neo-Islamic style, has a large dome and four watchtowers, and is surrounded by well-kept lawns and enormous date trees. Photography is prohibited.

Ajman Marina

The **harbour**, with its fully loaded dhows, water taxis (abras) and fishing boats, is situated at the northern end of Arabian Gulf Street, where the Khor Ajman leads into the Arabian Gulf. The hustle and bustle on the piers and on the water can be best observed from a nearby coffee house or restaurant.

★
Dhow yard

The dhow yard, where the traditional wooden ship are still built using ancient techniques and without any construction plans, opens a window on the past. Meanwhile, shipbuilders have also turned to fibreglass as a building material. At the yard, there are always ships at different stages of completion. The detailed dhow replicas made by yard workers in their free time, which are sometimes sold at the shipyard, make attractive **souvenirs**.

DUBAI

Area: 3,885 sq km/1,500 sq mi
Emir: Sheikh Mohammed Bin-Rashid
al-Maktoum (since 2006)

Population: 1,370,000

Of all the United Arab Emirates, Dubai attracts the most visitors: no other emirate offers more luxurious hotels or better shopping facilities. The choice of restaurants, serving both Arabic and international cuisine, is enormous; an endless row of hotels lines the Jumeirah beach.

The Emirate of Dubai, situated between ► Sharjah in the north and ► Abu Dhabi in the south, is the second largest emirate of the UAE, with 70km/43.5mi of coastline and an interior stretching 80km/49.7mi inland. The emirate owns **three exclaves** that are situated in the other sheikhdoms, the largest being ► Hatta. The eponymous capital of the emirate lies on both sides of Dubai Creek (Al-Khor), which is between 200 and 800 metres (219–875 yards) wide and stretches 12km/7.5mi into the sheikhdom.

Dubai is the most important trade centre in the United Arab Emirates, including the country's most significant harbours **Jebel Ali** and **Port Rashid**. Port Rashid can accommodate two cruise liners at the same time, thereby adding to the emirate's growing importance as cruise destination.

Home to 1,300 companies, Jebel Ali is by far the largest industrial site on the Arabian Gulf. With the Dubai World Trade Centre and more than 40 conventions per year, the emirate has also become the most important trade fair location in the Middle East. Dubai's most recent coup is underway: in order to create new sources of income besides petroleum, the free-trade zone **»Internet City«**, an »Arabian Silicon Valley«, has been established 20km/12.5mi outside the city.

History

2000 BC	First settlement of Al-Qusais
500 BC	Settlement of Jumeirah
7th/8th centuries	Dubai becomes important trade hub.
1833	The al-Maktoum family settles at Dubai Creek.
1971	Dubai becomes part of the United Arab Emirates.

← *Tradition and modernity meet at Dubai Creek.*

Dubai was colonized as early as in the 2nd millennium BC. Finds in Qusais, 13km/8mi north-east of Dubai, lead to the assumption that, even at this early stage, the region that is now Dubai was an influential **centre of trade**.

Around 500 BC, people settled in **Jumeirah**, where they constructed quite elaborate complexes of buildings. Among the finds are the remains of a building which was most likely used as a palace, as well as walls of a 20-room caravanserai. During the Umayyad Period (661–750), Dubai served as a resting post for caravans on their way from Oman to Mesopotamia.

Foundation of Dubai

Recent Islamic history of the Dubai sheikhdom begins in 1833, when the Bedouin tribe, the Bani Yas, moved from the Liwa oases to the coast under the leadership of **Sheikh Maktoum Bin-Buti al-Blofas**, and settled at Dubai Creek. In the early 20th century, more and more Persian merchants chose Dubai as their new place of residence and built spacious, multi-storey residences from coral limestone.

The blossoming metropolis of Dubai

During the first half of the 20th century, Dubai evolved into an industrial metropolis on the Arabian Gulf. In 1935, the **Deira Souk** already included more than 300 shops. As a transport hub, too, Dubai is gaining in importance: **Dubai International Airport** came into operation in 1971 and soon became the largest airport on the Arabian Peninsula. In 2000, the opening of the **Burj al-Arab** luxury hotel, the tallest hotel building in the world (►Baedeker Special p.190), attracted international attention.

★ ★ Dubai

F 3

Population: 950,000

All over Dubai construction work is taking place, with cranes towering over every part of the city. Even some buildings from the 1970s and 1980s have been torn down and are being replaced by new ones. The city has been extended with new districts and artificial islands.

The souk at the historic Bastakiya quarter has been authentically restored.

Dubai Creek splits the city into two halves. The actual heart of this western-looking metropolis is the landing stage for water taxis, the **abras**, ancient wooden boats connecting the two parts of the city. The **Al-Shindagha tunnel** and a pedestrian tunnel cross beneath the estuary of Dubai Creek over to Bur Dubai. In recent years, Dubai has become astonishingly green: thanks to an underground irrigation system, the median strips of city highways blossom with magnificent date trees and bougainvilleas, roses and oleander bushes. The splendid residential palaces of the local upper class lie hidden behind high walls. The harbour is constantly being expanded. The **Westside Marina** is a new building project on the coast of Al-Sufouh: a yacht harbour, hotels, parks, supermarkets, offices and residential buildings are built along a 3km/1.9mi-long manmade lagoon.

Thriving city on the Gulf

Highlights Dubai

Dubai Museum
National museum in a restored fort.
▶ page 183

Burj al-Arab
Luxurious city icon
▶ page 190

Shindagha
Restored old town
▶ page 188

Jumeirah Mosque
Illuminated at night
▶ page 194

Gold Souk
Here, all that glitters is, in fact, gold.
▶ page 197

● VISITING DUBAI

INFORMATION

Government of Dubai Department of Tourism and Commerce Marketing
National Bank of Dubai
12th floor
Bani Yas Road
P.O. Box 594
Dubai
Tel. 04 / 2 23 00 00, fax 2 23 00 22
Open:
Sat–Thu 8am–2pm
www.dubaitourism.co.ae

Tourism Information Centre
Bani Yas Square
(Pavillion in the city centre)
Dubai
Tel. 2 28 50 00
Open: daily 9am–10pm

Tourism Information Centre
Sheikh Zayed Road
(Road to Abu Dhabi)
Tel. 8 84 68 27
Open:
Sat–Thu 8am–2pm

SHOPPING

The wide range of souks and malls in the shopping paradise of Dubai can quickly use up visitors' holiday budgets. However, don't miss out on a stroll through the three-storey Bur Juman Centre. Its numerous designer boutiques are primarily aimed at wealthy locals (Trade Centre Road, tel. 3 52 02 22; open: Sat–Thu 10am–10pm, Fri 4pm–10pm). Other well-known shopping complexes in Bur Dubai are the Al-Wafi Shopping Mall and the Karama Shopping Area.
Some of the largest shopping malls in town are in Deira: the Al-Ghurair Centre (Al-Riqqa Road), the Hamrain Centre (Abu Baker Siddique Road) and the City Centre (Bani Yas Road).

CITY TOURS

An open-topped double-decker bus drives from Wafi Centre to the most prominent sights, from Bur Dubai to Deira, including a total of eight stops (The Big Bus, Tel. 324 41 87, www.bigbus.co.uk, May–Sept daily 3pm–8pm, Oct–April daily 10am–8pm; fares: Adults 75 AED (£10), children 45 AED (£6), families 195 AED (£26.50).

A-Wafi Shopping Mall – one of Dubai's more than 30 shopping paradises

INTERNET CAFÉ

Al Matrix.com Café
Metropolitan Hotel
Sheikh Zayed Road
P.O. Box 3 74 14
Dubai
Tel. 3 43 00 00
www.methotels.com

Al-Jalssa Internet C@fe
Al Ain Center
P.O. Box 31 61, Dubai
Tel. 3 51 46 17

WHERE TO EAT

► Expensive

⑤ **Al-Dawar**
Hyatt Regency Hotel
Corniche Road
Deira
Tel. 2 09 11 00
This revolving restaurant on the 25th
floor of the Hyatt Regency Hotel
offers a large buffet with international
specialities.

Aquarium
Dubai Creek Golf &
Yacht Club, Deira
Tel. 2 82 57 77
Exquisite fish restaurant in the 35m/
115ft-high clubhouse; elegant, exclu-
sive atmosphere.

► Moderate

⑦ **Al-Boom**
Al-Boom Tourist Village
Tariq Bin-Ziad Road
Tel. 3 96 18 85
Several dhows, some anchored, some
used for dinner cruises on the creek,
offer Arabic cuisine; mainly fish.

② **Danial**
Twin Towers
3rd floor
Baniyas Road
Tel. 2 27 76 69

Fine Iranian cuisine. Try the kebab
special for two or more people. They
also offer fish dishes and one inexpensive daily dish.

► Inexpensive

① **Bayt al Wakeel**
Souk al Kabeer (Bur Dubai)
Tel. 3 53 11 14
The trading house from 1935 lies at
the abra landing stage at the creek;
Arabic and Western cuisine.

China Times
Jumeirah Plaza Centre
Jumeirah Beach Road
Tel. 3 44 29 30
This Chinese restaurant has an ex-
tensive menu and delicious dishes.
Ideal for families with children.

Baedeker-recommendation

► Inexpensive

③ **Food Court**
Twin Towers
Baniyas Road
The most beautiful food court in town is
situated on the 3rd floor of the Twin Tower
shopping complex by the creek. Choose
between the air-conditioned hall and the
large balcony with a great view of the
activities on the water.

A romantic dinner alongside the creek

④ **Apple**
Twin Towers
Baniyas Road
Tel. 2 27 44 46
Romantic restaurant on the third
floor of the shopping complex, with
good Arabic fish dishes. Excellent
balcony view of the creek. Offers
water pipes.

⑥ **Popeye**
Baniyas Road
Tel. 2 22 55 57
Indian restaurant with outdoor seating directly by the creek. They also
serve sandwiches and freshly squeezed
fruit juices.

WHERE TO STAY
▶ **Luxury**
① *Burj Al-Arab*
▶ p.190

Al-Maha Desert Resort
P.O. Box 76 31
Margam Village, tel. 3 42 22
www.al-maha.com, 40 suites
How to get there: road no. 66 to Al
Ain, after 65km/40.4mi between the
exits 50 and 51 (Margam and Muqab)
10km/6.2mi of dirt road. The bungalows, designed as a Bedouin encampment, are built on desert sand.
Approximately 70km/43.5mi south-
east of Dubai, this luxury residence is
surrounded by barren landscape (▶
p.201).

② *Royal Mirage*
Al-Mina Al-Siyahi Street
Jumeirah Beach
P.O. Box 3 72 52
Tel. 3 99 99 99
Fax 3 99 99 98
www.royalmiragedubai.com
253 rooms
The hotel, with its minarets, more
than 1,000 palm trees, marble halls
and Moroccan antiques, seems to
come directly out of an oriental fairy-
tale world. The spacious lobby, with
golden frescoes and lighted ceiling, is
crowned by a large dome. As the
name suggests, the hotel is owned by
the royal family; it is run by Sun
International. If there happens to be a
yellow Ferrari – unobtrusively
guarded – parked outside at the
entrance, it means that the owner,
Sheikh Mohammed Bin-Rashid al-
Maktoum, is in the house.

③ *The Ritz-Carlton*
P.O. Box 2 65 25
Tel. 3 99 40 00
Fax 3 99 40 01
www.ritzcarlton.com
138 rooms and suites
At this luxury hotel, situated 25km/
15.5mi south of the city centre on
Jumeirah Beach, guests are looked
after by as many as 350 employees.
Equipped with several restaurants,
bars, a cigar room, a beach club, three
pools, a kids' pool and club, a 300m/
328yd stretch of private beach, tennis
and squash courts and a fitness room,
this hotel provides a mixture of
European luxury and oriental flair.

▶ **Mid-range**
Radisson SAS
Baniyas Road, Deira
Tel. 2 22 71 71
www.radissonsas.com
301 rooms
This hotel encompasses a shopping
arcade with fashion and antique
stores, as well as several restaurants, of
which the »Fishmarket« is not only
the most beautiful, but also has rather
an unusual concept: diners take a
shopping basket and wander along an
enormous counter laden with fresh
fish, shell fish and vegetables. The
choice of food is then prepared as
requested while guests enjoy the view
of the illuminated creek and Bur
Dubai.

Marco Polo
Al-Mateena Street
P.O. Box 2 55 70
Tel. 2 72 00 00
126 rooms
The former Novotel is situated close
to the Al-Ghurair Shopping Mall.
Includes a French, Indian and Tex-
Mex restaurant, an English pub, a
nightclub and discotheque.

Golden Sands Apartments
Al-Mankhool Street
(opposite the Ramada)
P.O. Box 91 68
Tel. 3 55 13 33, fax 3 51 63 28
www.goldensandsdubai.com
419 apartments
Moderately priced apartments, each
with kitchenette and pool. Ideal for
self-caterers or longer stays.

▶ **Budget**
④ *Sands*
Naif Roundabout, Deira
P.O. Box 2 80 56
Tel. 2 27 31 00
36 rooms
This hotel is located on a corner of the
busy centre, which makes it slightly
noisy. Relatively comfortable rooms.
Includes a Filipino and an Indian
restaurant.

⑥ *Royalton Plaza*
Clocktower Roundabout
P.O. Box 3 32 14
Tel. 2 95 91 71
Fax 2 95 83 77
E-mail: rtonplz@emirates.net.ae
136 rooms
Each room is equipped with air-
conditioning, TV, telephone and fax
machine, internet access, and some
have a balcony. The pool can be found
on the rooftop. Includes a Greek
restaurant and Irish pub.

⑤ *Riviera*
Dubai Creek Corniche
P.O. Box 13 88
Tel. 2 22 21 31, fax 2 21 18 20
Email: riviera@emirates.net.ae
109 rooms
The hotel, with its marvellous view of
the creek, is located next to the Twin
Towers complex. It has a simple but
good restaurant, serving Arabic as
well as Thai and Japanese cuisine.

What to See in Dubai

Bur Deira
The district Bur Deira, situated north of the creek, is Dubai's modern city centre. Lined by several luxury hotels, the wide Bani Yas Road along the creek turns into the city's cultural and social focal point after dark. The majority of sights on the Deira side can be visited on foot starting at **Bandar Talib Abra Station**, the landing stage for water taxis. Take a look at the building of the Etisalat telephone company, with its roof antennae shaped like a gigantic golf ball. The postmodern Municipality Building is made of shiny marble and granite, and standing next to it are the recently built high-rise buildings of steel and glass which shape the skyline of the city. **Dubai International Airport** is on the eastern edge of the city and opposite, right next to the creek, is the famous **Dubai Creek Golf & Yacht Club**.

Deira Souk ▶
Deira Souk is situated in the far west of Deira, near the creek and the tip of the mainland, Al-Ras, which leads into the estuary from here. The souk is split into the **Gold Souk**, which numbers among the emirate's biggest attractions, and the vending streets reserved for fish, meat, spices, vegetables, textiles and household goods.

Bur Dubai
The Bur Dubai district is located on the south-west side of Dubai Creek. From Dubai International Airport, it can be reached via the Al-Garhoud Bridge or, further north, via the Al-Maktoum Bridge. More stylish and far more pleasant is taking a water taxi after dark and crossing the creek to the Bastakiya district, where time seems to have stood still: dimly lit lanterns faintly illuminate the narrow alleys, lined with old coral-stone houses. At the busy souk, just a few steps away from the landing stage of the water taxis, the air is filled with the smells of curry, incense and coriander. The souk alley and several buildings along the landing stage have already been restored, 60 more historic houses on the verge of decay are also intended for reconstruction.

Bastakiya
Bastakiya is Bur Dubai's **oldest district**. Until the mid-20th century, most of the multi-storey houses were inhabited by wealthy merchant families from Iran and India. Coral and shell limestone was used as a construction material. The larger houses had two reception rooms with separate entrances, one for the man of the house and one for his wife or wives. Many of the newly restored houses have elaborately carved wooden doors and window screens. One or more wind towers on the rooftop channel cooler wind into the living rooms below.

An old dhow in »dry dock« outside the Dubai Museum

Today these houses are surrounded by high-rise buildings and seem endearingly low and small. Most are no longer accessible to the public.

Dubai's first office and administrative building, Bait Al-Wakeel is located not far from the water taxi landing stage. Constructed in 1934 by the former ruler **Sheikh Rashid Bin-Saeed Al-Maktoum** and elaborately restored in 1995, it also houses a Maritime Museum dedicated to the emirate's shipping trade, pearl diving (►Baedeker Special p.242) and fishing history.

On the right side, the souk arcade, built in traditional style using old construction materials, sells textiles, arts and crafts, ceramics and spices.

The old Al-Fahidi Fort, located directly in the centre of the Bastakiya district, was built in 1787. The over 40m/44yd-long and 33m/36yd-wide complex was used as a monitoring and observation station for protection against foreign attacks. The square north-west tower was erected in 1799, and stored cattle and gunpowder. In the 20th century, the fort served as a police station and prison.

The Al-Fahidi Fort was elaborately restored in 1971. Now it is home to the **National Museum**. The massive, nail-studded wooden en-

Bait Al-Wakeel

◄ Maritime Museum

◄ Souk arcade

Al-Fahidi Fort

**
Dubai Museum

The National Museum: recreated scenes of historic life in Dubai

trance gate, flanked by two cannons, is originally from Sheikh Saeed's house in the Shindagha district. The ground floor displays pearl-diving exhibits including tools, scales, measuring devices and sieves as well as 3,500-year old grave finds from Qusais. In the basement, which was added in the 1990s, life-size figures re-enact historical scenes from Dubai, enhanced by atmospheric light and sound effects: sparkling stars shining above the white tents of a Bedouin encampment; men sitting around an open fire, closely listening to the tales of a storyteller. A few steps further, there's the workshop of an iron smith, and boys sitting around the small wooden tables of a Qur'an school reading from the Holy Book to the rhythm of the teacher's stick (open: Sat–Thu 8.30am–7.30pm, Fri 2pm–8pm).

New Diwan Across from the museum stands the **administration building** of the Emir of Dubai, also called New Diwan, which is not open to the public. The entrance is flanked by two massive wind towers. Built in 1990, the traditional-style construction includes hundreds of arches decorating the many windows, arcades and hallways. The wrought-iron bars lend the building a very special charm.

★ ★
Grand Mosque The Grand Mosque of Dubai stands next to the Diwan. While the 70m/230ft-high minaret tower is visible from a distance, the nine large and 45 smaller colourful, lead-glazed domes dominating the mosque's appearance are no less striking. The original Grand Mos-

A coffee break at the Heritage Village

que, built here in 1900, served as the architectural model for the newer building. As **Bastakiya's landmark** and the emirate's most prominent Islamic place of worship, the Grand Mosque has room for 1,200 people and attracts a particularly large number of believers. Although virtually none of the mosques in the UAE are accessible to non-Muslims, this magnificent building is an exception. The Sheikh Mohammed Centre for Cultural Understanding, an organization founded in 1999 and dedicated to the promotion of Muslim culture, offers **guided tours** of the Grand Mosque on Sundays, Tuesdays and Thursdays. Visitors not only gain insight into the hand-crafted details of the interior design, but are also given an introduction to the basics of Islamic practices (for bookings see p.30).

◀ Guided tours

Diving Village

Diving Village and Heritage Village opened as part of the Dubai Shopping Festival in 1997. A **museum village** with small palm-leaf houses in old Arabian style was built in Shindagha on the creek's estuary; an aquarium provides a glimpse of the underwater world of the Arabian Gulf. At Diving Village, visitors can experience a 19th-century fishing and pearl-diving village and receive entertaining information on the flora and fauna of the Arabian Gulf. The ancient dhows, some of which are still being built today, are a reminder of Dubai's centuries-old seafaring tradition (open: see Heritage Village).

★★ **Heritage Village**

It is just a quick walk from Diving Village to Heritage Village (Al-Tourath). In this recreated traditional souk, **arts and crafts** are exhibited and offered for sale, while potters and weavers can be watched at work. The small stands of the village market sell almond and date sweets, served with tea from small handleless cups.

Dubai Plan

Arabian Gulf

0,5 mi
©Baedeker

AYAL NASIR

Bohri Mosque
Naif Fort
Police St.
Post Office

AL-SABKHA

Al-Ghabiba Roundabout
Shindagha Tunnel
Heritage Village
Market
AL-DAGHAYA
Deira Gold Souk
Bazaar
Al-Ahmadiya School
AL-SHINDAGHA
Sheikh Saeed House
Bait Public Library
Al-Wakeel
Bus Station
Deira Old Souk
Bus Station
Post Office

Al-Khaleej

Al-Abra Corniche
Nhor Street
Al-Shindagha Rd

AL- RAS

BASTAKIYA

Market
AL-GHABIBA
Abre Docks
Dubai Old Souk
Grand Mosque
Ben Yas Rd.
Al-Bin-Abi Talib Rd.
Al-Fahidi Roundabout

Port Rashid

Textil Souk
AL-RIFAA
Al-Ghabiba Road
Al-Khaleej Road
Al-Fahidi St.
Al-Fahidi Fort
Dubai Museum
AL-MUSALLA
BUR DUBAI
Al-Fahidi Roundabout
Post Office
AL-HAMRIYA

Falcon Roundabout
Al-Rifaa St.
Al-Nahda St.

Al-Rola Street
Al-Saidiya Roundabout
Khalid Bin-Al-Waleed Road

AL-BALOOSH

ZARIBAT DOIE

Mina Road

Al-Mankhool Road

TAWI AS SAIGH

MANKHOOL

Al-Adid Road

Musalla Al-Eid

Mina Road

Ruler's Beach House
Diyafah Roundabout
Jumeirah Beach Rd.
Al-Wasl Road
Ad Diyafah Rd.
Al-Satwa Roundabout
AL-KIFAF
Al-Mankhool Road
Al-Adid Road
AL JAFLA HOUSING
Al-Qataiyat Road
Trade Center Road

① ② ③
Jumeirah Mosque
AL-HUDEIBA
Post Office

World Trade Centre

Where to stay
① Burj al-Arab
② Royal Mirage
③ Ritz-Carlton
④ Sands
⑤ Riviera
⑥ Royalton Plaza

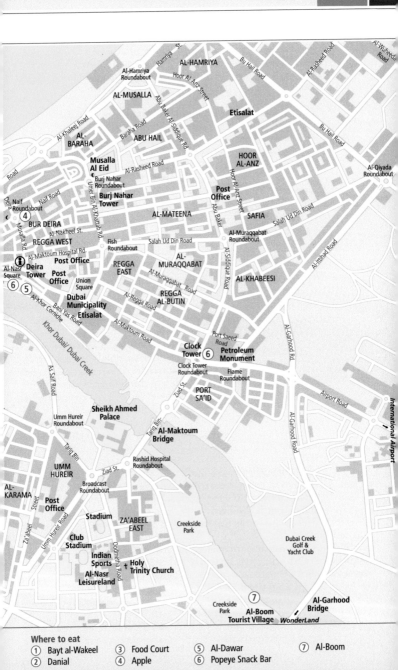

AL-HAMRIYA
Hamriya St.
Al-Hamriya
Roundabout
Hoor Al-Anz Street
Bu Hail Road
Al-Rasheed Road
Al-Wuheeda Road

AL-MUSALLA

Abu Baker Al-Siddique Rd.
Baraha Road
Al-Khaleej Road
Etisalat
Bu Hail Road

AL-
BARAHA
ABU HAIL
HOOR
AL-ANZ
Al-Qiyada
Roundabout

Road
Musalla
Al Eid
Al-Rasheed Road
Burj Nahar
Roundabout
Burj Nahar
Tower
Umm Bin Al-Khattab Rd.
Naif Road
Naif
Roundabout
Post
Office
Abu Baker
Hoor Al-Anz Street

(4)
BUR DEIRA
AL-MATEENA
SAFIA
Salah Ud Din Road
Al-Ittihad Road

Al-Nakheel St.
REGGA WEST
Fish
Roundabout
Al-Muraqqabat
Roundabout
Al-Maktoum Hospital Rd.
Salah Ud Din Road

Deira Rd.
Musalla Rd.
(i)
Al-Nasr
Square
Deira
Tower
Post Office
Post
Office
Union
Square
REGGA
EAST
AL-
MURAQQABAT
Al-Muraqqabat Road
AL-KHABEESI
Al-Siddique Road

(6)(5)
Al-Khor Corniche
Bani Yas Road
Dubai
Municipality
Etisalat
REGGA
AL-BUTIN
Al-Regga Road
Al-Maktoum Road

Khor Dubai/Dubai Creek
As Saif Road
Port Saeed
Road
Al-Garhood Rd.
Clock
Tower (6)
Petroleum
Monument
Clock Tower
Roundabout
Flame
Roundabout
Airport Road
International Airport

Sheikh Ahmed
Palace
Umm Hureir
Roundabout
Ziad St.
Tariq Bin
PORT
SA'ID
Al-Maktoum
Bridge
Al-Garhood Road

Tariq Bin
UMM
HUREIR
Ziad St.
Rashid Hospital
Roundabout

AL-
KARAMA
Za'abeel Street
Umm Hureir Road
Post
Office
Broadcast
Roundabout
Stadium
ZA'ABEEL
EAST
Oodmeina Road
Creekside
Park

Club
Stadium
Indian
Sports
Al-Nasr
Leisureland
Holy
Trinity Church
Dubai Creek
Golf &
Yacht Club

Creekside
Park
(7)
Al-Boom
Tourist Village
WonderLand
Al-Garhood
Bridge

Where to eat
① Bayt al-Wakeel
② Danial
③ Food Court
④ Apple
⑤ Al-Dawar
⑥ Popeye Snack Bar
⑦ Al-Boom

⊕ During the winter months there are regular theme events, for example folk dance performances or a re-enactment of a Bedouin wedding (opening hours of the Diving Village and Heritage Village: Oct to April daily 4.30pm–10.30pm, May–Sept daily 5.30pm–10.30pm, admission free).

✳
Sheikh Saeed House

The residence of **Sheikh Saeed al-Maktoum**, ruler of Dubai from 1912 until 1958 and grandfather of the current emir, was erected in 1896 in traditional Islamic style and completely restored a number of years ago. It is situated on the Shindagha spit, the northern side of the creek estuary. The wind towers of the building, the elaborate carving works, the balconies and inner courtyards leave an impression of the splendour in which houses were decorated even before the oil boom.

Sheik Saeed's House in Shindagha

Many of the approximately 40 rooms present various **exhibitions** and collections, including a collection of coins from the United Arab Emirates, the oldest dating back to the end of the 18th century, and 19th century stamps of the »Trucial States« (▶ History p.47). The **Al-Maktoum wing** exhibits some particularly interesting historical black-and-white photographs of the ruling family and personalities of the emirates dating back to the first third of the 20th century, as well as rare photographs depicting life in Dubai between 1948 and 1953. The oldest shots show the Fahidi fort, which was built to guard Dubai, and the Al-Ahmadiya School, the emirate's first school.

The **Marine Wing** is dedicated to the Arabian Gulf and exhibits photographs of pearl divers and ancient dhows, true-to-scale replicas of abras, fishing boats and dhows, and old tools for pearl diving. Another room is dedicated to the social, cultural and religious life in ⊕ 1950s Dubai (open: Sat–Thu 8.30am–9pm, Fri 3pm–10pm).

✶ ✶
Shindagha Cultural and Heritage Project

In the palace surroundings, the Shindagha Cultural and Heritage Project is currently underway: **32 traditional houses** – including the Sheikh Saeed Majlis, the emir's former office, the Sheikh Juma Bin-Majid House and the Obaid Bin-Thani House – are to be reconstructed to revive the past splendour of the district. Many of the historical **wind towers** will also be rebuilt.

A promenade is also being built on the banks of the creek, where several traditional cafés will offer Arabic specialities and water pipes.

Have a dip at the WonderLand family theme park.

This park, completed in 1995, is one of the favourite projects being carried out by Dubai's ruling Maktoum family in their effort to turn the emirate into a green oasis. The new design of the western side of the creek cost approximately 100 million AED. On more than 2km/1.2mi of land between the Al-Maktoum Bridge in the north and the Al-Garhoud Bridge in the south, planners from all over the world have created an attractive centre for leisure and **relaxation**. An amphitheatre with a capacity for 1,200 spectators hosts regular theatre plays and concerts. Creekside Park also has a **children's museum**, with a focus on natural history and science, promoting interactive learning experiences.

★
Creekside Park

On 18ha/45ac of land at the southern end of Creekside Park, this **leisure and amusement park** offers a »Main Street«, a »Theme Park« and »Splashland«, a water park with gigantic slides, wave riding and surfing. Special attractions are the water tornados and a water cinema, where films are projected onto a water surface. There are also numerous restaurants, snack stands, bars and live music. Prices for rides and shows vary and are paid for with vouchers from a voucher book (open: daily 10am–11pm, Wed women only, Thu families only).

★
WonderLand Family Fun Park

The **amusement park** situated next to WonderLand Family Fun Park was designed in traditional Arabic style and features replicas and exhibitions on Dubai culture. It also includes several restaurants. In the evening, creek boat trips are offered for about 100 AED (£13.50) (open: daily 9am–1am, admission free).

Al-Boom Tourist Village

The lobby – a dome of light and gold

The billowing sail the »Arabian Tow on its island

BURJ AL-ARAB – PURE LUXURY

The Burj al-Arab Hotel is a technological masterpiece and the latest symbol of modern-futuristic Dubai. The »Arabian Tower«, rising 321m/1,053ft into the air, is the most spectacular and, despite opening only recently in 2000, the most famous luxury hotel in the world.

It does not fall short on superlatives: »tallest hotel in the world«, »monument to luxury«, »Allah's earthly garden« – journalists from all corners of the world were stunned and amazed when they travelled to Dubai for the opening of the Burj al-Arab to write about the latest symbol of this rich and modern state.

The helicopter pad looks out from the »dhow sail«.

Its own island

Built on an artificial island 300m/ 328yd off Dubai's Jumeirah Beach, the Burj al-Arab rises up into the sky like the sail of an old Arabian dhow. The building is stabilized by 800 concrete pillars driven 40m/131ft deep into the ocean floor. It took more than 3,500 workers to complete the hotel in time for the national holiday on 2 December 1999.

According to the owners of the hotel, including the Emirates national airline – the majority of which belongs to the ruling Al-Maktoum family – the building costs of approximately **US$1 billion** are well invested; after all, the Burj al-Arab helps position Dubai as an exclusive city destination and also spreads the fame of the small emirate.

Dome of light and gold

No expense has been spared: the 180m/591ft atrium lobby is a dome of light and gold. Golden canopies extend from columns covered with 0.001mm of thin gold leaf; a water

fountain, omnipresent in the Emirate of Dubai, sends water jets 50m/164ft into the air.

£5,700 – not including breakfast

The suites have a minimum size of 170 sq m/203 sq yd and cost approximately £600 per night.

canopy bed, grandiosely decorated in gold and purple.

The **other rooms** also feature gold leaf decoration. A baroque mirror hangs from the ceiling over every double bed. The two levels of the suite are connected by a lift. The bathroom is decorated with mural paintings, and the mirrors can't steam up, due to a

Dubai's new trademark cost the little sheikhdom about GBP 1,015,000,000.

The bill for the two 780 sq m/933 sq yd royal suites **on the 25th floor** comes to approximately £5,700 per night – not including breakfast, though with a butler service.

A total of 1,200 employees look after 202 suites. On each floor, there is one room for the butler and one for a bodyguard.

Luxurious design

A private lift takes guests up to the world of superlatives, which caters to the tastes of the Arab customers used to luxury: the suites are equipped with state-of-the-art communications technology and a revolving four-poster

sophisticated cooling fan. The vase on the floor is illuminated from inside, and the video room is almost as big as a cinema.

Interior design

The interior design was just as important as the unmistakable exterior of the hotel – which ranks among the world's top city landmarks along with the Eiffel Tower in Paris or the Sydney Opera House.

»Once in a lifetime«

Chief designer Khuan Chew called the project a »once in a lifetime« assignment, and it took years of planning

Dinner in an aquarium: the underwater »Al-Mahara« restaurant

and preparatory work. Each room was built according to individually designed colour sketches.

Every room was assigned a **colour scheme** of five shades based on two

Exotic woods from Sumatra, blue granite from Brazil

main colours, to prevent an overload of colour with the chosen materials.

The rooms and suites were decorated by the interior designers of KCA International Designers, who used materials from more than three dozen countries.

Rare types of marble were bought from shut-down quarries, the exotic woods were imported from Sumatra and Java, and blue granite was acquired in Brazil for £878 per square metre.

Underwater dining

The underwater restaurant »Al-Mahara« is accessed via a lift which is shaped like a submarine. Dinner is served in a futuristic-looking dining room, reminiscent of the science fiction novels by Jules Verne.

Huge panes of bullet-proof glass reveal the underwater world of the Arabian Gulf. It is a stunning presentation of a marine paradise, with

specially designed coral gardens and tropical fish that are fed regularly by hotel staff.

Royal relaxation

The small Juna Lounge in the mezzanine creates an intimate atmosphere. Cigar fans will appreciate the first-rate selection.

The interior design of the gender-separated »Assawan Spa & Health Club« on the 18th floor is inspired by the Jordanian royal city of Petra. The rooms are designed in relaxing shades of blue, green and yellow; Moorish mosaics decorate the walls and pillars, and a simple beam ceiling creates a pleasantly unpretentious contrast to the luxury materials.

»Monument to luxury«

Even those not staying at the hotel can visit this luxury monument – for a fee of 200 AED (£27), which is then deducted from any purchase made at one of the hotel boutiques.

Occasionally, **members of the royal family** can be spotted driving up to the entrance of the Burj al-Arab. Sheikh Mohammed Bin-Rashid al-Maktoum, for instance, enjoys driving up in his yellow Ferrari, in the company of his Jordanian wife and surrounded by a dozen bodyguards, to have a strawberry milkshake at the bar.

The local **dhow yard** is situated in Jaddaf, 1km/0.6mi south of Al-Garhoud Bridge. Only in recent years has Dubai, the most modern of the emirates, decided to revive traditional trades, and few local shipbuilders still master the art of building the large Arabic trading ships without the use of construction plans using old-established methods. The boats, with a displacement of up to 250 tons, are built in between huge piles of teak wood imported from India (open: Sat–Thu 9am–12pm and 4pm–7pm). ⏱

Dhow building yard

The Al-Wafi Shopping Mall is situated a few side streets west of Creekside Park, in Umm Hureir. Modelled on American malls, this architecturally complex building houses dozens of boutiques. The shops beneath the glass roof – always perfectly clean – of the huge **pyramid** sell designer fashion from the US and Europe, French clothing for children and shoes from Italy and Great Britain. A stroll through the mall numbers among the most popular leisure activities for wealthy locals, while the hall with high-tech games on the third floor is mainly frequented by young people.

Al-Wafi Shopping Mall

The Karama Shopping Area, situated right in the middle of the residential area Al-Karama, is particularly popular among foreign visitors and guest workers. The small shops sell textiles, sporting goods, bags and shoes – although the majority of the goods on offer are replicas of famous brands and counterfeit designer goods. Prices are low, but please note that importing designer knockoffs into the EU is prohibited.

Karama Shopping Area

To this day, dhows are built by hand without construction plans.

Dubai World Trade Centre

Opened in 1979 in the presence of Queen Elizabeth II, the trade centre consolidated the emirate's reputation as a significant Arabian economic power. It is still one of the most prestigious business addresses in all of Dubai. Around 200 companies reside in the Dubai World Trade Centre; its tower is one of the city's **landmarks** and was its highest building before the completion of the luxurious Burj al-Arab (▶ Baedeker Special p.190). The 39 floors still tower over the Bur Dubai district, while the panoramic view from the observation platform on the 30th floor is absolutely spectacular (Trade Centre Road, on the corner of 2nd Zabeel Road; »Top of the Tower« tours: Sat–Thu 9.30am and 4.30pm).

★ Jumeirah Mosque

Visitors cannot possibly miss Dubai's most impressive mosque on Jumeirah Beach Road. Based on the medieval **Fatimid style** of the Egyptian caliphs, it is an outstanding example of modern Islamic architecture: two minarets tower over a majestic dome; high archways accentuate the main entrance, above which hang three heavy iron chandeliers. European stonemasons were hired for the filigree designs on the sandstone surfaces. The numerous diamond-patterned stone window grilles have an impressive effect. The ivory-coloured place of worship, where even members of the ruling family gather for Friday prayer, is encircled by spacious lawns.

Non-Muslims can access the mosque as part of a **guided tour** organized by the Sheikh Mohammed Centre for Cultural Understanding (for bookings see p.30; every Thu 10am).

Jumeirah Mosque – Dubai's most beautiful place of worship

The largest **water theme park** in the Middle East is situated directly next to the Jumeirah Beach Hotel and looks out on the spectacular Burj al-Arab luxury hotel. The park, which is designed like an oasis, provides a wide range of attractions: its water slide, »Jumeirah Sceirah«, is considered the largest and fastest in the world; figures from Arabian legends and fairy tales, such as Sinbad or Scheherazade create an atmosphere of excitement and fun. The various rides, shops and cafés at the **Wild Wadi** park provide all-day entertainment (open: daily 11am–7pm, reduced admission from 4pm).

Fun on the slide at »Wild Wadi«

Dubai Zoo on Jumeirah Beach Road is the oldest zoo in the United Arab Emirates. An Austrian engineer working in Dubai started building the private zoo in 1962: he leased land to keep smaller Gulf animal species in cages and enclosures. Today, more than 1,400 animals – mainly from the Arabian Peninsula – live in this far too small area, which is also why a new zoo, intended to comply with international standards, is being built next to Mushrif Park (open: daily except Tue 10am–6.30pm).

Also known as Majlis Al-Ghoraifa or Umm Al-Sheif Majlis, the former summer residence of **Sheikh Rashid Bin-Saeed al-Maktoum** was built in 1954 in the coastal town of Umm Suqeim in a traditional style using coral stone and plaster. It was made accessible to the public after its restoration. On the ground floor is a large, open veranda and a storage room beneath the stairs. The upper floor consists of a room decorated with rugs, lamps, floor cushions, guns and Arabic coffee pots. The summer palace also includes a garden with a replica of an old irrigation system (Jumeirah Beach Road, south of Jumeirah Beach Park, by the »No. 1 Supermarket«; open: Sat–Thu 9am–1pm, 3pm–8pm, Fri 2pm–8pm, free admission).

Jumeirah Archaeological Site

This archaeological site located on Jumeirah Beach Road between the Hilton Beach Club and the Dubai Art Centre can only be visited with a special permit. The area of over 20ha/49ac houses remains of a civilization that settled here in the 5th century. A building complex, magnificently decorated with stucco work and mosaics, is believed to have been a Governor's residence. Another 20-room building is thought to have been a caravanserai. Remains of a souk and several residential homes were also found.

About 20km/12.4mi south of the city centre the **Emirates Golf Club**, with an 18-hole course, even hosts international championships. The clubhouse, built and arranged like a group of Bedouin tents, is world famous. One of these concrete tents is owned by the ruler of Dubai.

? DID YOU KNOW ...?

■ that each of Dubai's four golf courses needs between 4.5 million and 7.5 million litres (1.19–1.98 US gal) of water every day? Therefore, an 18-hole golf course uses a minimum of 335 × 4.5 million litres per year, as there are hardly any overcast or rainy days when irrigation isn't necessary.

Water taxis are constantly underway on the creek.

Abra Docks   The landing stage for **water taxis** is located on the Al-Khor Corniche, the creek promenade. Abras, flat, wooden, diesel-powered boats with two rows of seats, come and go, transporting guests across the creek. The abras are a cheap and therefore an indispensable means of transportation for many Asian and Arab guest workers. For tourists, these wooden boats are an inexpensive and idyllic way to get to know Dubai from the water. Abras are operated from sunrise to midnight and leave as soon as there are enough passengers.

! *Baedeker* TIP

Abra tour

Those who are not so keen on an overcrowded abra and are more interested in a longer, individually planned tour across the creek can arrange an abra tour with the captain. The fee must be negotiated beforehand – approx. 100 AED (£13.50) per hour.

Directly adjacent to the Abra Docks, **three covered souks** provide plenty of shopping opportunities: the Al-Dhalam Souk selling household goods, the oldest souk on the Deira side offering foods, and the Spice Souk. The narrow alleys are crowded with sacks and pots containing exotic herbs and spices from the Middle East and Asia. The smells are truly beguiling, and there are plenty of promising opportunities for photographers. The handmade ceramic incense jars are a good buy: each one is different and unique.

Dubai Municipality   The postmodern **city hall** is located on the side of the creek, east of the Deira Souk. The construction consists of an open, square structure, covered with light marble, which again surrounds another round, red granite building. A tall, globe-shaped fountain complements this eye-catching ensemble. A monument, very much in the style of the United Arab Emirates, stands in front of the building: a dromedary balancing a chess board on its back – a reminder of the chess world championships held in Dubai in 1986.

A short walk away is the Gold Souk, one of Dubai's most prominent sights. 300 tons of gold are imported into the UAE each year, about 10–15% of the world production, with most of it ending up at the Gold Souk in Dubai or at the New Gold Building. Around 200 shops line both sides of the covered street. As soon as the sun sets, limousines with tinted windows stop at both ends of the pedestrian zone, and Arab women from neighbouring states and emirates, dressed in black, climb out and disappear immediately into the glittering jewellery shops.

✶ ✶
Gold Souk

The nearby New Gold Building houses the offices of the gold wholesalers. At the **Gold Centre** the continuous flow of the shining metal

◄ New Gold Building

Dazzling Dubai: one of around 200 shops at the Gold Souk

is distributed out to the emirates. At Dubai's Gold Souk, gold is sold according to weight – except for very light pieces of jewellery. One gram of 22-carat gold costs around 10 dollars, duty-free. Bargaining is often possible, especially when intending to buy several pieces at once. With larger purchases, customers receive small gold gifts as complimentary give-aways.

Al-Ahmadiya School

The oldest school of the emirate is located on Al-Ahmadiya Street in the Al-Ras district, not far from Deira Souk. The building, erected in 1912, was commissioned by the successful merchant **Sheikh Mohammed Bin-Ahmad Bin-Dalmouk**. Housed in a traditional clay building, the school consists of twelve classrooms surrounding an inner courtyard. Initially, only adult men were educated here; later, in 1926, boys were also accepted. The tall, cool former classrooms and the damaged Qur'an inscriptions decorating the walls have been restored (open: Sat–Thu 8am–7pm, Fri 3pm–7pm).

? **DID YOU KNOW …?**

■ Besides Jumeirah, there are two other archaeological sites in Dubai where excavation work and research is done, and which confirm that the region was not first colonized during the Islamization of the Arabian Peninsula, but already served as a trading hub centuries earlier. Tourists are currently not allowed to visit the sites individually; they can only be viewed as part of a tour booked through a travel agency, which obtains a permit from the museum in Dubai.

Not far from the Al-Ahmadiya School, a merchant's house built in 1890 has been elaborately restored and turned into a **Museum of Traditional Architecture** to show how 19th-century houses on the Arabian Gulf were decorated. The museum displays decoration techniques using plaster, wood, glass and sheet metal (open: Sat–Thu 8am–7pm, Fri 3pm–7pm).

Naif Fort

Sheikh Saeed was builder of the Naif Fort, a defensive fortification near the Naif Roundabout, which was meant to protect the Deira side from incursions. The building, which was built only in the 1930s, consists of an enormous tower overlooking the creek, and other long, expansive sections. After several decades, the police moved into the **Burj Naif**; today the ground floor houses a small police museum, documenting the history of the local police from the end of the 19th century until today.

Burj Nahar

One of the three watchtowers guarding the old district of Deira in the 19th century was reconstructed and surrounded by a small garden. The **watchtower** on Naif Road at the Burj Nahar Roundabout was erected in 1870. Originally built of clay and shell limestone, the round tower with a diameter of around 10m/33ft has two tiny windows at the top, surrounded by numerous narrow loopholes and bays. The roof of the tower is encircled by small battlements. It is a popular photo subject.

The **Dubai Creek Golf & Yacht Club** is situated on the eastern shore of Dubai Creek. The 18-hole golf course stretches over 80 hectares and has quickly evolved into a venue for highly remunerated championships. Only constant underground irrigation and the care of hundreds of foreign workers allow the course to retain the lush green grass on the dry desert ground. Even for non-golfers, a visit to this immaculately maintained facility is worthwhile. The clubhouse boasts an extraordinary architectural design: its 45m/49.3yd roof construction is shaped like the sails of a traditional dhow. The chrome and glass building houses swimming pools, fitness rooms and a café/restaurant. The no less spectacular clubhouse of the marina, which is designed like the upper deck of a luxury liner, is a quick walk away from the golf clubhouse.

Dubai Creek Golf & Yacht Club

Around Dubai

The camel racetrack in Nad Al-Shiba is just a few miles outside Dubai on Nad Al-Shiba Road, on the way to Al Ain and the Emirates Golf Club. Between October and March, camel races take place every weekend – i.e. Thursday afternoons and Friday mornings. Thousands of primarily male spectators from the Arabian Peninsula, but also an increasing number of Asian guest workers, come here especially for the races, blocking all major access roads. It is advisable to avoid these roads during race times.

Nad Al-Shiba

The excavations of **Al-Qusais**, an extensive ancient burial site, is located approximately 13km/8mi north-east of Dubai. The graves date back to around 2000–500 BC. Burial objects include spearheads and axes made of bronze for men, and make-up utensils for women.

Baedeker TIP

»Around Dubai in ten minutes«

An extraordinary way to view the sights of Dubai is to fly over the city in a helicopter. The name of the sightseeing flight says it all: »Around Dubai in just ten minutes«. The usual starting point is Creekside Park (reservations: Desert Air Tours, Dubai Airport, Terminal 2, tel. 2 29 44 41; Aerogulf Services, tel. 2 82 31 57; approx. 800 AED (£108) for up to four passengers).

Al-Sufouh district The Al-Sufouh district is situated between Sheikh Zayed Road and Al-Sufouh Road, which becomes Jumeirah Beach Road south of the Burj al-Arab luxury hotel. Archaeologists estimate the burial sites to be many thousands of years old, dating back to the Umm al-Nar Period (around 2700–2000 BC ► History p.43). The discovery of the site was quite sensational, as the round and above-ground communal grave with a diameter of over 8m/26ft is one of the largest of its kind. The grave finds, exhibited in the museum of Dubai, include finely wrought jewellery and ceramic vessels as well as bronze spearheads.

> **! Baedeker TIP**
>
> **Dubai winter sports**
>
> While even morning temperatures climb over 35°C/95°F, the shopping complex of the Hyatt Hotel on Corniche Road always stays pleasantly cool. Children, teenagers and adults meet here to ice-skate at the Galleria Ice Rink. Visitors to the new indoor ski resort Ski Dubai can glide downhill on one of five pistes (Mall of the Emirates, Sheikh Zayed Road, exit 39, www.skidxb.com).

✳ Khor Dubai Wildlife Sanctuary The Emirate of Dubai is a breeding and over-wintering region for hundreds of bird species. The southern end of Dubai Creek in particular has become a preferred **habitat for migrating birds**, as the shallows on the shores offer plenty of food. Between February and April, and again between September and November, the Khor Dubai Wildlife Sanctuary south of the city, near the end of the creek, is considered particularly well suited for bird watching.

Here the estuary widens to a shallow lake with several small islands, making it a paradise for waders. So far, 400 different bird species have been identified.

The most striking birds are the pink flamingos; Sheikh Mohammed bin Rashid Al Maktoum, ruler of Dubai, provides them with carotene-rich feed to keep their feathers nice and bright.

Mushrif Park Situated just under 10km/6mi beyond the airport, the **recreational park** is popular among locals and guest workers alike. Besides a restaurant, shady picnic areas and two swimming pools – one for women and one for men – there is also a funfair, an aviary, a deer park and facilities for pony and camel rides.

The »**World Village**« is known for its replicas of sights from around the globe. Miniature trains take visitors to all the attractions (open: daily 8am–11pm).

Al-Mamzar Beach Park The calm water at this **private beach club** north of Dubai, on the border with Sharjah, is ideal for families with small children. Changing rooms, showers, a large swimming pool and an open-air restaurant make for a relaxing day at the beach.

Wednesday to Saturday is reserved for women and children (Al-Mamzar Lagoon, Al-Khaleej Road, Hamriya; open: daily 8am to 10pm).

Al-Maha: an eco-resort in the middle of the desert

AL-MAHA DESERT RESORT

A unique combination of luxury hotel and closeness to nature: each air-conditioned suite, designed as a mixture between a bungalow and a Bedouin tent, is covered by a sun-shielding tent roof. Situated in the middle of the desert close to the village of Margam 50km/31 miles south-east of Dubai, the hotel is surrounded by sand for as far as the eye can see.

A refreshing swimming pool is set into the wooden sun deck of the suite, from which guests can observe antelopes, gazelles and zebras drinking from the artificial waterholes. The other side of the bungalows look out onto a blue lake surrounded by palm trees. The two salons of the main building, the majlis, are decorated with precious rugs and Arabic antiques.

High-class ecotourism

Staying in a luxury tent

The suite itself leaves nothing to be desired. Jewellery can be stored in a room safe, large sliding doors create a sense of space. The interior decor, using Arabic accessories, is simply overwhelming: heavy cushions with ornate pillowcases; doors and chests made of exquisite, elaborately studded wood. Antique rifles, saddles, bags and textiles decorate the walls.

Desert adventure

The Al-Maha Desert Resort cost over £10 million to build. Owned by Sheikh Ahmed Bin-Saeed al-Maktoum, also head of Emirates Airlines, the 25 sq km/9.7 sq mi area of fenced-in desert land accommodates plants and animals, including the rare Oryx antelope (Arabic: al-maha). A natural water reservoir provides the water for the animals' waterholes and the 30 pools for the hotel guests. Waste water is cleaned and reused for irrigating the soil.

No place in the Emirates is closer to the desert than this hotel. When the sun sets behind the Hajar Mountains, and the heat of the day quickly turns into a cool breeze, the desert reveals all of its beauty in shades of violet and pink.

Hatta

G 4

Population: 10,000

Hatta oasis and its extensive palm groves is surrounded by sand dunes and the Hajar Mountains. Tourists are attracted by the restored fort and the crystal clear water of the Hatta Rock Pools, situated in a wadi 17km/10.6mi south of Hatta.

Charming Dubai exclave Approximately 100km/61mi south-east of Dubai, the exclave of Hatta was once an important trading hub on the route between Oman in the north and the Arabian Gulf. For decades, Hatta has been a popular **weekend destination** among Dubai locals thanks to its moderate climate and particularly charming landscape.

The well-made road from Dubai leads to Hatta Road, past neat residential areas, mosques and small cubic houses – state-built accommodation for Bedouin families – as well as ever more impressive sand dunes reaching heights of 170m/558ft. At sunrise and sunset they almost glow bright red. Travel companies organize regular trips into the desert which meet all the expectations westerners have of the endless sea of sand. The area between Dubai and Hatta is also ideal for **sandskiing** and **sandboarding**. In the early afternoon, four-by-fours can be observed driving up the dunes.

The oasis village from the 16th century was restored true to the original; construction materials were produced according to traditional techniques: a mixture of sun-dried mud and straw. Missing doors and windows were brought in from the other emirates and Arabian countries, and thus the old fort, the historic mosque, two watchtowers and two dozen residential houses could be re-constructed. A stroll among the old houses leads to the **falaj channels** (▶Baedeker Special p.214) which irrigate the gardens.

 ▶ HATTA

WHERE TO EAT

▶ **Moderate**

Jeema
Hatta Fort Hotel
Tel. 8 52 32 11
The restaurant mainly serves Arabic cuisine. Those who find the temperatures a little cool here should go to the Gazebo Coffeeshop by the pool.

WHERE TO STAY

▶ **Mid-range**

Hatta Fort Hotel
P.O. Box 9277
Tel. 04 / 8 52 32 11, fax 8 52 35 61
www.hattaforthotel.com
50 chalets
The comfortable chalets are situated in a garden which features rich bird life. Includes a 9-hole golf course, pool, a tennis court and a facility for archery and clay pigeon shooting.

The fact that Hatta is a popular destination for weekend getaways means the settlement is increasing in size. The newly built houses feature traditional architectural details such as simple façades and small windows to keep out the heat. Colourful iron entry gates are decorated with traditional Arabic symbols – coffee pots, date trees, dromedaries – displaying the inhabitants connection with their past. To add to Hatta's development as a tourist town, a souk by the town entrance is currently in planning, offering handicrafts and souvenirs; also planned is a zoo, a recreational park, a chair lift into the mountains and a tourist information office.

Popular weekend getaway

What to See in and around Hatta

The **open-air museum** is a replica of a typical oasis mountain village: narrow alleys criss-cross a town of mud houses and barasti huts made of palm leaves. There is a small fort in the town centre, and a playground that was created next to the falaj water channels.
Another part of the museum is an exhibition of traditional ceramic works and weaving techniques, as well as Bedouin garments and camel equipment (open: Sat–Thu 8am–8pm, Fri 3pm–9pm).

Hatta Heritage Village

The Hatta Oasis has become a popular weekend destination.

The rulers of the Emirates with British governmental officials (circa 1960 in Dubai)

EMIR, SULTAN UND CALIPH

What's the difference between an Emir and a Sultan? What was a Caliph? Who is allowed to call himself a Sheik? Although these titles come up very frequently while reading on Arabia, their actual meaning is hardly ever explained.

Emir

At the beginning of the Islamic crusades in the 7th century, an emir was a military leader who often became a region's governor once it was captured. Later it became the official title for a regional governor or ruler of a province and had extensive administrative and financial power. In religious and judicial matters, however, he was subordinate to the caliph, the highest authority in Islam. The title emirate, the political territory of an emir, goes back to the Arabic word »amara« (= to order). Today, besides the seven emirates of the UAE, there are also the Emirates of Kuwait, Bahrain and Qatar.

Sultan

The word sultan« is Aramaic (»shultana«), meaning power or rulership. From early on, the caliphs were called sultans by the Abbasid caliphs who gradually transformed their religious power to absolute secular power. Eventually the rank of sultan was used everywhere in the Islamic world. Besides Sultan Qaboos of Oman and Sultan Hassanal Bolkiah of Brunei, there are only a few local sultans in Saudi Arabia.

Caliph

At the start of Islamization, the caliph was the highest leader. As a successor of the Prophet he had both secular and religious power. He was elected by an Islamic community, first from the direct descendants of Muhammad in Medina, later also from religious leaders not related to the prophet. When several Arabic dynasties titled themselves caliphate, it led to disputes until the title lost its significance; today it is no longer in use.

Sheikh

A sheikh, a »man of old age«, was originally an elected Bedouin tribal leader who also held the office of Chief Justice. Increasingly, sons of deceased sheikhs entered elections to become the successors of their fathers, and this led to sheikh becoming a hereditary title. Today not only the seven rulers of the UAE carry it, but also their many sons and grandsons.

17km/10.6mi south of Hatta lies one of the most impressive landscapes in the Emirate of Dubai: the Hatta Rock Pools are a group of
ravines carrying water all year round. Several travel companies as
well as the Hatta Fort Hotel organize half and full-day tours here.
However, with a four-by-four and decent maps, tourists can also visit
Hatta Pools by themselves.

✱✱
Hatta Rock Pools

From the roundabout on the street
from Dubai to Hatta, near the Hatta Fort Hotel, turn right and follow
the street south-east. At the local
police station about 3km/1.9mi
further on there is another small
roundabout. Turn south here and
pass the school with the colourful
mural paintings. The street first
leads to the small oasis villages of
Jeema, known for its mineral
water, and Al-Fay; continue then
along a dirt road, reaching Hatta
Pools after nearly 15km/9.3mi.

Along the road, several shady palm
trees make for an idyllic spot for a
picnic (which the Hatta Fort Hotel
is happy to put together). At Hatta
Pools, however, natural shade will
be sought in vain.

Around Hatta Pools, numerous
well-kept and restored falaj channels (► Baedeker Special p.214)
carry water along the sides of the
wadi into the groves and gardens
of the surrounding villages.

A refreshing swim in a canyon pool

FUJAIRAH

Area: 1,175 sq km/453.7 sq mi   **Population:** 130,000
Emir: Sheikh Hamad Bin-Mohammed
al-Sharqi (since 1974)

Fans of underwater sports appreciate the outstanding diving and snorkelling facilities off the coast of the Emirate of Fujairah. Although the emirate is still new to tourism, efforts have recently been made to extend the tourist infrastructure.

The Eastern part of the United Arab Emirates is marked by the impressive panorama of the rugged **Hajar Mountains**. This mountain range, running south from the northern Musandam Peninsula, has in the territory of the UAE a length of about 80km/49.7mi and a width up to 30km/18.6mi, and functions as a natural barrier between the east and the west coast. In the UAE, the highest elevations of the Hajar Mountains are 1,000m/3,281ft (3,000m/9,843ft in Oman), separated by deep, sometimes fertile valleys. Fujairah, the emirate situated on the **Gulf of Oman**, is different from the other sheikhdoms for various reasons. The emirate's territory includes three Sharjah exclaves. Nature lovers will appreciate the magnificent tours through the spectacular scenery of Fujairah's Hajar Mountains.

Emirate with impressive landscapes

For many years, there was hardly any contact between the inhabitants from the east coast and the people from the rest of the country. Only since 1976 have Dubai and Fujairah been connected by a paved road. With the extension of the international airport, which up until now was mainly used for importing and exporting goods, Fujairah is now competing with the other emirates for the favour of foreign tourists.

In Fujairah, neither oil nor gas has yet been discovered; Fujairah's expenditure is ensured only by generous donations from Abu Dhabi. Besides fishing, steady income is provided by the poultry and cattle farms, where the majority of the male population works. Fujairah's deepwater port, built in 1981, is the second largest in the UAE.

Economy

← *The Coffeepot Roundabout and the Mosque characterize the centre of the capital of this small emirate on the east coast.*

History

AD 632	Battle of Dibba
16th century	Portuguese build forts.
1903	Emirates declare independence.
1925	The British bombard Fujairah.
1971	Fujairah becomes part of the UAE.

First settlement
Finds from an early settlement on the east coast, including ceramic shards and jewellery – date back to the beginning of the Common Era. However, little is known about the early inhabitants of this region.

Battle of Dibba ▶
In 632, during the process of **Islamization**, Saudi Arabian Muslims defeated the inhabitants of the east coast in a battle near Dibba, in what is now the UAE; a burial site near Badiyah is proof of this event.

Coveted by foreign powers ▶
The Emirate of Fujairah was long coveted by foreign powers. Because the coast offered many protected harbours and also lay at an intersection of centuries-old seafaring routes, the inhabitants feared invasions from foreign sailors. For protection, they built watchtowers at the harbours of Dibba, Khor Fakkan and Fujairah. In the 16th century, members of the **Sharqiyin** tribe living in Fujairah resisted sev-

The mighty fort at Fujairah was built in 1670.

eral attacks by the Portuguese; nevertheless, the harbours were taken and the watchtowers were extended and turned into Portuguese forts. The Dutch took an interest in the east coast in the 17th and 18th centuries, the British in the 19th century. By the end of the 19th century, **Sheikh Abdullah Bin-Mohammed al-Sharqi** succeeded in uniting the continuously feuding tribal families in the common struggle for independence.

Fujairah, which was part of Sharjah, declared its independence in 1903, and the locals' resistance against British occupation increased. The conflict culminated in the bombardment of the city of Fujairah on 20 April 1925, during which almost the entire fort was destroyed. It wasn't until 1952 that the British finally recognized Fujairah as the seventh »Trucial State« (►History p.47).

◄ Independence

Fujairah

G 3

Population: 65,000

Wide streets traverse the city of Fujairah in which only a few buildings are more than 50 years old. Distances in the city are small, which makes walking far more practical than taking a car. The mosque in the centre of town may only be entered by Muslims.

The old town to the north of the mosque is little more than a few original houses and several ruins. The slightly elevated restored fort next to the palm gardens is also part of the historic town. In the past, it was the majestic date trees which added to the reputation and the modest wealth of the city. Today's status symbol is the Fujairah Hilton hotel, located directly at the beach.

A fort and palm gardens

► VISITING FUJAIRAH

INFORMATION
Fujairah Tourism Bureau
P.O. Box 829
Trade Centre
9th floor
Fujairah
Tel. 09 / 2 23 14 36
Fax 23 10 06

WHERE TO EAT
► Expensive
Sailor's
Hilton Hotel

Tel. 222 24 11
Overlooking the Indian Ocean, this restaurant primarily serves fish specialities.

► Moderate
① *Royal Cafeteria*
Corniche Road South
Tel. 222 66 88
Simple café and restaurant at the beach serving Arabic specialities. A view of the shipping traffic heading for the Strait of Hormuz.

▶ **Inexpensive**
Pizza Inn
Fujairah Trade Centre
Hamad Bin-Abdullah Road
Tel. 2 22 25 57
This pizzeria offers a wide range of pizza and tasty pasta dishes. Opens at 10am.

WHERE TO STAY
▶ **Luxury**
② *Hilton*
Beach Road
P.O. Box 231
Tel. 2 22 24 11
Fax 2 22 65 41
92 rooms
Very pleasant waterfront hotel, north of the Old Fishing Harbour near the coffee pot roundabout, with swimming pool, fitness centre and water skiing facilities.

① *Al-Diar Siji*
Al-Sharqi Road
P.O. Box 11 99
Tel. 2 23 20 00

Fax 2 23 21 11
Email: sijihotl@
emirates.net.ae
90 rooms
Central location by the Trade Centre. Includes health centre, pool, sauna, tennis court, beach club, cinema and a bowling alley as well as several restaurants and discos.

Baedeker-recommendation

▶ **Budget**
③ *Fujairah Beach Motel*
Port Road
P.O. Box 283
Tel. 2 22 81 11
Fax 2 22 80 54
Email: FBM@emirates.net.ae
100 rooms
Seaside location south of the harbour, or the northern edge of town. Includes a po restaurant, entertainment programme, di co and nightclub.

What to See in Fujairah

Old settlement
The old town is a historic mud house settlement situated north-west of Al-Nakheel Road, 2km/1.2mi from the city centre. In the 1980s, the houses, which were entirely washed away by the rain, consisted only of a few foundation walls in whose shadow goats fed on newspaper. In recent years, an effort has been made to reconstruct the historic town and restore the few remaining houses.

Fujairah Museum
Today, the former Emir's residence on the northern edge of the old settlement houses the Fujairah Museum. The massive fortification, built in 1670, still intentionally shows the signs of the city's bombardment in 1925. The multi-storey building consists of three main sections, a huge round tower and several large halls. Besides excavation finds from **Bithnah** and **Badiyah** – mainly ceramics and jewellery – there is also an ethnographic section displaying household goods, farming tools, traditional garments and guns (open: daily 8am–6pm).

Fujairah Plan

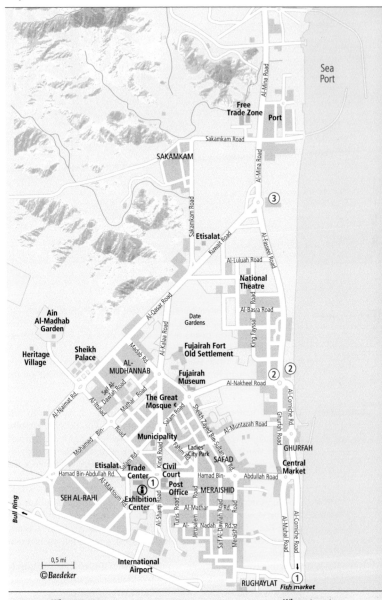

Sea Port

Free Trade Zone

Port

Al-Mina Road

Sakamkam Road

SAKAMKAM

Sakamkam Road

③

Etisalat

Al-Faseel Road

Kuwait Road

Al-Luluah Road

National Theatre

Al-Qasar Road

Al-Basra Road

Date Gardens

Ain Al-Madhab Garden

King Fayssal Road

Heritage Village

Sheikh Palace

Al-Kalaa Road

Modab Rd.

AL-MUDHANNAB

Fujairah Fort Old Settlement

Fujairah Museum

② ②

Al-Nakheel Road

Al-Comiche Rd.

Sef Al-Dawlah Road

Al-Ittihad

Mathar Road

The Great Mosque

Salam Road

Sheikh Zayed Bin-Sultan

Ghurfah Road

Al-Njamat Rd.

Municipality

Kindi Road

Fahim Rd.

Ladies' City Park

Al-Muntazah Road

GHURFAH

Mohamed Bin-   Road

Etisalat

Trade Center

Civil Court

SAFAD

Central Market

Hamad Bin-Abdullah Rd.

Salam Rd.

Post Office

Hamad Bin-Abdullah Road

Bull Ring

①

Exhibition Center

SEH AL-RAHI

Al-Maktoum Rd.

Al-Sharqi Road

Tunis Road

MERAISHID

Al-Mathar

Al-Dawlah Rd.

Al-Minal Road

Al-Comiche Road

0,5 mi

©Baedeker

International Airport

Jerusalem Al- Nadah Rd.

Saif Al-Dawlah Rd.

Meraishid Road

RUGHAYLAT   Fish market

①

Where to stay
① Al-Diar Siji
② Hilton Hotel
③ Fujairah Beach Motel

Where to eat
① Royal Cafeteria

This type of bullfight is a completely bloodless spectacle.

Souks

The **fish market** is situated on Rughaylat Road, south of the city opposite the fishing harbour. The daily catch is sold in auctions every morning. Right next to the fish market, numerous vending stalls offer a wide range of fruit and vegetables.

Fujairah's **main souk** (Central Market) can be found in the city centre on Hamad Bin-Abdullah Road (near the roundabout on the corner of Ghurfah Road).

Date gardens

The entire eastern border of the city of Fujairah, approximately one third, is covered by expansive **date gardens**. The people here also run fruit and vegetable gardens; the produce is sold at the local markets and transported to the neighbouring emirates. The rich supply of water here makes plants which cannot even survive in any of the other emirates thrive, e.g. bananas and mangos.

★ ★
Bullring

On the western edge of the city, the round and dusty **bullfight arena** hosts between ten and fifteen »Arabian bullfights« every Friday afternoon. But unlike the Spanish corrida, with picadores and toreros, the animals in Fujairah don't fight against people, but against one another.

With this type of bullfight, which originated in the Omani Batinah Plain, two strong Brahmin bulls – traditionally imported from India, as they are highly resistant to heat and lack of water – are brought together by their owners, held on a rope attached to the horns and through a nose ring. On command, the men loosen the ropes to let the enormous animals charge towards one another. Panting loudly, the bulls push each other back and forth with their heads. If neither of the bulls capitulates, a referee decides which animal wins.

Usually this type of bullfight passes without bloodshed. Should the animals, however, threaten to hurt one another, they are separated immediately. There is no prize money; instead the winning bull's value increases – they usually cost between 3,000 and 30,000 AED (about £4,000) – and with it the owner's reputation.

In 1997 a Heritage Village, similar to the ones in Dubai and Abu Dhabi, was built on the northern edge of the city at the end of Al-Ittihad Road. Two cannons flank the entrance to this spacious area which covers approx. 6,000 sq m/7,176 sq yd.

Heritage Village

The **open-air museum** houses several exhibitions recreating the recent past of the emirate: collections of old household goods, ceramic vases and bowls, which part of the rural population still uses today for storing dates, olive oil or cheese. Fishermen's tools are kept in trditional »arish« huts made of palm leaves.

The village's location is particularly charming, directly adjacent to the lush, green **Ain Al-Madhab Garden** which is irrigated by a sulphurous mineral spring – a very popular spot for walks and picnics (open: Sun–Thu 8am–1pm and 4pm to 6pm, Fri 2pm–6pm). ☺

The limestone houses at Hatta Heritage Village have been authentically rebuilt.

The Persians brought falaj-building techniques to the Arabian Peninsula over 2,500 years ago.

A well preserved system can be found near Al A

CONCRETE RIVERS

Only a few of the old water channels in the Emirates still exist or have been restored. They are called falaj, Arabic for »to distribute«. They stretch along the edges of wadis and pass through palm groves and gardens.

The layout of the aflaj (plural of falaj) system is rather sophisticated, and the forks and distribution points can be changed by repositioning the stones to direct the flow to other channels, i.e. different gardens. This is also how bath houses and cattle troughs are supplied with water.

The channels have a width and height of up to 20–50cm/8in–1ft 8in, and are made of brick clay and stones fixed with concrete. The shapes can vary; some channels are carved into rock. Approximately 2,500 years ago, Persians introduced this technology to the region of what is now the UAE and Oman.

King Solomon's water

According to an old legend, it was the prophet and king Solomon who tried to relieve the misery of the people living in the water-poor regions, ordering his helpers to create a system of stone water channels. There are two classifications of ain-aflaj systems (ain = spring), using either the more common surface channels (ghail-falaj) or underground channels (qanat-falaj). If a spring is located at a higher elevation, a basin is constructed next to the spring. The water flows into the channel and descends for miles into the villages and nearby fields.

Qanat-falaj

The construction of an underground qanat-falaj is far more difficult. Up in the mountains, water is collected from a groundwater spring and carried through a tunnel built within the rock. The stream here must also have a low gradient – otherwise the tunnel would have to be bigger and be much harder to build – so the falaj often runs for miles through the mountain. The maintenance work on the falaj is done by a wakil, who accesses the falaj via specially constructed shafts.

Water master

The wakil is in charge of the water supply and is elected by the village community. His task is to look after this precious resource. He changes the water distribution by repositioning the connections and forks according to a fixed schedule. Depending on the area to be irrigated and according to inherited rights and newly bought

wakil's, the water master, falaj book documents exactly who gets how much water and when.

shares, the water is channelled for different lengths of time.

Today in the UAE, there are hardly any remains of the old water system; this arduous method has been replaced by water desalination plants. In Oman, however, the tradition is still kept alive. Fields across the entire country are watered by functioning and well-maintained aflaj. One system well worth visiting is near Al Ain, at the oasis of Buraimi.

Water register

For centuries, falaj books have documented the exact distribution of water for each channel system, including details about the families living in the drainage area, the size of property and purpose for water access – household, garden or cattle.

In a land register, the wakil controls and enters the individual rights, the time of day and duration of water access, as well as its acquisition or sale. Because one channel supplies hundreds of families with water, his job requires discretion and conscientiousness, which has successfully prevented disputes from early on.

In fact, the history of the Arabian Peninsula is marked by battles over oases and water rights. These disputes have sometimes even resulted in the construction of massive fortifications around and over springs. There are strict rules about how the precious water may be used. The supply of drinking water has top priority: the water is channelled to the local fountain where the village people extract it, driven by a sense of responsibility for the community. Here, the falaj is often covered with a stone plate to protect the channel or water from pollution.

Then the water is directed to locations for bathing or cleaning, e.g. mosques, followed by the supply for cattle and irrigation of agricultural areas.

Around Fujairah

✳
Khor Kalba

Khor Kalba, which belongs to Sharjah and is located directly south of the city of Fujairah, is popular for its long, white sandy beaches. Visitors from the other emirates as well as foreign tourists enjoy spending a relaxing weekend by the sea in the Marine Hotel.

Al-Hosn
Museum ▶
🕐

The ethnographic Al-Hosn Museum in the Al-Hosn Area, situated in the northern part of town, exhibits traditional garments, coins and various commodities (open: Sat–Thu 8am–2pm and 4pm–8pm, Fri 4pm–8pm).

Old Fort ▶

The Kalba Old Fort stands south-west of the town centre, directly at the foot of the mountain range. Its current form dates back to the re-inforcement by the Portuguese in the 16th century. The fort lies amidst several derelict houses belonging to the old town of Kalba.

**Khor Kalba
Mangrove
Reserve Park**

South of Kalba, the Khor Kalba estuary stretches southward 4km/ 2.5mi inland, where it eventually turns into a swamp and mangrove landscape. Designated as a **nature reserve**, it is the northernmost

A little picnic on the expansive Corniche at Khor Kalba

mangrove region in the world and particularly appreciated by natural scientists. Due to a mix of ocean and fresh water, the Khor Kalba mangroves have optimal conditions for growth. Nowhere else in the United Arab Emirates are there as many plants, birds and marine wildlife as here. **Canoe tours**, operated by an environmentalist group, are an excellent opportunity to find out more about the ecosystem. Groups are accompanied by expert rangers and, with a bit of luck, visitors may sight the local dugongs (sea cows) living in the shallow waters off the coast.

! *Baedeker* TIP

Mountain trips
A trip to the Hajar Mountains is absolutely worthwhile. Alongside remote villages, the tour leads past mineral springs and even a waterfall. These mountain trips, however, definitely require a four-by-four; otherwise it's better to join an organized tour, which can be booked in the hotels.

The old village of Al-Hayl, including an old historic castle, is situated in the wadi of Hayl, 8km/5mi southwest of Fujairah. In the 19th century, this palace-like fort was the main residence of the emirate's ruling family and was used to fight off invaders from the neighbouring region of Oman. Although mainly built from mud, the building is still in good condition. The square, three-storey defence tower is also open to visitors. From the battlements on the rooftop there is a nice view of the palace, the surrounding abandoned village and the wadi, which carries water all year round.   **Al-Hayl**

26km/16.2mi south-west of Fujairah, on the border to Oman, the hot **mineral springs** of Ain Al-Ghamour, with surface temperatures of between 55–60°C/131–140°F, are used for healing purposes – and are a popular destination for weekend picnics.

Bathers relaxing at the Al-Wurayah Waterfall

In 1985, during agricultural work in a date grove, a horseshoe-shaped **grave from the Iron Age** was discovered about 15km/9.3mi north of Fujairah, on the northern border of the village of Qidfa. The approximately 3,000 year old grave contained burial objects such as jars, daggers, axes and jewellery, which are now on show at the Fujairah Museum.   **Qidfa**

The Al-Badiyah Mosque is the oldest of the Emirates.

✴ Al-Wurayah Near Zubarah, 5km/3.1mi north of Khor Fakkan, a road branches off from the coastal road and leads south-west toward the Al-Wurayah **waterfall**. Beforehand a road branches off to the Wurayah Dam, one of Khor Fakkan's two water reservoirs. After approximately 12km/7.5mi, the road ends shortly before the Wurayah waterfall, which supplies a flow of fresh spring water all-year round.

Badiyah 35km/21.7mi north of Fujairah, the small town of Badiyah is known for its enormous **Thursday Market** for agricultural produce, attracting buyers and sellers from the entire emirate.

★ ★ Al-Badiyah Mosque ▶ Close to Badiyah, tourists can visit a first-rate historical sight in terms of art and culture: the **oldest mosque of the UAE**, the Al-Badiyah Mosque. Experts give the most varied estimations of how old it actually is – between 1,300 years (beginning of Islamization) and 800 years. The building, which was most likely named after its sponsor Othman **Masjid Al-Othmani**, is not tall and has a floor space of only several square yards. The modest looking white-washed mosque is characterized by its four low domes, supported only by a single pillar. A double-winged wooden entry door, which is usually locked, leads to the house of prayer. Visits to the mosque are only possible when staff is present, which is very rare. North of the mosque, the ruins of the Badiyah Fort are visible in the mountains.

Dibba, 60km/37.3mi north of Fujairah, is a beautifully situated coastal town, appreciated by locals for its wide, sandy beaches. As there is no real tourist infrastructure to speak of, with the exception of some restaurants and tea salons, foreign visitors are rarely ever spotted here. The grey-green shimmering mountains of the Musandam Peninsula stretching into the distance are most impressive.

Dibba: a city in three parts

A fact hardly any visitor would notice at first: Dibba is split into three parts, shared between the Emirates of Fujairah and Sharjah and the Sultanate of Oman. Of course, in a small town such as Dibba there aren't any border controls or customs, so everyone is allowed to move freely between the southern UAE section and Bayah, the western Omani part of town. A closer look makes the difference in the architectural design of the quarters apparent: the houses in the Omani

> ! **Baedeker** TIP
>
> ### Spectacular view
> North of the Bithnah Oasis, on the road to Sharjah, the view of the old fort surrounded by date trees is absolutely stunning!

district are laid out in a more traditionally Arabic style, and the colourful iron gates carry typical emblems such as camels, coffee pots and water pipes.

The picturesque Bithnah Fort is situated in a small oasis valley 15km/9.3mi north-west of Fujairah, on the way to Dubai or Sharjah. Built in 1735, the fort guarded the strategic route of the **Wadi Ham** through the Hajar Mountains.

Bithnah

Excavations of the surroundings included several hints that the Bithnah oasis must have already been inhabited more than 3,000 years ago. The ceramics and metal items found in a T-shaped communal grave, used from approximately 1300 to 300 BC, document the former settlers' stage of cultural development. The Museum of Fujairah has a replica of the grave as well as an exhibition of the burial objects discovered inside. The excavation site itself is not publicly accessible.

◀ Excavations

RAS al-KHAIMAH

Area: 1,625 sq km/627 sq mi   **Population:** 170,000
Emir: Sheikh Saqr Bin-Mohammed
al-Qasimi (since 1948)

Rugged mountain peaks, green oases and simple fishing settlements: located on the Arabian Gulf, the northernmost sheikhdom of the United Arab Emirates has been a member of the federation since 10 February 1972. Like Fujairah, it possesses some of the country's most beautiful landscapes.

Ras al-Khaimah means »tip of the tent«. The assumption is that this expression refers to the emirate's steep mountains whose summits resemble the shape of tents – once the home of the nomadic inhabitants of Ras al-Khaimah. »**Tip of the mountain«**

The emirate is bordered by the mountainous Musandam Peninsula and the Strait of Hormuz. There are broad palm oases and agricultural areas, with the Hajar Mountains offering numerous springs.

The population still lives from **fishing** and **agriculture**, exporting its produce to the six remaining emirates. Due to the large mountain range, it rains here more than in the neighbouring emirates; the plains are used for growing crops and grazing cattle.

The first **agricultural research station** on the Arabian Gulf was set up in 1960 in Digdagga, not far from the capital; a training facility was added several years later. Today Digdagga supplies the emirates with poultry, eggs, milk and meat, dates, fruit and vegetables. ◄ Digdagga

In Ras al-Khaimah, **oil production** only began as late as 1984, with the opening of the **Saleh field**, situated on the Arabian Gulf. So far its yield has paid for the development of an industrial area north of the capital, as well as several infrastructural developments. Industrial production is mainly based on cement and construction materials. Other sources of income are an expanding free trade zone and Saqr Port, the Emirates main deep water port. Oil

← *Compared to the Gulf-metropolis of Dubai, the capital of the small Emirate of Ras al-Khaimah leaves a much less modern impression.*

History

2000 BC	Settlement of Khatt
13th century	Julfar's heyday
1819	The British conquer Ras al-Khaimah.
1971	The sheikhdom joins the UAE.
1984	First oil production in Ras al-Khaimah

First settlement The area of what is now Ras al-Khaimah was already colonized in the second millennium BC. During excavations on the slope of the **Ghallila Mountains**, an oval-shaped grave was found; in **Shimal** two elongated graves with several side graves. The oldest findings include stone bowls with engraved decorations, bones, fish hooks, stone beads, shell jewellery, ceramics, ship models, bronze arrowheads and spearheads, as well as stone markers – an indication of underground graves. Other 4,000 year old findings were discovered above the hot springs of **Khatt**, in the location of what might have once been an oasis settlement. The area of the **Wadi Qawr** is the site of 3,000 year old communal graves as well as remains of two settled villages from the same period.

Julfar The harbour town of Julfar, north of Ras al-Khaimah, is of legendary importance and was even praised by the explorers **Ibn Battuta** (►Famous People) and **Marco Polo**. Founded at the beginning of the Islamic Period, the town is also mentioned in the Qur'an. One of its famous navigators was **Ahmed Bin-Majid** (► Famous People), the »Sea's Lion«, whose logbooks were long used by Arab sailors.

British domination In the beginning of the 18th century, the British became increasingly active in the Gulf region and tried to extend their power. The **Qawasim**, based in Ras al-Khaimah, were still a thorn in the side of the British, as the Qasimi trading fleet and far-reaching trade relations competed with the interests of the British East India Company.

By the end of the 18th century, the Qawasim owned the largest trading fleet of the Indian Ocean, and controlled sea trade on both coasts of the northern Gulf region. In 1819, Major General **Sir William Grant Keir** conquered the city and the nearby Dhayah Fort. Based on the peace treaty between the British and the rulers of the nine sheikhdoms, signed in 1820, **Sheikh Sultan Bin-Saqr al-Qasimi** regained Julfar and the other Qasimi harbour towns, but only in exchange for British domination of the Gulf coast. In this way, the »Pirate Coast« became the »Trucial Coast«.

Ras al-Khaimah was part of the sheikhdom of Sharjah for most of its history. Apart from a brief period of independence from 1869-1900 it did not finally become independent until 1919 when Britain recognized it as a separate Trucial state.

Ras al-Khaimah

F / G 3

Population: 130,000

Ras al-Khaimah gives a far less modern and Western impression than, for instance, the metropolis of Dubai. The houses, architecturally simple buildings with one or two-storeys, were erected in the 1970s and 1980s. The old town still contains a few old houses in the traditional style.

Ras al-Khaimah is situated 100km/62mi north of Dubai, and stretches across the western side of the northern Musandam Peninsula along the flat coastal regions. An estuary separates the town into an Old Town in the west and a New Town (Al-Nakheel) in the east; the two sides are connected by a bridge and water taxis. Unfortunately, the Old Town is in a deplorable condition: many houses are deserted and on the verge of decay. More importance is placed on the new **Tower Links Golf Course**, an 18-hole course with a hotel and marina integrating an area of mangrove forest.

Coastal town on the Musandam Peninsula

What to See in Ras al-Khaimah

The emirate's historic fort was built during the Persian occupation between 1736 and 1749. Now only the square tower to the left of the entrance remains from this time, all other parts of the building having been built in the following centuries. It served as a palace for the

★
Old Fort

The mid-18th century fort served as the Emir's Palace until 1960. Today it houses the emirate's National Museum.

► VISITING RAS AL-KHAIMAH

INFORMATION

A tourist information office is located inside the National Museum of Ras al-Khaimah.

WHERE TO EAT

► Expensive

② *La Tour d'Argent*
Ras al-Khaimah Hotel
Eid Musallah Road
Tel. 2 36 29 99
The best restaurant in the emirate offering Asian and Arabic specialities.

► Moderate

③ *Hotel Nakheel*
Muntaser Road
Tel. 2 28 28 22
Due to exquisite cuisine, the hotel restaurant is always busy.

► Inexpensive

① *Pizza Inn*
Al-Feisal Road
(next to the post office)
Tel. 2 33 40 40
An »Italian enclave« with Arabic-inspired pizza and pasta dishes.

WHERE TO STAY

► Luxury

Al-Hamra Fort Hotel & Beach Resort
Al-Hamra Jazira
P.O. Box 14 68
Tel. 2 44 66 66

Email: hamfort@emirates.net.ae
83 rooms
Located on an island at the southern entrance of the city, this hotel was designed like an Arabic fort with wind towers. Many rooms have a balcony and a view of the ocean.

► Mid-range

② *Ras al-Khaimah Hotel*
Al-Khouzam Road
(RAK Corniche)
Khouzam
P.O. Box 56
Tel. 2 36 29 99
Email: rakhotel@emirates.net.ae
93 rooms
The hotel is situated on a hill overlooking the dhow harbour. It offers various water sports facilities, a pool, tennis and squash courts, sauna and workout room.

► Budget

① *Bin Majid Beach Hotel*
Bin Majid Road
P.O. Box 19 46
Tel. 2 35 22 33
52 chalets
The very inexpensively priced chalets are located on the edge of town on a hill overlooking the beach. Includes two restaurants, a bar and discotheque, two pools, a private beach, a playground and a gym.

③ *Al-Nakheel*
Muntaser Road
Nakheel
P.O. Box 53 33
Tel. 2 28 28 22
Fax 2 28 29 22
55 rooms
Hotel situated east of the lagoon, in the centre of the New Town, with a pub and restaurant.

ruling al-Qasimi Family – first **Sheikh Salim Bin-Sultan al-Qasimi**, grandfather of the current emir, then his successor **Sheikh Sultan** and finally the current ruler **Sheikh Saqr**. When Sheikh Saqr had a new palace built for himself in 1960, the fort served as police headquarters, then as a prison. Since its renovation in the 1980s, the fort has been home to the **National Museum**.

Ras al-Khaimah Plan

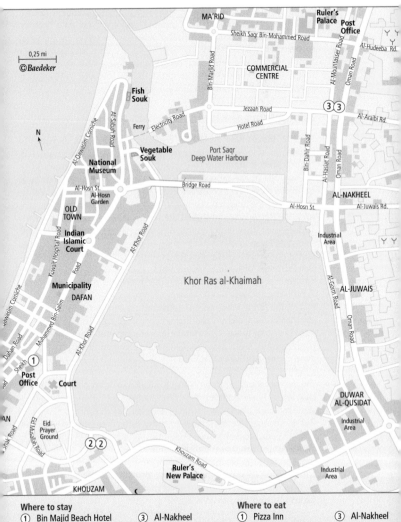

0,25 mi
©Baedeker

N

MA'RID

Ruler's Palace
Post Office

Sheikh Saqr Bin-Mohammed Road

Bin-Majid Road

Al-Mountasser Road

Oman Road

Al-Hudeeba Rd.

COMMERCIAL CENTRE

Fish Souk

Jezaah Road

Al-Araibi Rd.

Al-Qawasim Corniche

Al-Sabah Road

Electricity Road

Ferry

Hotel Road

Vegetable Souk

Port Saqr
Deep Water Harbour

Bin-Dahir Road

Al-Hasiat Road

Oman Road

National Museum

Bridge Road

AL-NAKHEEL

Al-Hosn St.
Al-Hosn Garden

Al-Hosn St.

Al-Juwais Rd.

OLD TOWN

Indian Islamic Court

Kuwait Hospital Road

Al-Khor Road

Khor Ras al-Khaimah

Industrial Area

Al-Gorm Road

Oman Road

AL-JUWAIS

Municipality

DAFAN

Qawasim Corniche

Mohammed Bin-Salim

Al-Khor Road

Dafan Road

Post Office

Court

DUWAR AL-QUSIDAT

Industrial Area

Eid Prayer Ground

Eid Musallah Road

Khouzam Road

Ruler's New Palace

Industrial Area

KHOUZAM

★
National Museum of Ras al-Khaimah

The museum consists of an ethnography and archaeology department, with exhibits and finds from Ras al-Khaimah, as well as a natural history department with an extensive shell collection and numerous fossils. The oldest piece of the archaeological collection, a stone knife, dates back to the third millennium BC. The majority of the collection is comprised of finds from the archaeological site of Shimal. Also interesting is the collection of silver coins, which were discovered in 1965 during excavation work on an old well. They have been attributed to the Persian Samanid and Buwayhid tribes, and date back to the period between 920 and 981. An additional 124 silver coins were found in 1985, minted under Persian rule between 1010 and 1023 in Sohar, in what is now Oman. Other exhibits feature finds from the former harbour town of Julfar, mostly from the 16th and 17th centuries, including bronze coins, Chinese porcelain, ⏲ mugs from Thailand and ceramics from Vietnam (open: daily 10am–5pm, Thu women only).

Around Ras al-Khaimah

★
Julfar

In 1272, **Marco Polo** visited the harbour town of Julfar, beyond the lagoon on the northern edge of Ras al-Khaimah, and praised its beauty. **Ahmed Bin-Majid** (▶Famous People) was born here in 1432. He was one of the most famous navigators of Arabia and author of 40 works on geography and navigation. He is also believed to be the inventor of the magnetic compass. Toward the end of the 15th century, the Portuguese controlled the region around Julfar; in the early 16th century, they built a garrison, a tollhouse and two forts to guard the coastal region. At the beginning of the 17th century, British and Dutch colonialists challenged the position of the Portuguese, and destroyed both Portuguese forts in 1633.

Visitation ▶
Situated in the hills above a bay, this historical site is about 2km/1.3mi long and 300 to 400 metres (328 to 438 yards) wide. In other places, the foundation walls of 14th-century residential buildings and streets were uncovered, and further dwellings from earlier times exposed beneath those. The foundations of a mosque from the early Islamic period have also been identified (open: daily except Tue ⏲ 9am–12pm, admission free).

Sheba's Palace

The historically important ruins of the »**Palace of the Queen of Sheba**«, most likely built in the 16th century, are situated on a freestanding rock above the town of Shimal, 3km/1.9mi north-east of Ras al-Khaimah. In reality however, the ruins date back to a hill fort and are completely unconnected to the legendary queen who lived in South Arabia about two millennia before the fort was even built. Today, all that is left of the fortification are a few foundation walls. It is still possible to see the remains of a **drinking water cistern**, which was equipped with a barrel-shaped roof to keep the water clean and protect it from the sun.

In the second millennium BC, copper deposits were found in what is now Northern Oman. The copper was extracted and transported along the caravan route to Shimal, 5km/3.1mi north of what is now Ras al-Khaimah, and shipped from there to Mesopotamia (now Iraq). The archaeological site extends over more than 3km/1.9mi and includes a settlement and the remains of a large burial site. These burial sites consisted of large, over-ground communal graves, as well as individual graves up in the mountains, which increased in number beginning in the 2nd millennium BC. One of the graves held about 40 bodies and contained valuable burial objects, including ceramic pots, stone-carved jugs, silver earrings and numerous pearls.

The openly accessible excavation site is hard to find, so visitors with an interest in archaeology should hire a local guide. The walk up the rocky, steep trail to the graves is strenuous.

Shimal

Ruins of a medieval fort near Shimal

Up until the second half of the 20th century, the wide and easily accessible **Al-Qor Wadi** was a preferred caravan route for traversing the Hajar Mountains. Pack camels transported the merchants' goods from the Gulf coast to the Batinah desert in Oman. Only with the development of a road between Hatta and the Batinah coast did the old route lose its significance.

A tour through the Al-Qor Wadi not only passes through beautiful landscape, but also enters a region which was inhabited thousands of years ago. Archaeologists have found a horseshoe-shaped communal grave built deep within the rock. The discovery of a grave situated near Naslah (east of Huwaylat) caused a sensation; more than 2,000 burial objects were found: elaborately worked vases, jugs and storage vessels made of easy-to-process soft stone from the surrounding area. Near **Rafaq**, the ruins of a fortified village were found on both sides of the wadi. Based on ceramic shards, the settlement has been dated to the 2nd millennium BC.

◄ Wadi tour

The best way to reach the Al-Qor Wadi is to leave from ►Hatta. At the Hatta Fort Hotel, take the asphalt road that turns into a dirt road leading to the wadi.

Wadis in the Hajar Mountains:
green pearls surrounded by a raw, grey-brown rocky landscape

Huwaylat Huwaylat, an **old oasis** located in the wadi, was once a traditional transit town for caravans on their way to the Batinah coast. Today Huwaylat is a **popular weekend destination**, and its streets are lined with numerous holiday homes. The old resthouse and a general store, which sells tea and coffee, are reminders of earlier times. Falaj channels (▶Baedeker Special p.214) outside the town and parallel to the wadi conduct water to the gardens of the oasis inhabitants.

Munay From Huwaylat, an approximately 8km/5mi stretch of road leads northward to the small oasis town of Munay and the magnificent **palm gardens**. Here, time seems to have stood still: men in long white garments promenade leisurely down the street, meeting for tea or a game of cards. All women are veiled and scurry hastily away when they encounter a stranger. The **ruins of an old fort** and a watchtower remain from earlier centuries.

✱
Wadi Asimah A trip into the mountains along the lush, green Wadi Asimah is very popular with the locals. Accessible via the village of Al-Ghayl, it is situated on the road traversing the Jiri plain, between Ras al-Khaimah and Manama. The dusty road leads through quaint mountain valleys and past steep ravines.

Green
paradise ▶ This must be paradise: lush green leaves on tall date trees, juicy red-green mangos hanging from the branches, deliciously scented fruit

Final preparations before a race at the Digdagga camel track

trees cast shade along the paths leading to the adjacent gardens. The landscape around Asimah is not just stunningly beautiful; it also bears evidence of ancient settlements.

In 1972, the remains of nearly 20 graves from the 2nd millennium BC were found, which were furnished with an abundance of burial objects. Among the most significant and precious finds, all of which can be viewed at the museum in Ras al-Khaimah, is an approximately 4,000 year old filigree bronze mug, as well as several gold necklaces from the 1st century AD. It is only possible to visit the fenced-in excavation site as part of a tour booked with a local travel organization.

◄ Excavations

◄ Visits

Fans of the sport consider the camel race track in Digdagga, 10km/ 6.2mi south of Ras al-Khaimah, to be the most picturesque. Situated in beautiful surroundings, it has managed to maintain its charm by forgoing ugly concrete terraces. Every Thursday and Friday during the racing season, between October and April, hundreds of dromedaries are to be seen here. Fed on a diet of fresh hay, honey, dates, eggs and barley – quite unlike the pack animals and the animals for slaughter – and kept under constant veterinary supervision, the racing dromedaries are ready to run at the age of three or four (►Baedeker Special p.230).

Camel race track in Digdagga

The owner drives alongside the track during the training of his racing camels.

VENGEFUL SHIPS OF THE DESERT

Of all mammals in the United Arab Emirates, camels cope best with the extreme dryness. Fatty humps help the animal survive without water for several days; in emergencies, they will even drink salt water.

Wide foot pads allow the camel to walk in deep sand without sinking. Long eyelashes and closable nostrils prevent sand from getting into the camel's eyes and nose.

The art of survival

In extreme heat, a camel can increase its body temperature to 42°C/107°F to avoid losing too much water by sweating. Likewise, on cold desert nights, the animal can lower its body temperature to 34°C/93°F so that it doesn't freeze or catch a cold. Camels are able to survive without eating or drinking for long periods of time, and when they do they can drink 100 litres/26 US gal of water within a mere 15 minutes, a supply which will last them for up to three weeks when they are working, and up to 10 months when they are only grazing. Camels are herbivores and feed on shrubs, thorn bushes and desert grass. Camels can cover up to 50km/31mi per day and carry loads of up to 250kg/550lb. However, these animals are not completely robust. They quickly fall sick from polluted water, and if they are not given enough rest

after a strenuous tour they can suddenly drop dead.

It takes a very long time before camels accept their owners. These extremely vengeful animals will remember bad treatment for their entire lives, and will take revenge with kicks or bites even years later.

Desert joy

In order to get the calves accustomed to humans, the Bedouins used to take the young with them into their tents. For these sons of the desert, camels were their most precious and important property. They had hundreds of poetic pet names for their four-legged companions. Camels with whom they had a particularly close relationship would be named »miracle of beauty«, »dauntless courage« or »desert joy«.

Not just a meat animal

These frugal animals have been known on the Arabian Peninsula for 4,000 years. It is no exaggeration to claim that the settlement of the region was only possible due to camels. The word »camel«, however, is not entirely correct, for it is the single-

humped dromedary, the »gamal«, which is domesticated on the Arabian Peninsula.

In former, less prosperous times the animals were particularly valued for their milk and meat; their dung served as heating material, their

ruling family are fans of the sport and own several hundred racing camels, some of which are worth two and a half million dirham (£340,000).

Each race involves around three dozen camels. The jockeys wear headphones through which they re-

Even the head of state appears at especially important and high-stakes races.

leathery hide was processed to make sandals and water jugs, and their hair and fur was used to make tents, rugs and clothing. Even their shoulder blades served as writing boards for children.

Status symbols

Today camels mainly function as status symbols. A young camel costs as much as a used car: between 7,500–25,000 AED (£1,000–£3,375). Visitors can often observe large herds grazing behind the fencing along motorways or in the desert.

Camel races

Attending one of the many camel races during winter is quite an experience. Members of Abu Dhabi's

ceive instructions from the camel owners following them in their jeeps alongside the racetrack.

Racing can be quite tricky as camels are very hard even to steer in a desired direction, let alone getting them to trot or gallop. Some won't budge at the start of the race, while others run in the wrong direction or backwards. Every now and again, a camel leaving the racetrack can cause an accident – either by running straight into a camera team by the side of the track or into the camel owners' vehicles. A trot or gallop can really only be achieved if the jockey constantly hits the animal with his whip, particularly the sensitive body parts. Laws prohibit the use of boys younger than 16 years and weighing less than 45 kilograms (99 pounds).

SHARJAH

Area: 2,600 sq km/1,004 sq mi
Emir: Sheikh Dr. Sultan Bin-Mohammed al-Qasimi (since 1972)

Population: 750,000

Sharjah is a modern emirate, though in comparison to Abu Dhabi and Dubai it has a much simpler infrastructure. The old fishing village of Al-Khan, for example, with its unsurfaced roads, narrow paths and houses made of coral limestone and mud, is situated at the western edge of the eponymous capital south of the Al-Khan lagoon.

As the third largest emirate of the United Arab Emirates, Sharjah contains several geographically distinct areas. The capital of the same name, 15km/9.3mi north of Dubai on the west coast of the United Arab Emirates, covers the major part of the emirate. Besides this there are exclaves on the Gulf coast of Oman – including Dibba, Khor Fakkan and Khor Kalba – and two larger islands in the Arabian Gulf. The large industrial areas are located in the south-west. Sharjah makes up 30% of all industrial activity in the UAE. The city is traversed by two estuaries: the Khalid Lagoon in the east rea-

ches far into the city, with a coastal road stretching along its eastern side, which is lined by several hotels. In the lagoon itself there are several islands, including Jazeerah Park. The Al-Khan Lagoon in the western part of the city splits into three estuaries separated by sandbanks. The southern border is where Al-Wahda Street leads into the city from Dubai. Due to Sharjah's extremely strict ban on alcohol, the emirate has to find something to offer as an alternative to its easy-going neighbour Dubai in order to promote tourism. In recent years Sharjah has become the **»cultural capital«** of the UAE: the city centre has been restored and many historic buildings have been turned into museums. Today, Sharjah has more museums than all the other emirates combined.

◄ Cultural stronghold

Sharjah is run by **Sheikh Sultan Bin-Mohammed al-Qasimi**, who is considered the most intellectual of the seven emirs of the UAE. The Ph.D. agricultural economist actively promotes agriculture in the emirate. He has also written two novels and several historical books on the Gulf region.

Agricultural economist in power

← *The view over Al-Ittihad Square in the centre of the Sharjah city*

Economy Sharjah only has moderate petroleum resources, and gas reserves have not yet been developed, which is why the emirate has concentrated its energies on **industry**, **trade** and **tourism**.

History

4000 BC	First settlement in Sharjah
1820	Peace treaty with Great Britain, Sharjah becomes a British base.
1971	Sharjah joins the UAE.
1972	Oil fields are discovered in the emirate.

First settlement The first colonization of Sharjah happened some 6,000 years ago. The people of the ancient town of Sarcoa lived from maritime trade and fishing; later also agriculture and pearl diving (►Baedeker Special p.242).
The major part of its history, however, is still largely unknown due to a lack of archaeological excavation work.

16th century: the Portuguese erect forts Beginning in 1507, the **Portuguese** built forts in Khor Fakkan, Khor Kalba and Dibba to control the spice trade. After around one hundred years they were driven away by the Dutch. In the 17th century the British arrived and began to trade with the **Qawasim** tribe, the ancestors of the current ruling family.
In the 18th century, the Qawasim were the prevailing sea power in the southern Gulf, with harbours in Ras al-Khaimah and Sharjah.

19th/20th century: under British rule In 1803 **Sheikh Sultan Bin-Saqr al-Qasimi** became Emir of Sharjah and ruled the sheikhdom for 63 years. The relationship with the British suffered when they held the Qawasim responsible for pirate raids on British ships, which led to the first British attack on Ras al-Khaimah in 1819 and ended with the destruction of the entire settlement. However, several peace treaties, the first concluded in 1820, secured British supremacy in the Gulf for 150 years.
From 1853, the coast was referred to as the »**Trucial Coast**« or »Trucial States«. Between 1823 and 1954, Sharjah was the only British base on the southern Gulf, and they established their first airport here as early as 1932 for the state-owned Imperial Airways, used for stopovers on the way from England to India. When the British withdrew from the gulf in 1971 Sharjah joined the newly formed United Arab Emirates.
In 1972, after the emirates came together in a federation, oil and later gas were found in the **Mubarak Field**, 80km/49.7mi off-shore on the island of Abu Musa, which eventually instigated the emirate's modern development.

✦ Sharjah

Population: 450,000

The first impression of this modern city is that of spacious gardens and parks. In the city centre, there are districts with perfectly restored Islamic buildings, including many museums. »Smile, you're in Sharjah« is the city's welcome slogan.

Sheikh Sultan Awal Road starts at the mouth of the estuary and leads all the way to Sharjah's harbour and Corniche, which is lined by the beach hotels of the city. The modern centre is located south of the harbour, around Arooba Street, while suburbs and industrial areas are found further south.

Modern metropolis

What to See in Sharjah

The old residence of the ruling family on Al-Boorj Avenue was built in 1822 by **Sheikh Sultan Bin-Saqr al-Qasimi**. All political decisions concerning the emirate were made at this two-storey mud-brick building, and it was used until the mid-20th century. In 1969, the entire building was torn down, except for the 12m/39ft Al-Mahalwasa tower. Twenty years later, the loss of this historic building was so much regretted that the fort was reconstructed true to the original on the initiative of the current emir, **Sultan Bin-Mohammed al-Qasimi**. Today the main portal is adorned with a door from the original building.

✶ ✶ Al-Hisn Fort

Since 1997, the Al-Hisn Fort has served as Sharjah's **history museum**. The exhibitions give an insight into pearl diving on the Arabian Gulf (►Baedeker Special p.242) and shed light on the history and development of the city. The museum's pride and joy are its historical maps of the Gulf region as well as the country's oldest rifle, named Abu Fatilah (»father of the muzzle-loader«).

◄ City Museum

Highlights Sharjah

Heritage Area
Perfectly restored historic buildings
► page 237

Souk Al-Arsah
A stroll through the past
► page 240

Islamic Museum
Precious writings and sacred art
► page 237

Blue Souk
The UAE's most photographed building
► page 245

▶ VISITING SHARJAH

INFORMATION

**Sharjah Commerce &
Tourism Development Authority**
11th floor, Crescent Tower
Al-Arooba Street
P.O. Box 2 66 61
Sharjah
Tel. 06 / 5 56 27 77
Fax 5 56 30 00
www.sharjah-welcome.com

MUSEUMS

The museums and historic buildings
are usually open between 8am and
1pm and between 4pm and 8pm.
Museums are closed on Mondays;
Wednesday afternoons are reserved
for women. On Fridays the opening
hours are restricted, from 5pm to
8pm. With the exception of the
Natural History Museum and the
Science Museum, the admission to all
museums is free.

SHOPPING

Shopping in Sharjah is a special
experience. The Blue Souk is the most
stunning and largest souk in the
entire country, while the new Al-
Majarrah Souk is another highlight of
neo-Islamic architecture.

WHERE TO EAT

▶ Expensive

③ **Caesar's Palace**
Marbella Resort
Khalid Lagoon Corniche
Tel. 5 74 11 11
The elegant restaurant with a mag-
nificent view of the lagoon serves
international cuisine, with a focus on
Italian specialities.

Baedeker-recommendation

▶ Moderate

② **Fishermen's Wharf**
Hotel Holiday International
Khalid Lagoon Corniche, Al-Majaz
Tel. 5 73 66 66
This rustic, marine-style restaurant serves
fish and shellfish, which is prepared
according to the wishes of the guests.

▶ Inexpensive

① **Sanobar**
Al-Khan Road
Tel. 5 28 35 01
Popular restaurant serving delicious
stews

WHERE TO STAY

▶ Luxury

① **Holiday International**
P.O. Box 58 02
Khalid Lagoon (Buheira)
Corniche, Al-Majaz
Tel. 5 73 66 66
255 rooms
All rooms of this particularly family-
friendly hotel have a balcony over-
looking the lagoon or the city.

*The Blue Souk: a shopping experience with
over 600 shops*

► Mid-range

③ *Carlton*

Sheikh Sultan Al-Awal Road
Al-Khan Corniche
P.O. Box 11 98
Tel. 5 28 37 11
Email: Carltonh@emirates.net.ae
260 rooms
The hotel includes three restaurants, a large fitness area and a 200m/218yd beach.

⑥ *Radisson SAS*

Corniche Road
Tel. 5 37 11 11
www.radissonsas.com
300 rooms
This hotel, directly located on the Corniche, is especially popular with European package tourists. Includes several restaurants, a private beach and various options for water sports.

② *Nova Park*

Al-Wadah Street
(on the corner of King Feisal Street)
Al-Qasimia
P.O. Box 35 88
Tel. 5 72 80 00
www.novaparkhotel.com
256 rooms
Comfortable hotel with swimming pool and fitness room; shuttle bus to the city centre and Dubai.

► Budget

⑤ *Beach Hotel*

Al-Khan Corniche
P.O. Box 59 77
Tel. 5 28 13 11
www.beachhotel-sharjah.com; 131 rooms
The beach hotel with a pool and entertainment for children is located 5km/3.1mi from the city centre. Free transport to the airport and city.

⑦ *Coral Beach Hotel*

Corniche Road
Al-Muntaza
P.O. Box 55 24
Tel. 5 22 10 11
www.ebmanage.com/coralbeach
156 rooms
This beach hotel features a tennis court, a sauna and pool. Free shuttle service five times per day to Dubai and Sharjah, as well as to the airports of Dubai and Sharjah.

④ *Summerland Motel*

Al-Khan Corniche
P.O. Box 60 06
Tel. 5 28 13 21
Email: bustansh@emirates.net.ae
44 rooms
Simple hotel on Sultan Al-Awal Road. All rooms equipped with air conditioning, bathroom and TV.

Literature Square

Some of the historic buildings west of the fort in the **Heritage Area** have been dedicated to Arab and local writers. The triangular cottage in the middle of Literature Square provides coffee for visitors. The **House of Poetry** features an extensive collection of Arabic poetry.

★
Islamic Museum

West of Literature Square, the Islamic Museum can be found in the former residence of **Saeed Bin-Mohammed al-Shamsi**, owner of a famous trading house. The exhibits – all of which are on loan from the private collection of Sheikh Sultan al-Qasimi – include a replica of the embroidered curtain covering the Kaba door in Mecca. Also

Sharjah Plan

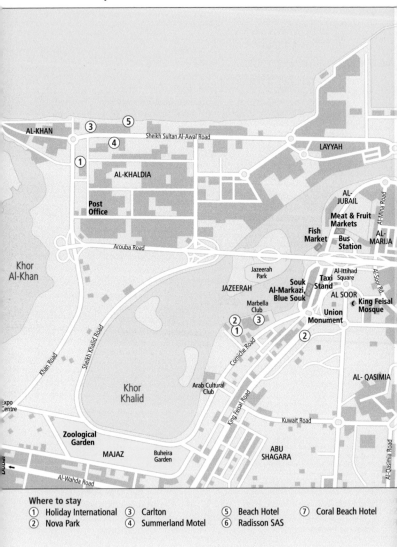

AL-KHAN

Sheikh Sultan Al-Awal Road

LAYYAH

AL-KHALDIA

Post
Office

Arouba Road

AL-
JUBAIL

Meat & Fruit
Markets

Fish
Market

Bus
Station

AL-
MARIJA

Al-Mina Road

Khor
Al-Khan

Jazeerah
Park

JAZEERAH

Souk
Al-Markazi,
Blue Souk

Taxi
Stand

Al-Ittihad
Square

AL SOOR

King Feisal
Mosque

Al-Soor Rd.

Marbella
Club

Union
Monument

Sheikh Khalid Road

Khan Road

Khor
Khalid

Corniche Road

Arab Cultural
Club

King Feisal Road

AL- QASIMIA

Kuwait Road

Expo
Centre

Zoological
Garden

MAJAZ

Buheira
Garden

ABU
SHAGARA

Al-Qasimia Road

Al-Wahda Road

Where to stay

① Holiday International   ③ Carlton   ⑤ Beach Hotel   ⑦ Coral Beach Hotel
② Nova Park   ④ Summerland Motel   ⑥ Radisson SAS

on view is a world map from 1099 and numerous editions and calligraphies of the Qur'an, up to 900 years old. A special exhibition is dedicated to **Islamic archaeological finds** in Sharjah.

The former residence of Obaid Bin-Isa Bin-Ali al-Shamsi, also known as Naboodah, whose trading business made him a wealthy man, is situated north of the Islamic Museum. Built in 1845, the Na-

Obaid Bin-Isa Bin-Ali al-Shamsi

boodah family lived there until 1980. The impressive architecture, built out of coral limestone and African hardwood, was restored and turned into a **museum of regional history**. The two-storey building has a large inner courtyard and a revolving, shady gallery on the first floor. The rooms exhibit silver jewellery, toys and garments – including the »working clothes« of pearl divers. The replica of a historic boat, partly woven from palm branches and ropes, is displayed in the courtyard (Fireij Al-Souk, Al-Gharb).

The restored historic **Souk Al-Arsah** is situated in the old town in the square between Bait Al-Naboodah and Majlis Al-Naboodah. »Arsah« is the term for an open space or courtyard between buildings. Accessible through four different gates, this souk is well worth visiting for its authentic centuries-old market atmosphere. The shops with elaborately carved entry doors offer high-quality arts and crafts. The smells of incense and spice oils are everywhere. The narrow alleys reveal some great opportunities for finding souvenirs: silver goods from Oman and Yemen, pearl necklaces from Dubai and hand-woven textiles from India (market hours: daily except Fri morning 9am–1pm and 4.30pm–10pm).

Al-Midfa Majlis The house of the **Midfa family** with an unusual, round wind tower can be found in a quiet area north of the souk. It was built in the early 20th century by Ibrahim Bin-Mohammed al-Midfa, who in 1927 founded the first newspaper called *Oman* in what is today the United Arab Emirates. Later, the building was restored and made accessible to the public. Besides personal items of the former inhabitants, exhibits include tools for pearl trading and small storage trunks as well as scales and antique writing utensils.

Art quarter The art quarter located east of Al-Boorj Avenue stretches nearly all the way down to Corniche Road. Here, at Arts Square, the modern Sharjah Art Museum has been built. Five 19th-century buildings have also been restored and adapted for artistic purposes: the Sharjah Art Centre, the House of Sheikh Mohammed al-Qasimi, the Very

Sculptures by Arabic and foreign contemporary artists in the Art Museum's courtyard

Special Arts Studios, the Building of the Emirates Fine Arts Society and the Sharjah Art Galleries.

The three-storey building houses the **largest art exhibition in the UAE**, primarily featuring paintings by Arab artists. A majority of the exhibited paintings, historic maps and objects come from Sheikh Sultan Bin-Mohammed al-Qasimi's private collection. Eight permanent exhibitions show 300 works with the Middle East as their subject, including lithographies by **David Roberts** (1796 – 1864). Among the contemporary artists whose works are shown here are **John R. Harris**, **Ali Darwish**, **I. Gilbert** and **Abdel Kader al-Rais**. The museum is particularly proud of its possession of the old documents on the al-Qasimi's resistance against the British colonial power in the 19th century. Local artists are given free studio space, which also gives museum visitors the chance to watch the artists and painters at work (Al-Boorj Avenue, Shewhain; open: daily except Mon and Fri morning 8am–1pm and 4.30–8.30pm).

★ ★
Sharjah Art Museum

☉

Until 1960, the Bait Al-Serkal was owned by the father of the current emir. Then it was converted into an American hospital, and finally used as an art museum from 1995 until 1997. The three-storey city palace now houses the regional **art school** and can be visited on request (tel. 5 51 12 22).

Sharjah Art Centre

A jeweller proudly presents a selection of his precious merchandise.

A fascinati... variety of pearls

OYSTER HARVEST

The museums in Sharjah, Dubai and Abu Dhabi are highly dedicated to the history of pearl diving, and for a good reason: until the discovery of crude oil and the emergence of Japanese cultured pearls, trade with pearls was one of the most significant economic activities on the Gulf coast.

Around 1900, the heyday of the pearl-diving industry, the Sheikhdom of Abu Dhabi had the largest pearl diving fleet on the Arabian Gulf – with more than 400 boats. However,

Pearls – the most important source of trade in the Gulf sheikhdoms before the oil boom

pearl diving was already being practiced 1,000 years ago.

Oyster banks at depths of up to 30m/98ft were located off the Gulf coast. Pearl divers went out to sea between May and September, when the ocean was calm and storms unlikely.

At sea with prayer leader and cook

On board every boat were around ten divers and the same amount of helpers. A cook and often a prayer leader accompanied the crew. The captain's task was to find a suitable diving

ground. Once an oyster field was discovered, all other boats were notified as well. Oyster fields of up to 200 sq km/77 sq mi ensured a rich harvest.

Gloves and nose clips

Equipped with leather gloves, a wooden nose clip and a rope tied around the hips, the men dived down to the bottom of the sea to collect oysters into a basket. Each dive lasted approximately three minutes. On command, the helpers would then pull the divers up from the depths. A working day, starting at sunrise and ending at sunset, comprised up to 100 dives. The boats only returned to their home harbour at the end of a pearl diving season.

Harvests were stored in precious teakwood chests with ivory intarsia. The quality and size of the pearls was determined with a magnifying glass, scales and other mechanical devices specially built for this purpose. Traders sold the precious pearls to India and Europe. In the 1920s, jewellers from as far away as New York sent requests to purchase the highly valued pearls from the Arabian Gulf.

The wealth created from pearl exports led to a building boom in the sheikhdoms – sandy hut villages evolved into small harbour towns. The 1930s, the Great Depression and competition from Japanese cultured pearls marked the decline of the pearl diving industry. Eventually, the Second World War made the export of pearls impossible.

Nevertheless, pearls from the Persian Gulf are still considered to be the best in the world – and are priced accordingly.

The Al-Majarrah Souk, recognizable from a distance by its shining, golden dome, houses over 50 shops.

Emirates Fine Arts Society The Emirates Fine Arts Society, based opposite the Sharjah Art Museum, organizes the Emirates' entire art scene: it hosts exhibitions, produces catalogues and promotes artistic activity.

Sharjah Art Galleries The Sharjah Art Galleries are accommodated in the Obaid Al-Shamsi House. Those interested may be able to observe the artists at work in their **studios**, which are arranged around an inner courtyard. Their artworks are exhibited and sold in the galleries (open: daily except Mon and Fri 8am–1pm and 4pm–8.30pm).

Al-Majarrah Souk Easily recognisable from its golden dome, one of Sharjah's most artistically sophisticated souks is situated at the old dhow harbour on Corniche Road. The building houses about **50 shops** whose Islamic architecture is well worth seeing.

The structure of this expansive sandstone building is marked by several implied arches, embedded in variously sized window openings. The front end features impressive arches, several metres high, decorating the main entrance which is covered by an enormous golden dome. Wrought-iron lamps make the building particularly stunning after dark.

The shops mainly cater to locals, offering colourful textiles, golden shawls and exotic fragrant oils.

A stroll around some of the nearly 600 shops in the Blue Souk is an alternative to taking in Sharjah's cultural sights.

The famous **Souk Al-Markazi**, also known as the Blue Souk, can be found between Khalid Lagoon and Al-Ittihad Square. The six elongated buildings decorated with blue tiles and superimposed wind towers make this construction from 1978 look much like a Belle Époque train station. The souk is the most photographed building of the Emirates and is considered the main **landmark of Sharjah**. Around 600 shops offer cosmetics, textiles and electronic devices, prayer rugs and household goods, mainly to suit the tastes of locals and Asian guest workers. Lovers of antique shops should visit the open gallery on the first floor. The souk is surrounded by lawns and gardens, and is a particularly popular picnic location among locals (Al-Majaz, southern end of the Buheira Corniche).

★ **Blue Souk**

The **Grand Mosque** on Al-Ittihad Square, with elaborately decorated mosaics and calligraphies, was a gift from the Saudi Arabian King and duly named after him. In presenting this gift and offering further financial support, the Saudi Arabian King was allegedly trying to convince the Emir of Sharjah to reintroduce the ban on alcohol in the emirate.

King Feisal Mosque

On Al-Ittihad Square, between the mosque and the souk, the tall and slender Ittihad monument rises as a symbol for federation and union. The shells at the foot of the column stand for the seven emirates, while the bowl-shaped top holds a pearl.

Ittihad Monument

WIND TOWERS

In the 19th century, Persian traders passed on their knowledge of wind tower technology to the desert dwellers of what is now known as the United Arab Emirates. Simple technology with impressive efficiency: buildings exposed to the blazing heat could from then on be ventilated – without the use of electricity. In addition, wind towers create a far more pleasant room climate than modern air-conditioning systems.

① **Concave funnel**
Four concave funnels capture even the slightest wind – regardless of its direction – and compress the wind in the top section of the tower.

② **Shaft system**
The air cools as it is channelled downward through a sophisticated shaft system.

③ **Bottom funnel**
The cooled air is directed to the rooms. Every now and again, the wind sweeps over a water basin on the ground, which provides further cooling from evaporation, thereby creating a pleasant indoor climate.

Pleasant climate without sophisticated technology: wind towers in the United Arab Emirates.

Near the King Feisal Mosque rises the Ittihad Monument, a symbol of the seven emirates' unity.

Khalid Lagoon This lagoon was artificially enlarged and encircled by a 5.5km/ 3.4mi corniche with numerous hotels, restaurants and cafés as well as gardens and parks. The connection to the sea has been maintained so that boats can still come and go. A 60m/197ft-high fountain is featured at the centre of the lagoon. At the shore, **dhow trips** are offered, which last between 15 and 60 minutes.

Jazeerah Park ▶ Jazeerah Island in the Khalid Lagoon is easily accessible via Al-Arouba Road. A 10ha/25ac park includes an area for children, a small zoo, two swimming pools and a manmade waterfall. A miniature train transports visitors to the various attractions and the picnic grounds.

Cultural Square This square, located in the Halwan district at the crossroads of Green Belt Road and Al-Qasimi Street, is visible from afar due to the enormous marble monument in the shape of an open book. The Science Museum and the Archaeological Museum, two of the most prominent museums of the emirate, are located here, as well as the Cultural Centre, which offers exhibitions on the history and culture of the emirate along with theatre and folklore performances.

Sharjah Science Museum Surrounded by palm trees, this expansive museum, which also houses a **planetarium**, was built in 1996 in neo-Islamic style. The white building is entered through an elaborately carved door. The museum is divided into three sections: the Exhibition Hall, the **»Learning Center«**, and a lounge area with a café and souvenir shop. The Exhibition Hall is seen as a **science museum**, primarily aimed at children to help them grasp – literally – scientific and technical contexts by playing and experimenting with 50 interactive exhibits.

The topics include building and construction, media, the human body and sports. A »motorway« and miniature cars teach children how to drive, while an »educational supermarket« provides »shopping practice« for youngsters.

The Learning Center teaches everything there is to know about computers and their technical applications (Cultural Square, next to the television station, tel. 5 66 87 77).

The **Sharjah Archaeological Museum**, which opened in 1997 directly next to the Science Museum, owns an excellently presented and didactically outstanding collection of exhibits and takes visitors on a journey through time, from the first settlement of the Gulf region to the present.

The museum features replicas of 3,000 year old settlements as well as finds from several excavation sites, including precious burial objects. A walk through the exhibition provides insight into the emirate's 6,000 year old history. Its trade relations with Mesopotamia are illustrated with shells, necklaces and ceramics. The tools of shepherds, farmers, hunters and fishermen show the lifestyles of people over the last few thousand years (Al-Hizam Al-Akhdar Road, on the corner of Sheikh Zayed Road, Cultural Square, tel. 5 36 64 66).

! Baedeker TIP

Sharjah Women's Club

A paradise of relaxation for women, who come here with their children to drink tea, chat, read, attend the courses on offer (from language lessons to make-up classes) or take part in the fitness programme. Although the Sharjah Women's Club is directed at both local and foreign women, it is attended mainly by locals (Ajman Road, next to the Emir's Palace).

Around Sharjah

Halfway between Sharjah and Al-Dhaid stretches the spacious area of the Sharjah Desert Park. The nature reserve began as a small protection area for endangered lizards, and was established by Sheikh Sultan Bin-Mohammed al-Qasimi in 1992. At the **Natural History Museum**, accommodated in a large modern building, visitors can learn more about the fauna and flora of the United Arab Emirates. One exhibition room illustrates the human impact on desert landscapes, while the geology of the region is exhibited on two floors, featuring fossils and sparkling crystals. The museum is especially proud of its **herbarium**, with its almost complete documentation of all plants found in the United Arab Emirates.

★
Sharjah Natural History Museum & Desert Park

At the Children's Farm, located across from the museum, kids can observe and feed sheep, lambs, goats, ponies and chickens.

◄ Children's Farm

Reptile House ► The Reptile House exhibits both common and rare species of snakes, lizards and insects.

Arabian Wildlife Centre ► The enclosures of the Arabian Wildlife Centre accommodate desert foxes, jackals and porcupines. Visitors can observe the animals through the large windows of an air-conditioned hall, which provides various information panels for orientation.

The **Breeding Centre of Endangered Wildlife** is not open to the public. As the name suggests, the centre is dedicated to the breeding of endangered species such as the striped hyena or the Oryx antelope (Sharjah Airport Road, Dhaid Highway, Junction no. 8; open: Sat–Wed 9am–6pm, Thu 11am to 6pm, Fri 2pm–6pm).

! **Baedeker TIP**

Searching for shells in the desert

Turning off at the first roundabout in Al-Dhaid, and driving 12km/7.5mi toward Al-Madam, the road eventually leads to Mileiha where »Fossil Rock«, a rugged limestone rock, rises above the golden desert. The short, yet strenuous hike is rewarded with a stunning view. Also, take a look at the maritime fossils inside the rock – 100-million year old sea snails and shells. Please note that it is illegal to collect them!

The **Al-Dhaid** oasis, situated 50km/ 31mi east of Sharjah, has been deemed the Emirates' fruit basket. The city is surrounded by numerous springs and groundwater reserves which are used to irrigate large agricultural areas. More than 4,000 farms are located here, producing cattle, fruit and vegetables and grain. The large souk in the city centre sells ceramics, rugs, spices and various kinds of dates. The **Old Fort** stands at the northwestern edge of the city. During winter, the **camel race track** on the road to Sharjah hosts races every Thursday and Friday morning.

Khor Fakkan

G 3

Population: 11,000

Khor Fakkan's beautiful location between the northern Hajar Mountains and the sea has turned the town into a popular bathing resort. Visitors attracted by beaches and dive areas appreciate the calm and tidy atmosphere here.

Important harbour city in the UAE For the government, this city is strategically important, since a harbour on the east coast of the UAE would allow the Emirates to continue import and export activities even if the Strait of Hormuz were to be threatened or closed. The harbour is always occupied with huge, up to 300m/984ft-long ships transporting oil and goods containers. It is in the middle of a massive expansion programme, which is intended to double the length of its quay.

⟩ VISITING KHOR FAKKAN

WHERE TO EAT

▶ Expensive
Al-Ghargour
Oceanic Hotel
Corniche
Tel. 2 38 51 11
The round rooftop restaurant of the
Oceanic Hotel serves international
cuisine. Spectacular view of the ocean,
harbour and mountains. No alcohol
served.

▶ Moderate
Irani Pars
Corniche
Tel. 2 38 77 87
Persian cuisine with Arabic
influence, always well attended.

▶ Inexpensive
Taj Khorfakkan
Corniche Road
(opposite the Safir Centre)
Tel. 2 37 00 40
Excellent promenade location. This
Indian restaurant offers inexpensive
lunch deals (12pm–3pm) and dinners
from 7pm. The fish and prawn curries
are absolutely delicious!

WHERE TO STAY

▶ Luxury
Oceanic Hotel
Corniche
P.O. Box 1 04 44
Tel. 09 / 2 38 51 11
www.oceanichotel.com
162 rooms
Comfortable hotel with beautiful pri-
vate beach and plenty of water sports
facilities, including a dive platform.

▶ Mid-range
Holiday Beach Motel
Dibba – Khor Fakkan Highway
P.O. Box 14 33
Tel. 09 / 2 44 55 40
41 bungalows
In Al-Fuqait, north of Khor Fakkan
and 5km/3.1mi from Dibba, the row
of bungalows of this new motel is
located between the steeply rising
Hajar Mountains and the beach. The
small houses arranged around a pool
are equipped with one or two bed-
rooms, a living room, terrace, kitchenette and bathroom. Includes a
restaurant, bar and nightclub. The
hotel-owned PADI diving centre offers 4-day diving courses (with cer-
tificate).

Khor Fakkan, the »creek of two jaws«, is located in a softly rounded
bay at the foot of the Hajar Mountains. The landmark of Khor Fakkan, an emir's palace, stands high above the city. Below the palace,
which remains empty for most of the year, is the popular Oceanic
Hotel. Several small cafés and restaurants line the **seaside promenade**, which landscape architects designed as a park. Several years
ago, the rising number of visitors led to the construction of a traditional-style souk selling food and textiles as well as electronic devices
and arts and crafts. The main shopping street is Sheikh Khalid Road,
off Corniche Road, near the roundabout.

»Creek of two
jaws«

Small fishing boats bobbing in the harbour at Khor Fakkan

History   In the 16th century, Khor Fakkan became one of the most significant hubs for dhow traffic; from here ships left for Africa and India. The Portuguese established a base here in the 16th century and built several watchtowers, of which only one still exists today.

What to See in Khor Fakkan

Rifaisa Reservoir   The Rifaisa Reservoir is situated further inland in the mountains. Locals say that there is a sunken village at the bottom of the lake that can be seen when the water is clear…

Oceanic Hotel   The Oceanic Hotel, located at the northernmost end of the bay, is central to the city's tourist and social life. The circular louvre houses a restaurant; hotel guests come here for the calm atmosphere and for the relatively low prices compared to Abu Dhabi and Dubai. Between the palm trees and the white sandy beach there are several tennis courts and a swimming pool. A rock emerges from the water of the bay, which is protected from heavy swells, making for ideal snorkelling conditions.

Returning to Hotel Oceanic from a dive

A diving club directly next to the hotel even has offers for beginners ◄ Diving club
to explore the Gulf's rich underwater world and observe morays,
butterfly fish or hakes. Dive spots include the Anemone Gardens, the
Martini Rocks, the Hole in the Wall and all around the small Shark
Island, a short boat ride off-shore. Those interested can either book
an organized tour at the hotel or a travel agency, or ask a fisherman
for a ride.

UMM al-QUWAIN

Area: 750 sq km/290 sq mi   **Population:** 45,000
Emir: Sheikh Rashid Bin-Ahmed al-Moalla
(since 1981)

The country's second smallest emirate is situated north of Ajman, between Sharjah and Ras al-Khaimah on a long and narrow sandy spit on the Arabian Gulf. Architecturally, the sheikhdom is the most untouched of all the emirates.

Umm al-Quwain means »mother of two powers«, and refers to the citizen's long seafaring tradition. The eponymous capital is situated at the end of a land spit, which gives a small-town impression quite

»Mother of Two Powers«

unlike the metropolises of the Emirates of Abu Dhabi, Dubai or Sharjah. Funds for constructing new buildings or for renovating old ones are modest.

There are only few high-rise buildings and the industry is still being developed. The population has always survived on meagre incomes from fishing and trade.

Economy

The oasis town of Falaj al-Moalla, located 55km/34.2mi south-east of the capital in the Emirate of Sharjah, also belongs to the sheikhdom of Umm al-Quwain, which stretches 40km/24.9mi between the coast and the hinterland.
The local farmers profit from the rich supply of water to cultivate date trees and grow fruit and vegetables. Cows provide the emirate with milk and dairy products, and a poultry farm produces chicken; surplus produce is exported to the remaining emirates.

Falaj al-Moalla

In 1976, small deposits of **oil** as well as larger **gas deposits** were dis-covered 22km/13.7mi off shore. According to an agreement with Du-bai, Umm al-Quwain supplies the wealthier emirate with gas, which is needed for one of the industrial plants in the Jebel Ali free-trade zone.
But the emirate continues to expand its economic base by inviting investors and establishing its own free trade zone.

Oil and gas resources

← *Umm al-Quwain's old fort, once the Emir's Residence, is now used as a museum.*

✳ Umm al-Quwain

F 3

Population: 25,000

All interesting tourist attractions, such as the tourist centre, the fruit and vegetable market, the fish market, the dhow yard and the marine club, can be found near the lagoon. The old town, including the fort surrounded by date trees, is definitely worth a visit.

 VISITING UMM AL-QUWAIN

INFORMATION
UAQ Tourist Centre
at the Flamingo Beach Resort
Tel. 06 / 7 65 11 85

WATER SPORTS
The tourist centre at the tip of the peninsula offers a restaurant, boat and surfboard rental and diving. The local dive area is near a small rock island off the coast. The lagoon, which provides a habitat for a large variety of birds, can be explored with pedalos or small sailing boats. The shores of the small lagoon islands are equally fascinating; some of them are surrounded by mangroves.

WHERE TO EAT
► **Moderate**
① *Flamingo Beach Resort*
UAQ Tourist Club
Tel. 7 65 11 85
The hotel restaurant is open until midnight.

③ *Umm al-Quwain Beach Hotel*
Umm al-Quwain Corniche
Tel. 7 66 6778
The hotel restaurant offers simple Lebanese cuisine; on Fridays there is live music.

► **Inexpensive**
② *UAQ Marine Club*
UAQ Lagoon
Tel. 7 66 54 46
The simple club restaurant may also be visited by non-members.

WHERE TO STAY
► **Mid-range**
① *Flamingo Beach Resort*
UAQ Tourist Club
Tel. 7 65 00 00, fax 7 65 00 01
www.uaqtourist.com
48 rooms
The leisure and water sports club on the northern tip of the peninsula includes a pool and a beautiful garden.

► **Budget**
② *Umm al-Quwain Beach Hotel*
Umm al-Quwain Corniche
P.O. Box 158
Tel. 7 66 67 78, fax 7 66 72 73
96 rooms
When driving onto the Umm al-Quwain Peninsula, the beach to the left of the road is lined by several palaces belonging to the members of the emirate's ruling family. The Beach Hotel has managed to maintain its location between them, and consists of small beach bungalow apartments.

Umm al-Quwain *Plan*

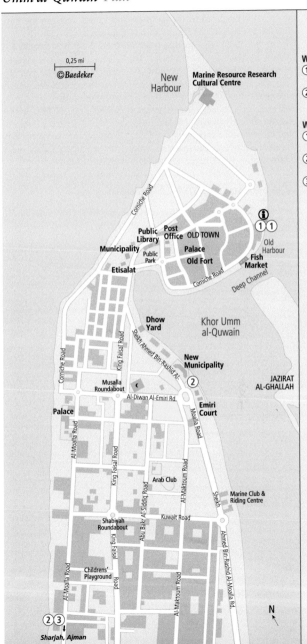

Where to stay
1 Flamingo Beach Resort
2 Umm al-Quwain Beach Hotel

Where to eat
1 Flamingo Beach Resort
2 UAQ Marine Club
3 Umm al-Quwain Beach Hotel

0,25 mi
©Baedeker

New Harbour

Marine Resource Research Cultural Centre

Corniche Road

Public Library
Post Office
OLD TOWN
Old Harbour

Municipality
Palace
Public Park
Old Fort

Etisalat
Corniche Road
Fish Market

Deep Channel

Dhow Yard
Khor Umm al-Quwain

Sheikh Ahmed Bin-Rashid Al-

King Faisal Road

New Municipality

JAZIRAT AL-GHALLAH

Corniche Road

Musalla Roundabout

Al-Diwan Al-Emiri Rd.
Emiri Court

Moalla Road

Palace

Al-Moalla Road

King Faisal Road

Al-Maktoum Road

Arab Club

Abu Bakr Al-Siddiq Road

Sheikh

Marine Club & Riding Centre

Kuwait Road

Shabiyah Roundabout

King Faisal Road

Ahmed Bin-Rashid Al-Moalla Rd.

Al-Moalla Road

Childrens' Playground

Road

Al-Maktoum Road

N

2 3
Sharjah, Ajman

City on the largest lagoon in the UAE
The capital of the emirate is situated on a peninsula that reaches into the sea. It is bordered by the Arabian Gulf to the west and the Emirates' largest lagoon, the Khor Umm al-Quwain, to the east.

During the 1980s, the northern part of the lagoon was extended to create a harbour for fishing boats. The reclamation of land changed the scope of the quickly expanding city, which is split into two sections: the Old Town in the northern part of the peninsula, with its narrow winding alleys, and the New Town in the south.

Recently constructed administration buildings and modern houses line the perfectly straight roads.

Numerous small shops, cafés and simple restaurants lie along King Feisal Road, which runs several miles from north to south and is subdivided by the Musalla and the Shabiyah roundabouts.

What to See in Umm al-Quwain

✴ **Old Town**
Lazimah, the old town of Umm al-Quwain which covers the northern tip of the peninsula, is well worth visiting. The streets are filled

The placid, sandy beaches of Umm al-Quwain are ideal for those seeking relaxation.

with old, derelict houses, traditionally built with coral and shell limestone. Some even still have the wooden-framed window openings. Umm al-Quwain doesn't possess the necessary funds to build new houses, which is why the old buildings remain standing. As the awareness for the beauty and unique historical value of traditional architecture was heightened in the wealthy emirates of Dubai and Abu Dhabi, new traditional-style houses were erected everywhere – not least to satisfy the tourists' perception of old Arabia – and Umm al-Quwain now also plans an extensive restoration of its old town. Unfortunately, the high city wall, which once surrounded it, doesn't exist anymore; three old watchtowers are all that is left.

Baedeker TIP

A dip in the lagoon?
The big lagoon, Khor Umm al-Quwain, allows all kinds of water sports, and the tourist centre near the fish market provides the necessary equipment. Spontaneous travellers should therefore consider setting a few hours aside for a dip when visiting the old town.

The historic Old Fort is still in good condition, due to restoration in recent years in order to turn it into a police station. Erected from mud bricks in the mid-18th century, the building was long used as **emir's residence**. Today the fort houses a small museum (open: daily except Fri 9am–12pm and 4pm–7pm). | **Old Fort**

The lagoon Khor Umm al-Quwain is habitat to numerous (aquatic) birds. Bird life is particularly manifold when flocks of migrating birds from European regions come here for the winter.
Thanks to the United Arab Emirate's increasing environmental awareness, the entire lagoon is now a protected area. | **Khor Umm al-Quwain**

At the dhow yard, south of the old town, shipbuilders still employ traditional techniques to make the wooden ships which centuries ago secured the Arabs' maritime supremacy.
Workers don't mind being watched by visitors (► Baedeker Special p.260). | ★ **Dhow yard**

The 85 sq km/32.9 sq mi Siniyah Island is situated in the Arabian Gulf opposite the city. Ceramic finds suggest that Siniyah was already colonized in the 7th century – during the time of Islamization. The island is privately owned by **Sheikh Rashid Bin-Ahmed al-Moalla** and houses a private zoo. | **Siniyah**

Around Umm al-Quwain

In pre-Christian times, Al-Dhour (»the houses«) had one of the biggest harbours of the region. The settlement used to be situated on the coast, but due to sand drifts the coast line has changed so that | **Al-Dhour**

An old dhow rests outside the Dubai Museum.

Dhows are sti by hand, with construction p

ARABIC DHOWS

Arabs have been sailing the seas for thousands of years. As early as 2500 BC they dominated the transfer of goods across the Indian Ocean. After the spread of Islam and the associated creation of a world empire, Arab sailors established trade routes to Canton.

A return trip took around 18 months – one of the longest sea journeys at that time. Even today, the Emirates' ports are almost like a picture from the past: dozens of anchored dhows are loaded with electronic goods, food or furniture.

Under full sail...

Centuries-old shipbuilding tradition

The name »dhow« was coined by Europeans and used to denote the various types of traditional Arab wooden ship. Eventually the term was adopted in Arabic.

Even in pre-Islamic times, dhows were built entirely from wood and without the use of nails; instead the ship's planks were sewn together with coconut fibre.

The round-shaped hull and relatively short keel are characteristic of a large dhow. Further distinct features are the forward leaning main mast and a vertical mizzen mast. Three differently sized, trapeze-shaped sails were taken on a voyage and exchanged according to the wind conditions. Some ships carried an additional triangular fore sail.

Ocean-going sambouks

There are several types of dhow: pearl divers and pilgrims to Mecca mainly used sambouks with a square stern. Sambouks were approx. 25m/27yd long and 6m/6.5yd wide and known

to be particularly fast and agile. The cabins for the captain and crew were in the elevated rear deck area. To this day, these ocean-going vessels are used as freight ships.

Booms and baghalas

The largest Arab dhows with an average length of 30m/33yd and a width of approx. 7m/7.7yd were called booms. Narrowing at the bow and stern, the most characteristic feature of a boom is the rounded extension of the stern.

In the rear third of the ship, there was another elevated deck, the poop. This was where the coxswain stood, and where particularly important goods were stored.

The most magnificent dhow is the baghala, an ocean-going trade ship of up to 40m/44yd in length and with a loading capacity of up to 500 tons. The carved false galleries attached to

the side of the stern have a merely decorative function and – along with the high poop deck and the richly ornamented transom stern – reveal the influence of 18th century European shipbuilding.

By the middle of the 20th century, the two or three sail baghala was traded in for the faster and cheaper boom due to the baghala's elaborate and costly manufacture.

Dhow building

Today the shipyards of Abu Dabi, Dubai and Ajman mainly hire carpenters from India and Pakistan. Fewer and fewer craftsmen have mastery of the art of traditional dhow building for there were never – and still aren't – any tutorial books, all knowledge being orally conveyed.

Also, dhows are now equipped with diesel engines and modern radio and radar systems.

Believe it or not, one of the region's biggest harbours could be found here in Al-Dhour around 2,000 years ago.

the **archaeological site** is now about 3km/1.9mi east of Umm al-Quwain, on the road to Ras al-Khaimah. Among the most precious
finds are coins from the 2nd century BC, the economic heyday of
Al-Dhour. Ceramic shards, possibly stemming from the same vessels
as once produced in Rome, are an indication of early trade relations.
The approx. 1 x 3km (0.6 x 1.9 mile) archaeological site is openly accessible. It is not in good condition, as locals tend to use it as a picnic
ground. Further excavations are theoretically planned, but cannot be
realized due to a lack of funds.

Falaj Al-Moalla   The centre of Umm al-Quwain's agricultural production is the oasis
of Falaj Al-Moalla. Situated 55km/34.2mi south-east of the capital in
the Emirate of Sharjah, the oasis nestles in a valley and is surrounded
by bright red sand dunes. Visitors are primarily attracted by the valley, known as **Wadi Al-Batha**, whose impressive, enormously high
mountains of sand begin to glow copper red with the rising and setting of the sun.

Falaj Al-Moalla is a modern oasis. The town, characterized by its
well-trimmed parks and wide roads, is especially proud of the local
camel race track, where the men gather to attend the races during
the winter months. People here live in simple houses built several
decades ago. The most significant employer is one of the largest
poultry farms in the United Arab Emirates: the **National Company
for Poultry and Foodstuffs**, founded in 1977, has been modernized
several times at a cost of millions of dirham.

In 1980, Friesian and Jersey cows were imported to start a dairy farm in Falaj Al-Moalla. When the keeping of the animals was deemed unproblematic, the herds were increased and several farms established. Since then, several thousand litres of milk have been produced every day. Eventually a pasteurization and filling plant was established on an area of almost 100ha/247ac. In recent years, agricultural productivity has been significantly increased thanks to the use of fertilizers as well as efficient water extraction and the use of high performance pumps to pump water out of the ground and transport it directly to the farms.

 Baedeker TIP

Dreamland Aqua Park

The Emirate's biggest current attraction is situated on the coast, 14km/8.7mi north of the city: Dreamland Aqua Park, featuring various pools and slides, monster waves and baby pools, restaurants, cafés and picnic areas. As beautiful as Wild Wadi in Dubai, but not as crowded or pricey (open: daily 10am–8pm, Fri from 2pm; tel. 06 / 768 18 88).

INDEX

LIST OF MAPS AND ILLUSTRATIONS

PHOTO CREDITS

PUBLISHER'S INFORMATION

Illustrations etc: 198 illustrations, 21 maps and diagrams, one large city plan
Text: Dr. Manfred Wöbcke and Birgit Müller-Wöbcke
Editing: Baedeker editorial team (John Sykes)
Translation: John Sykes
Cartography: Christoph Gallus, Hohberg; Franz Huber, Munich; MAIRDUMONT/Falk Verlag, Ostfildern (city plan)
3D illustrations: jangled nerves, Stuttgart
Design: independent Medien-Design, Munich; Kathrin Schemel

Editor-in-chief: Rainer Eisenschmid, Baedeker Ostfildern

1st edition 2008

DEAR READER,

Dear Reader,We would like to thank you for choosing this Baedeker Allianz travel guide. It will be a reliable companion on your travels and will not disappoint you.This book describes the major sights, of course, but it also recommends hotels in the luxury and budget categories, and includes tips about where to eat, beaches, shopping and much more, helping to make your trip an enjoyable experience. Our authors Dr Manfred Wöbcke and Birgit Müller-Wöbcke ensure the quality of this information by making regular journeys to the United Arab Emirates and putting all their know-how into this book.

Nevertheless, experience shows us that it is impossible to rule out errors and changes made after the book goes to press, for which Baedeker accepts no liability. Please send us your criticisms, corrections and suggestions for improvement: we appreciate your contribution. Contact us by post or e-mail, or phone us:

► **Verlag Karl Baedeker GmbH**
Editorial department
Postfach 3162
73751 Ostfildern
Germany
Tel. 49-711-4502-262, fax -343
www.baedeker.com
E-Mail: baedeker@mairdumont.com

Baedeker Travel Guides in English at a glance:

► Andalusia	► New York
► Dubai · Emirates	► Portugal
► Egypt	► Rome
► Ireland	► Thailand
► London	► Tuscany
► Mexico	► Venice